Competitive Spirits

COMPETITIVE SPIRITS

Latin America's New Religious Economy

R. Andrew Chesnut

OXFORD
UNIVERSITY PRESS

2003

OXFORD
UNIVERSITY PRESS

Oxford   New York
Auckland   Bangkok   Buenos Aires   Cape Town   Chennai
Dar es Salaam   Delhi   Hong Kong   Istanbul   Karachi   Kolkata
Kuala Lumpur   Madrid   Melbourne   Mexico City   Mumbai   Nairobi
São Paulo   Shanghai   Taipei   Tokyo   Toronto

Published by Oxford University Press, Inc.
198 Madison Avenue, New York, New York 10016

www.oup.com

Oxford is a registered trademark of Oxford University Press

Library of Congress Cataloging-in-Publication Data
Chesnut, R. Andrew
Competitive spirits : Latin America's new religious economy /
R. Andrew Chesnut
    p.   cm.
Includes bibliographical references and index.
ISBN-13 978-0-19-531486-1
ISBN 0-19-531486-7
1. Religious pluralism—Latin American. 2. Latin America—
Economic conditions. 3. Economics—Religious aspects. I. Title.
BL2540.C48 2003
200'.98'090511—dc21   2002012188

9 8 7 6 5 4 3 2

Printed in the United States of America
on acid-free paper

Acknowledgments

The academic, moral, and financial support of a number of individuals and institutions enabled me to conduct the research for and write this book. In Brazil, anthropologist Anaiza Vergolino, who had contributed much to my first book, brought me up to date on Umbanda in the Amazonian city of Belem. Down the coast in Recife, historian Paulo Sipierski provided me with contacts among both the Catholic Charismatic and Xango communities. In the megalopolis of São Paulo, scholars Ricardo Mariano and Brenda Carranza, respectively, shared their latest research on neo-Pentecostalism and the Catholic Charismatic Renewal. Father Edward Dougherty (Padre Eduardo), one of the two founders of the Charismatic Renewal in Brazil, gave me a tour of his production studio in the Paulista city of Campinas, as well as a first-hand account of the birth of the movement. Likewise in Rio de Janeiro, Father José Luiz Jansen de Mello Neto (Padre Zeca), the surfer priest, gave me an insider's account of the growth of the Renewal. Also in Rio, Luiz Alberto Gomes opened the doors of Centro de Estátistica Religiosa e Investigações Sociais (CERIS) to me, while historian Ralph Della Cava helped with living arrangements in the carioca city. Finally in Brazil, sociologists María das Dores (Dodora) Machado and Cecilia Mariz shared their insights on women and religion in the South American nation.

By the late 1980s, Pentecostalism had found its most fertile Latin American soil in Guatemala. My own research (conducted in Guatemala in the late 1990s) revealed a religious economy as vibrant as Brazil's, which I had first studied years earlier in graduate school. Fathers José María Delgado Varela and Hugo Estrada proved valuable informants on the Charismatic Renewal in Guatemala as they related the movement's history to me. Sheny de Góngora, a lay leader of the Renewal, described the contours of the movement at the national level. Presbyterian missionary Dennis Smith and Pentecostal pedagogue Samuel Berberian both gave me unfettered access to their personal libraries.

Despite my family ties to the country, I had not conducted any serious research in Mexico before the studies that resulted in this book. Several individuals helped me negotiate the religious landscape of the country. Charismatic lay leader Miguel Ramirez provided key information on the Renewal in Mexico City and also connected me with other Charismatics. At the archdiocese, Alfredo Colin provided me with a comfortable workplace and hot coffee as I sifted through three decades of Mexican church history. Sociologist Carlos Garma updated me on Mexican Pentecostalism, while historian Roberto Blancarte discussed Catholic history with me and provided additional academic contacts. Many of these visits—especially to hitherto unknown parts of Mexico City— would have been difficult without the aid of my brother-in-law, Bertrand Hernández.

Here in the United States, scholars Virginia Garrard-Burnett, Rodney Stark, and Wade Clark Roof provided valuable comments on the book manuscript. I am especially grateful to Virginia, who has offered intellectual and moral support from the very beginning of my career. At the University of Houston, my fellow Latin Americanist historians John Hart, Susan Kellogg, and Thomas O'Brien enthusiastically supported the book project from its inception. Two faculty grants, a Research Initiation Grant grant and a faculty small grant, from the University of Houston supported my research in Latin America. And Cynthia Read and Theodore Calderara at Oxford University Press provided invaluable assistance in transforming the manuscript into a book. Finally, my wife, Viviana, and parents, Robert and Janet Chesnut, supported me in countless ways. All translations from the Portuguese and the Spanish are my own.

Contents

Competitive Spirits

Introduction

The New Temples of Religious Pluralism

L atin America's religious revolution continues to radically transform the spiritual economy of the most Catholic region in the world. In my previous study of the Pentecostal boom in Brazil, I argued that Charismatic Protestantism is remaking the socioreligious landscape of Latin America. Since the proliferation of Pentecostalism among the popular classes of Ibero-America was my exclusive focus, I was unable to capture the full magnitude of the religious revolution. At the beginning of the twenty-first century, Pentecostalism continues at the vanguard of Latin America's religious revolution, but now it is supported by a corps of Charismatic believers that has played less visible but nonetheless pivotal roles in the historic transformation of the religious economy of the region. Thus, while Pentecostal churches, such as the Assemblies of God (AD) and the Universal Church of the Kingdom of God (IURD), continue to be the main architects of the new religious landscape, a new generation of non-Pentecostal spiritual entrepreneurs has emerged to join in the demolition of the edifice of religious monopoly and to begin construction of the myriad temples of religious pluralism.

Of even greater social, political, and religious significance than the recent Pentecostal boom is Latin America's historic transformation from a monopolistic religious economy to an unregulated one in which faith-based organizations, like commercial firms, compete for religious consumers.[1] In the new free market of faith, Latin Americans are at liberty to choose among the hundreds of religious products that best suit their spiritual and material needs. After four centuries of religious monopoly in which the main choice for the popular classes was either to consume the Catholic product or not to consume any religion at all, impoverished believers, and indeed all Latin Americans, can now select from among a dizzying array of religious options that range from the African-Brazilian religion of Umbanda to the New Age group known as the Vegetable Union ("União do Vegetal" in Portuguese).

In a competitive religious economy, such as the one that has developed in Latin America over the past half-century, there is no place for the type of questionable product that indolent religious monopolists produce for a market guaranteed by state coercion. The invisible hand of the free market is as unforgiving with religious firms as it is with their commercial counterparts (Finke and Stark 17). If, for example, religious consumers demonstrate a strong taste for more participatory types of faith (as they actually have), those religions that restrict lay participation will either have to modify their products or face marginalization, even extinction. In order to thrive in the new religious economy, Latin American spiritual firms must develop an attractive product and know how to market it to popular consumers. If Pentecostalism, Charismatic Catholicism, and African diasporan religions are thriving at the beginning of the century, it is because they have learned to compete effectively in a pluralistic environment. In contrast, if Catholic Base Christian Communities (CEBs) and mainline Protestantism are stagnating, it is primarily because they lack competitive products of mass appeal and are not skilled marketers.

My purpose in this book, then, is to examine the development of Latin America's new religious economy by focusing on those spiritual firms that have prospered over the past five decades. In contrast to the few existing comparative studies of Latin American religion, this one seeks to comprehend the dynamics of religious competition and the nature of spiritual production. That is, what type of religious products are popular among spiritual consumers, and how do successful religious firms go about marketing their goods to target audiences? A focus on the success stories of the region's new religious economy then means examining those groups that have experienced significant numerical growth since the 1950s, when the free market effectively began to operate.

Since a global study of all prosperous religious groups in Ibero-America would require several volumes, this book concentrates on the main spiritual organizations that have thrived in the popular marketplace of faith. The popular religious marketplace is where the popular classes of Latin America's impoverished majorities produce, market, sell, and consume spiritual goods. Thus, in focusing on the popular marketplace, the religious economy of the region's privileged classes is of little concern. Kardecist Spiritism, for example, which has strong roots in the Brazilian middle and upper classes, will not be considered here in any depth. Nor will neo-Christian groups be discussed at length. Organizations such as the Jehovah's Witnesses have made impressive gains among the popular classes but lack the pneumacentrism (centrality of the Spirit or spirits) of the largest and most successful groups.

And finally, perhaps the most glaring omission, in the view of some, are the CEBs, which, more explicitly and self-consciously than any other Latin American religious group adopted a "preferential option for the poor." Their political importance aside, Base Christian Communities have not fared well in the new religious economy. A recent survey of religion in Brazil revealed that by the mid-1990s, the Catholic Charismatic Renewal (CCR) had twice as many members as the CEBs (Prandi 14). Other studies show that in Brazil, where they found their most fertile soil in Latin America, approximately two-thirds of the CEBs that still exist operate in rural areas (Adriance 167). Given that 70 percent of Brazilians and most Ibero-Americans are urbanites, the CEBs' concentration in the countryside is further evidence of their lack of mass popular appeal. The only type of liberation theology that will be analyzed in this book is the kind practiced by Pentecostals and Catholic Charismatics in which liberation (*liberación* in Spanish) is conceived of not as freedom from socioeconomic and political bondage but as deliverance from demonic spirits, or exorcism.

The Winning Spirit

With the exclusion of several religious groups from the pages of this book for their lack of either mass appeal or pneumacentrism, this introduction to Latin America's new religious economy can now focus on the main winners of the increasingly stiff competition for market share among popular souls. Two Christian groups, one Protestant and the other Catholic, and the religions of the African diaspora have proven to be the most skilled competitors in the unregulated religious economy that has developed over the last half-century. Pentecostalism, the Catholic Charismatic Renewal, and African diasporan religions such as Brazilian Candomblé and Haitian Vodou have emerged as the most profitable religious producers. The great majority of believers from the popular classes who practice their faith in an institutional setting do so in the temples and *terreiros*[2] of these three religious groups.

Although distinct doctrines and practice separate the three faiths, the common element of pnuemacentrism unites them in their success in the free market of faith. Deriving from the Greek word for "soul" or "spirit," *pneumatics* is the branch of Christian theology that is concerned with matters of the Holy Spirit. Expanding the definition beyond its traditional Christian boundaries, I consider pneumatic religion to be any faith-based organization that puts direct communication with the Spirit or spirits at the center of its belief system. Thus both Pentecostalism and the CCR are pneumacentric in that their emphasis on the role of the third person of the Trinity distinguishes them from non-Charismatic Christian denominations. Similarly, the African diasporan religions, which are often denominated "possession cults," place the relationship between human believers and divine spirits at the core of their practice. In fact, the ritual dances in which spirits such as the Cabocla Mariana possess believers and lead them into a trancelike state are the sine qua non of diasporan religion in Latin America.[3] Therefore, despite the fact that both the CCR and the Pentecostals consider diasporan religions to be demonic and have even launched a minor holy war against them in parts of Brazil, the primacy of the pneuma unites the three in their mass appeal to Latin American religious consumers. A strong preference for pneumacentric religion on the part of popular religious consumers has greatly boosted the stock of these three competing groups.

Religious Economy

Some readers who are not familiar with the application of microeconomic theory to the study of religion may be surprised or even disconcerted by the description and analysis of religious phenomena in economic terms. Indeed, the application of microeconomic theory to religious activity is a fairly recent development in the sociology of religion. North American sociologist Peter Berger pioneered the practice in the early 1960s by applying microeconomic principles to his analysis of ecumenism. A few years later in his classic book, *The Sacred Canopy*, Berger illuminated the dynamics of both monopolistic religious economies and free-market ones through the employment of microeconomic theory. Berger's dynamic model demonstrated, for example, that in a pluralistic religious environment, the faith that was once imposed as the product of a monopoly now must be marketed and sold to customers who are free to purchase the goods that most appeal to them (138).

While Berger's subsequent work veered off in a different direction, another North American sociologist of religion, Rodney Stark, began to analyze the vibrant U.S. religious economy by employing the theoretical tools of microeconomics. One of his greatest contributions to the field is the discovery that rates of participation in religious activities are greater in unregulated spiritual economies than in monopolistic ones (Finke and Stark 18). Thus, historically, a higher percentage of North Americans than Latin Americans have attended religious services and engaged in ecclesial activities. The application of microeconomic theory to the sociological study of religion is now commonplace in research conducted in the United States but remains rare in scholarly work on religious activity in Ibero-America.

In the Latin American context, religious economy is little known and those who are acquainted with it tend to oppose it. What little debate that exists among Latin Americanists on the subject has been limited to a website offering a one-sided discussion of the field's only significant application of religious economy, Anthony Gill's *Rendering unto Caesar*.[4] While some scholars of Latin American religion acknowledge that faith-based organizations compete with each other in the new pluralist economy, the dynamics of such competition are often obscured by a rather nebulous conception of the religious economy as an "arena" or "field." This approach typically rejects the market model for its alleged reduction of "trajectories through the religious arena" to "purely opportunistic efforts to solve concrete problems" (Burdick 8). In what is otherwise one of the most illuminating comparative studies of Latin American religion over the past decade, anthropologist John Burdick reduces the market model of religious competition to spiritual opportunism. But Burdick and other North American students of Latin American religion need only look at the religious "arena" in their home country to realize that the world's largest and most competitive spiritual market not only offers opportunities to solve personal problems but also provides faith communities with legitimation of secular status and other rewards. That believers seek such rewards, including the resolution of concrete problems, in an open religious market in no way makes them spiritual opportunists. Is it opportunistic for an impoverished *favelada* (or slum-dweller) in Rio de Janeiro to choose the Assembly of God over participation in a local CEB because the former offers faith healing and other gifts of the Spirit while the latter does not?

Religious economy offers a powerful theoretical paradigm for understanding why certain faith-based organizations thrive while others stagnate and fail. In contrast, a vaguely conceived religious "arena" in which religious groups may or may not compete with each other cannot adequately explain the rise of certain religions and the decline of others. Ironically, it is the economic model with its emphasis on religious competition that reveals the importance of religious organizations as personal problem-solving agencies, especially among the popular classes. For example, popular religious groups that do not put faith healing at the center of their praxis will have no mass appeal in Latin America. In other words, the economic model reveals that there is strong consumer demand for the production of divine healing, and those religious firms that produce it most efficiently and market it attractively will be the ones to prosper.

Thus, while studies in religious economy are standard fare among social scientists analyzing North American spiritual enterprises, Latin Americanist scholars have generally either ignored or eschewed the market model. To date, political scientist Anthony Gill is the only major scholar in the field to have applied microeconomic theory to the analysis of Latin American religion. His deft application of the market model to the political orientations of the Catholic episcopacies in Latin America clearly revealed what some in the field had long suspected. In *Rendering unto Caesar*, Gill demonstrated that above all it was religious competition from surging Protestantism that led bishops in such countries as Brazil and Chile to adopt a preferential option for the poor and then to oppose military dictatorships as anathema to what they perceived to be the interests of the popular classes. Conversely, Gill showed that where Protestant growth was much slower, as in Argentina, episcopacies not only failed to opt for the poor but often actively supported the generals in their authoritarian rule. Hence, the preferential option for the poor in nations with high levels of Protestant competition was essentially a member-retention strategy aimed at those segments of the Catholic community that were most likely to convert to Pentecostalism. Not surprisingly, Gill's work has proven extremely polemical, especially among the community of scholars who have written sympathetically on liberationist Catholicism in Latin America.

While Gill has broken academic ground in skillfully applying microeconomic theory to the analysis of episcopal politics, he understandably ignores the matter of religious production. That is, since his focus is primarily political, he does not perceive the problematic religious product offered by the CEBs. In fact, Gill concludes his book with a naïve prescriptive for the Latin American bishops to more vigorously promote CEBs, which he correctly describes as very close approximations of Protestant forms of organization. However, what Gill fails to perceive is that the CEBs are very similar to *mainline* Protestant denominations and not Pentecostal churches, which comprise approximately 75 percent of Latin America's total Protestant population. Had he been interested in issues of religious production, he would have recommended the CCR and not the CEBs to the episcopacies of the region. This book, in contrast, is more interested in the nature and dynamics of religious production. Church-state relations, while not absent, are not the primary focus.

Religious Monopoly

To understand the nature of the new free-market economy in faith, it is imperative to first comprehend the fundamental principles of a monopolistic economy. Ibero-America, after all, has experienced only half a century of robust religious pluralism while it lived four-and-a-half-centuries of de jure and de facto spiritual monopoly. Perhaps the most important principle of religious monopoly is that the monopolist depends on state coercion to enforce its hegemony (Stark 194). In Latin America, for example, Catholicism was first the established religion of the Iberian colonies and then continued to enjoy state-sanctioned monopolies under the independent Latin American nations until the latter half of the nineteenth century and even, in a few cases, into the first decades of the twentieth. Without access to the legal, economic, and political resources of the state, aspiring religious monopolists are very rarely able to impose the faith on their own.

With a market guaranteed by the state, the religious monopolist, like its commercial counterpart, is under no pressure to supply a quality product. In a monopoly, the only choice religious consumers have is either to consume the official product or not to consume at all. Of course, in monopolistic economies where coercion is so great that consumers are compelled to consume the official product through forced attendance at religious services, nonconsumption is not a viable option. Whatever the degree of coercion, the fundamental principle is that religious monopolists are naturally lazy (Stark and McCann 113). The absence of competition in a state-secured religious market provides no incentive for the monopolist to produce high-quality goods that meet consumer demand. Consumer tastes and preferences are largely irrelevant in a regulated religious economy.

Since no single religious firm can satisfy the varied tastes of consumers who may differ in age, gender, ethnicity, or class, the logical result is a substantial degree of apathy and indifference among religious consumers. More precisely, monopolistic religious economies will produce large numbers of nominal believers—those who feel culturally connected to the hegemonic faith but do not regularly participate in official religious services or activities (Stark and McCann 113). The religious economies of Ibero-America perfectly illustrate this basic sociological principle. Although Latin America is considered the world's most Catholic region, historically not more than 15 percent of the population have been active practitioners of the faith, attending mass and other ecclesial activities on a regular basis. While the figure seems astoundingly low, it is but the logical result of four centuries of no religious competition. Interestingly, in the United States and Canada, where Catholicism has always been a minority religion competing in a free-market economy, there are proportionately ten times as many priests as in Latin America (Stark and McCann 114). Moreover, whereas close to half of the padres serving in Ibero-America are foreign, the great majority in the United States and Canada are North American. Until very recently with the development of the CCR, Latin American men have shown little interest in the priestly vocation. In the same vein, recent surveys of religious activity in Latin America have revealed that active Catholics tend to be disproportionately concentrated in the middle and upper classes (R. Fernandes). This, of course, is the natural result of the church, for the past four centuries, having focused on those who had the largest amounts of capital, both religious and financial. Thus, in the monopolistic religious economy of Latin America, nominal Catholics have far outnumbered active practitioners.

The final significant postulate of a monopolistic economy is that the religious hegemon's main strategy for exercising its influence is through political channels. Since its hegemony is guaranteed by the state, the monopolist must invest significant institutional capital in maintaining and cultivating good relations with representatives of the state. It follows, then, that the chief executive officers of a religious firm that enjoys a monopoly would devote much more of their time and energy to currying favor with politicians than to designing attractive spiritual products and devising innovative ways to market them. For it is the representatives of the state and not religious consumers who hold the power to dissolve the firm's monopoly through disestablishment. Once again, the history of the Catholic Church in Latin America offers convincing evidence of the validity of this principle. During the three-century colonial era, the clergy and episcopacy were essentially state bureaucrats whose salaries were paid by the Iberian crowns. Since it was the state that paid their bills, priests, and especially bishops, had every incentive to maintain harmonious relations with government officials. Thus bishops, whose appointment to office ultimately depended on the Spanish or Portuguese crown and not the pontiff, spent far more time in the company of colonial officials than ministering to the spiritual needs of their humble parishioners. Humble parishioners do not appear on the episcopal radar until the middle of the twentieth century, when millions begin to withdraw what little religious capital they had in Catholic accounts to reinvest it in the rapidly rising stock of Pentecostalism.[5]

In short, monopolistic economies are characterized by large numbers of nominal believers (apathy), questionable religious products, and state coercion. Reflecting dissatisfaction with the monopolistic product, most consumers, where attendance at religious services is not compulsory, simply choose not to consume the official religious goods. Therefore, the origin of Latin America's vast flock of nominal Catholics is firmly rooted in four centuries of religious monopoly.

Faith in the Free Market

Having explored the type of religious economy that predominated in Latin America until five decades ago, I now examine the new type, the free market in faith that has developed rapidly since the 1950s. Of course, the development of a pluralistic economy depends on legal and constitutional guarantees of religious liberty. While Stark argues that a free-market religious economy is the "natural" type, the history of the West during the last millennium demonstrates pluralism to be the exception to the norm of spiritual monopoly. In any case, it is only in those societies in which the state does not favor any one religious organization over others and all enjoy the same legal rights that free-market economics will develop.

In Latin America, it was only during the period that spans the mid-nineteenth century to the first quarter of the twentieth that liberal constitutions disestablished the Catholic monopoly and declared freedom of worship. By the 1920s, from Chile to Mexico, Latin Americans enjoyed the legal right to affiliate with religions other than Catholicism. It should be noted that African diasporan groups generally did not benefit immediately from constitutional guarantees since the ruling elites considered religions such as Umbanda to be closer to witchcraft than to religion. Indeed, it was as late as the 1960s, ironically under military rule, when African-Brazilian religions were accorded full legal status, and the persecution of their practitioners and desecration of their *terreiros* ceased (Brown).

With the legal framework in place, a free market in faith will develop in which religious firms compete with each other for the loyalty of spiritual consumers. The will to compete in a free market is predicated on the premise of "member maximization." That is, religious firms, especially those belonging to proselytizing faiths, such as Islam and Christianity, prefer more followers than less. A larger membership base means more souls saved and greater resources for the spiritual organization, which must depend on tithes and donations from believers in the absence of state subsidies (A. Gill). Nonproselytizing religions such as the African diasporan groups do not possess the same will to compete as Christian denominations, but the prestige and livelihood of the *maes-de-santos* ("mothers of the saints," or priestesses) of Umbanda and Candomblé largely depend on the number of ritual clients and the amount of their payments or donations for services rendered.

In turn, competition for religious market share introduces the crucial element of consumer tastes and preferences (Berger 145). Religious monopolists naturally need not concern themselves with producing and marketing an attractive product. In a free market, however, religious firms ignore consumer preferences at their own peril. If Pentecostals, Charismatics, and African diasporan groups have prospered in the new economy, it is because they have developed religious products in accord with popular consumer preferences. Father Edward Dougherty, one of the North American founders of the CCR in Brazil, even conducts market surveys to "determine what the customers want" (Dougherty, personal communication, July 16). Those groups without appealing products will either be driven to the margins of the market (where they might survive by supplying a small niche of consumers) or be forced out of the business of religious production altogether.

In addition to consumer preferences, the free market introduces the rationalization of religious enterprises (Berger 139). Religious specialists must devise cost-effective ways to produce, market, and deliver the spiritual goods to the greatest number of consumers possible. And as in secular society, bureaucracy is the main expression of such organizational rationalization. A division of religious labor takes place in which bureaucratic officers specialize in different aspects of the spiritual enterprise, such as production and marketing. Having been conceived in the world's greatest unregulated religious economy during the era of industrial capitalism, Pentecostalism in Latin America has enjoyed a significant competitive advantage over its Catholic rival, which did not have to worry about rationalizing ecclesiastical structures until pneumacentric Protestantism forced it to.

Rationalization not only results in the division of labor within religious firms but also produces product specialization (Finke and Stark 20–21). The one-size-fits-all approach of the religious monopolist gives way to a multiplicity of products that are designed to appeal to specific sectors of society. Nowhere is religious specialization as great as in the vast U.S. market where religious organizations produce a vertiginous array of products for the world's most heterogeneous society of religious consumers.

In the emerging market of Latin America, neo-Pentecostal churches exemplify the degree of specialization that characterizes the region's new religious economy. Whereas classic Pentecostalism, best represented by the Assemblies of God, offered a rather generic form of faith healing, neo-Pentecostal churches, led by the Universal Church of the Kingdom of God, have tended to specialize in exorcism, a specific type of faith healing (Chesnut). Moreover, neo-Pentecostalism introduced prosperity theology to the Protestant market. Now Pentecostals—who believe they are entitled to material, as well as spiritual, blessings—can attend services that focus on financial prosperity. In a free religious market where hundreds if not thousands of spiritual firms compete for consumers, the logic of unfettered competition leads to a situation in which organizations must develop specialized products that consumers can distinguish from those of the competition.

Another major facet of the free-market economy is the privatization of religion. Religion in monopolistic economies constructs a common Weltanschauung that binds society together and gives ultimate meaning to social life (Berger 134). In marked contrast, religions of the competitive market provide meaning to and address the spiritual concerns not of society in general but of individuals. Thus religion operates predominantly in the private sphere, often far removed from its locus in the public arena of monopolistic economies. It follows, then, that the most successful firms in a free-market economy will tailor their production and marketing of religious goods to the exigencies of private life (Berger 147). Again, the Latin American market offers a clear example of privatization. In addition to their common element of pneumacentrism, the prosperous Pentecostals, Charismatics, and African diasporan groups share a strong emphasis on faith that addresses matters, particularly afflictions, of private life. Almost in diametrical opposition, the anemic CEBs have tended to give privilege of place to matters of public life, such as working to construct more just Latin American societies. As Burdick demonstrated in his study of CEBs on the outskirts of Rio de Janeiro, the small ecclesial groups often do not provide opportunities for members to discuss individual afflictions, such as alcohol abuse, domestic discord, and illness. Particularly in the popular Latin American religious marketplace, the relegation of such private concerns to the margins practically guarantees that an organization will fail to attract substantial numbers of adherents.

The final salient characteristic of the unregulated religious economy is its vibrancy. Challenging decades of accepted sociological theory, Stark has convincingly demonstrated that pluralistic religious economies are more dynamic than monopolistic ones. A comparison of Latin American and North American religious economies confirms Stark's thesis. Until the emergence of the free market in faith in the 1950s, Latin Americans regularly participated in church life at one-third the rate that North Americans did. If Latin America currently appears to be experiencing a religious renaissance, it is because institutional religious participation has greatly increased across the board. Of course, there are still winners and losers in a competitive economy, but even the former religious monopolist has witnessed a recent surge in participation, especially in its most popular movement, the CCR. Thus, equipped with the theoretical tools of religious economy, the student of Latin American religion and society will be able to better comprehend the dynamics of religious competition and understand why certain spiritual firms prosper while others stagnate or are driven out of the market.

Recipe for Success

As my main focus of this book is on the success stories in Latin America's new religious marketplace, the task at hand is to identify and analyze the factors that have propelled the CCR, Pentecostals, and diasporan groups to the top of the religious charts. Pneumacentrism has already been indicated as one of the most important products shared by all three successful groups. Indeed, the widespread popular appeal of spirit-centered religion in Ibero-America accords it near hegemonic status in the popular marketplace. Nevertheless, pneumacentrism is not the only important product supplied by the profitable firms. These three pneumacentric groups also happen to be organizations that put faith healing, in its myriad manifestations, at the center of their theologies and praxis. Indeed, in my recent study of Pentecostalism in Brazil, I argue that the Assemblies of God and others have proliferated on the basis of faith healing and its dialectical relation to poverty-related illness (the pathogens of poverty). Catholic Charismatics and practitioners of African diasporan religions share the Pentecostal emphasis on healing believers of their earthly afflictions through divine intervention. Given the greater incidence of all types of physical, psychological, and spiritual afflictions among the Latin American popular classes, the mass appeal of the product of *cura divina* (divine healing) should surprise few. Hence, the ways in which the three successful religious entrepreneurs produce and market their pneumacentric and faith-healing products will illuminate the reasons for their prosperity.

While possession of a salable product is the most important determinant of a religious organization's success or failure, it is not the only factor. In their groundbreaking study of the historical winners and losers in the U.S. religious economy, Stark and Finke demonstrate that the fate of religious organizations in a free-market economy also depends on their marketing, sales representatives, and organizational structure. Translating economic terminology into the ecclesiastical idiom, Stark and Finke posit that the success or failure of religious groups in a pluralistic environment depends on evangelization techniques, clergy, polity, and doctrine (17). Their narrow pairing of the religious product with doctrine, however, requires amplification. The religious product is not only an organization's set of beliefs and principles but also the practice of such beliefs in the form of worship or liturgy. For example, if the Charismatic Masses of the CCR are filling Catholic churches throughout Latin America, in large measure it is because of the appeal of its particular form of worship. Hence, incorporation of worship into the definition of the religious product will allow for a more complete understanding of the nature of spiritual goods. Analysis, then, of how the three prosperous religious groups have developed, marketed, and sold their products to popular consumers will provide a clearer picture of the formulas for success in Latin America's new religious economy.

Market Analysis

In this book I do not provide a comprehensive survey of religion in Latin America but, rather, an in-depth examination of the development of the region's new religious economy through focus on the most competitive religious firms. The focus on Pentecostalism, the Catholic Charismatic Renewal, and African diasporan religions allows the student of Latin American social science and humanities to better comprehend the most significant transformation of the region's socioreligious landscape in the past five centuries of history. While Latin

America in general is the focal point of the book, Brazil, Mexico, and Guatemala receive preferential treatment because of the size and dynamism of their religious economies. The two regional giants, Brazil and Mexico, account for more than half of Latin America's total population, while Guatemala is the most populous Central American nation and, along with Brazil, claims the region's most varied and vital religious market. I conducted field research for the book in these three countries in the late 1990s, using a wide array of resources, such as episcopal pronouncements, church journals, apologetic tracts, interviews with clergy and laity, observation/participation, and other literature written on the subject.

Before proceeding to examine the three most successful firms in the free market of faith, we need a fuller understanding of the four-and-a-half-centuries of Catholic monopoly. In chapter 2, I survey the major social, political, and religious components of Catholicism's historical hegemony in the region. While many historians of the Latin American church emphasize ecclesiastical debilities, my account stresses Catholicism's success in maintaining a legal monopoly for roughly four centuries, depending on the nation, and then another five to seven decades of a de facto corner on the religious market. This discussion of the Catholic monopoly focuses primarily but not exclusively on the period from the 1870s to the 1950s when the great majority of Ibero-American nations disestablished the church from its status as official state religion, thus forcing it to develop new strategies to preserve its influence in society.

In chapters 3 through 5, I examine each of the three major successful religious firms in the region's free market of faith. Chapter 3 covers Pentecostalism, the popular religion that contributed more than any other to the development of a competitive religious economy in Ibero-America. It was only with the proliferation of Pentecostal churches, beginning in the 1950s, that popular religious consumers in most countries had any culturally appropriate religious alternatives to Catholicism. As with the other two major religious traditions, consideration of Pentecostalism involves analysis of its products, sales representatives, marketing strategies, and organizational structures.

Pentecostalism's unparalleled success among popular religious consumers has resulted in the Pentecostalization of Latin American Christianity, of which the CCR is the most successful non-Pentecostal organization. The Catholic version of Pentecostalism is the subject of chapter 4. While academic spotlights shone on the more politically correct CEBs, the Catholic Charismatic Renewal was busy winning millions of adherents from Ciudad Juárez to Santiago de Chile. This chapter brings the CCR out of academic shadows and into the limelight it deserves as the largest and most vibrant Catholic lay movement in contemporary Latin America. Particular attention is paid to the CCR's role as the Catholic Church's most effective response to surging Pentecostal competition.

Departing from the Christian sector of the new religious economy, in chapter 5 I look at the elements of success of African diasporan religions. In the Caribbean and Brazil, religions of primarily West African origin have been flourishing since the middle of the twentieth century and in doing so have given religious consumers a popular non-Christian alternative. In fact, Brazil's premier African-origin faith, Umbanda, has even outgrown its original national border over the past two decades, expanding to neighboring Uruguay and Argentina, countries with minuscule populations of predominantly African ancestry. African-Brazilian religions, because of their size among the diasporan religions, receive preferential treatment.

If these three pneumacentric groups are thriving, it is also due to their appeal among those consumers who constitute the vast majority of the religious consumer market: women. Given that women comprise at least two-thirds of active spiritual consumers, religious firms must develop products that satisfy the special tastes and preferences of female consumers. Since, for example, it is Latin American women in their roles as wives and mothers who are chiefly responsible for the health of their children, in addition to their own, it is no coincidence that faith healing should be the sine qua non of success in the religious marketplace. In chapter 6, I explore the ways in which the three religious groups shape their products and marketing strategy, according to the distinct spiritual exigencies of female religious consumers. Finally, in the conclusion, I synthesize the principal arguments in the book by engaging in the debate on religious economy and looking beyond the religious landscape to the historical development of pluralist societies in Latin America.

One True Faith

Four Centuries of Religious Monopoly

A New World Monopoly

The Iberian conquest and colonization of the New World in the sixteenth century gave the Roman Catholic Church a new lease on life. As a result of the Protestant Reformation, the church had lost its millennial monopoly on religious production in Western Europe. The reformers—Zwingli, Luther, and Calvin—provoked an irreversible schism in the One True Church in which significant parts of Germany, France, and Switzerland and all of England, Scotland, and Scandinavia became Protestant territory. By the mid-sixteenth century, the Roman Catholic Church had lost its uncontested dominion over European souls and would now have to compete with Protestant churches for believers. Catholic navigators Columbus and Cabral and their respective discoveries of the Caribbean islands and Brazil meant, however, that as the European continent was lost to religious competition, an entire New World was won for reconstruction of the Catholic monopoly on faith. As Protestantism claimed Geneva and London, the alliance between the Iberian crowns and the Vatican guaranteed Catholicism's religious control over the indigenous peoples and African slaves, as well as Portuguese and Spanish colonists from São Paulo to San Francisco. Thus the Spanish and Portuguese conquest of the indigenous peoples and colonization of their lands meant that just as the Roman Catholic Church was being forced to contend with nascent Christian pluralism in Western Europe, it was able to corner the religious market in South, Central, and a significant part of North America for at least three centuries and well beyond in many areas.

In most Latin American countries, the decoupling of religious and national identity has only taken place since the 1950s. Before then, religious identity was inextricably intertwined with national and even regional and local representations of community and self. During the colonial era, all subjects of the Iberian crowns, whether creole and peninsular or Indian and African, were required to be Catholic.[1] Independence and the construction of Latin American nation-states changed little. To be Mexican, Peruvian, and Brazilian was to be Catholic. For those whose regional or ethnic ties superseded any sense of nationalism, to be Oaxacan or Aymaran, for example, implied believing in the saints and Virgin Mary, the twin pillars of popular Catholicism. Of course, Protestants, Spiritists, and practitioners of African diasporan faiths appeared on the religious landscape well before the 1950s, but it was not until then that a critical mass of non-Catholics had developed, which enabled individual believers to declare their faith without fear of persecution or having their patriotism questioned.

The wedding of religious identity with local, regional, and inchoate national identities during the three-and-a-quarter-centuries of Iberian colonial rule was a reflection of the fusion between church and state. Taken together, the construction of a hegemonic religious identity and the integration of church and state constituted the foundations of a model of church and society known as Christendom. In diametrical opposition to modern or postmodern societies, Christendom made very little distinction between the sacred and secular. In fact, as it operated in Europe and then Latin America, Catholic Christendom called for the church to comprehensively permeate all sectors of society and state (Bruneau 12). The goal was total religious coverage in which the church rode alongside the *conquistadores* and then instructed the *conquistados* (the conquered) in the ways of the faith, and of European culture as well.

At the level of the state, a series of agreements between the Vatican and the Iberian crowns established the legal basis for Christendom in the New World. Under the royal patronage system (*el patronato real*), the Vatican conceded considerable control over the New World church to the Spanish and Portuguese monarchs in exchange for a monopoly of faith in the colonies. A series of papal bulls issued between 1455 and 1518 formed the basis of the royal patronage in granting the following four privileges to the Iberian crowns: selection and sending of clergymen to the Americas, exclusive possession of the Americas, collection of ecclesiastical tithes, and establishment of new dioceses and determination of their geographical boundaries (Prien 119; Dussel 39).

While the *patronato* appeared to be inimical to ecclesiastical interests, it cannot be forgotten that the series of accords granted the church a religious monopoly over the better part of two continents and their peoples. Until the mid-twentieth century, only small pockets of Protestant populations dotted what was a Catholic landscape that stretched from Tierra del Fuego to Tijuana. Indubitably, the church became the junior partner in its joint venture with the state under the terms of royal patronage. The relinquishment of control over ecclesiastical appointments and finances meant a significant loss of institutional autonomy to the state. However, considering the fact that the Vatican did not possess the resources to establish the church and evangelize on a continental scale (A. Gill 21), its unequal partnership with the Iberian crowns must be regarded as an ingenious example of long-range planning. Had the Vatican not conceded the *patronato* and not accompanied the Iberians to the New World, it is possible that Catholicism would have remained a predominantly European religion and never would have attained the global presence it enjoys today. Thus, while the patronage system undeniably subordinated the church to the state, it also laid the political and legal foundations for over four centuries of Catholic hegemony in Latin America.

Tools of Monopoly in the Colonial Era

Determined to build "Catholdom" in the New World as it disintegrated in the Old, the Roman Catholic Church employed various strategies to secure its monopoly over Latin American souls and extend its influence throughout the body politic and colonial society. Chief among its instruments of ensuring religious hegemony was the political arena. For it was in state coffers that the clergy would find the funds and material resources needed to run the ecclesiastical institution. Indeed, the state's collection of the compulsory tithe compelled church officials to invest significant political capital in lobbying for their right to the full 10 percent, much of which colonial administrators skimmed for the royal treasuries. Since the Indians, African slaves, and many Iberian colonists were not property owners, the institutional church had no reason to expend valuable political capital on its impoverished parishioners.

As the religious organ of the colonial governments, the church not only had direct access to high political office but also was able to develop its own institutions of secular power, such as universities in Spanish America and the Inquisition. Throughout the three-century colonial era, clerics simultaneously served cross and crown in such elevated administrative posts as ministers, captains-general, viceroys, and regents. In fact, the first people appointed to the Council of the Indies, one of the two Spanish governmental organs charged with the administration of the New World colonies, were clergymen. The many priests and bishops who donned the secular hats of political office bolstered the temporal power of their church by further embedding it into the

Cathedral of Cuenca, Ecuador

organs of colonial rule and by increasing ecclesiastical access to the material re-sources of the state. Even the many clerics who did not hold political office were de facto civil bureaucrats since the Iberian crowns paid the salaries of parish (secular) priests and bishops.

Beyond incorporation into the state, the church erected its monopoly on the political, social, and economic pillars of education, the Inquisition, and control over capital and labor. The church's virtual monopoly on education at all levels in Latin America was one of its most powerful tools of extending ecclesiastical influence through the ranks of elite Iberian colonists and their native-born sons. Always at the vanguard, the Jesuits led the way in imparting both secular and sacred knowledge to the boys and young men who were to become the powerbrokers of colonial society. The church presumed that one of the most ef-ficacious ways of perpetuating Catholdom was to mold the minds of the movers and shakers of tomorrow. Having been taught most of what they knew about the world, both sacred and secular, by Jesuits, Dominicans, and Franciscans, the future lawyers, priests, and government bureaucrats of colonial society would presumably become powerful defenders of the faith. That the church in many countries was able to maintain its legal monopoly until a half-century after independence from Spain and Portugal is testament to the efficacy of its ed-ucational enterprise. It should be of little surprise that the colonial church spent precious few resources on educating the Indians, Africans, mestizos, mulattoes and poor Iberians who constituted the great majority of the Catholic faithful.

Since these parishioners were mere deckhands on the ship of the colonial state, the church strategically chose to invest its limited educational capital in the captains whose navigational skills would provide far higher returns.

In that it sought to prevent the circulation of potentially subversive ideas, the Inquisition constituted the opposite side of the ecclesiastical coin of knowledge control. In other words, as Jesuit brothers imparted sacred and secular knowledge that would fortify Catholdom, inquisitors attempted to censor information that was viewed as threatening to the church's privileged social, political, religious, and economic position. King Philip II exported the Holy Office to Spain's American colonies in 1570 and 1571 when the first Tribunals were established in Lima and Mexico City, respectively (Mecham 34). In contrast to its vigorous Spanish cousin, the Portuguese Inquisition in Brazil was anemic. The Portuguese church, unlike the Spanish, never established the Holy Office as an institution in Brazil. Rather, the Inquisition operated through Brazilian bishops and a mere three visitations, one per century, from the sixteenth to the eighteenth centuries. The bishops customarily returned those accused of offenses in Brazil to Portugal for trial (Pike 11).

Since the lines that divide the sacred from the secular were blurred in colonial Latin America, the Inquisition functioned as both a religious and a political institution. It was officially charged with combating religious heresy on the part of Jews, "New Christians," Protestants, and practitioners of pagan rituals, but the alliance between cross and crown meant that heretics were often regarded as political subversives, if not traitors, and vice versa (Prien 324). The Inquisition's prosecution of the fathers of Mexican independence, Miguel Hidalgo and José María Morelos, illustrates the dual nature of the institution. For the secular, or parish, priest Hidalgo's leading role in the war for independence from Spain, the Holy Office charged him with promoting Lutherism, having denounced certain popes, and condoning fornication. Even more gravely, inquisitors also accused the revolutionary cleric of declaring war on God, his religion, and the patria. The Tribunal in Mexico City defrocked Hidalgo before handing him over to Spanish authorities for execution by firing squad in 1811.

Fellow parish priest Morelos picked up the fallen torch of independence and suffered the same fate as his revolutionary and clerical confrere. After a four-year military campaign in central Mexico, Morelos was captured by the royal army and imprisoned at Holy Office headquarters in the Mexican capital. Inquisitors charged the mestizo priest with myriad crimes, of which being an "enemy of Christianity and traitor to God, king and pope" was the most serious. Morelos's two-day trial and death sentence at the hands of the Tribunal not only made him a martyr for Mexican independence but also reserved a unique place for him in church history as having experienced one of the Inquisition's shortest trials on record and being the last heretic that it put to death in Mexico

(Mecham 54–55). While the Inquisition ultimately was not able to prevent subversive philosophies emanating from the Enlightenment from reaching Latin American shores, the ecclesiastical enforcement agency effectively protected the church from religious competition throughout the colonial era.

Beyond banning books and persecuting real and imagined heretics, the church reinforced its spiritual monopoly through its great material interests. Through the tithe, *encomiendas* (an "entrustment" of indigenous labor and/or tribute) awarded by the state, bequests from wealthy parishioners, and banking operations, the Catholic Church had become the dominant economic force in colonial society by the end of the seventeenth century. Religious orders and dioceses were the principal creditors in colonial society, extending loans at interest rates of 4 to 6 percent. So rich had the ecclesia become that on the eve of independence in New Spain, it owned one-half of all productive real estate in the colony and almost two-thirds of the 3,397 houses in Mexico City (Mecham 39). In fact, as the colonial period came to a close, the church had eclipsed the state as the economic locomotive. Thus, the church's economic activities allowed it to reinforce its spiritual hegemony through the financial dependence of its parishioners.

At the upper echelons of colonial society, privileged *peninsulares* (Spanish-born) and criollos seeking loans had little choice but to procure them through ecclesial lenders, such as the Santa Casa de Misericordia, a lay brotherhood in Brazil that functioned as a bank, orphanage, hospital, and burial society. At the bottom of the social pyramid, African slaves and Indians contributed their labor, not interest payments, to church coffers. During the first half-century of Iberian rule, ecclesiastical officials forced the Indians to work on church-owned haciendas until the New Laws were implemented in 1542. The abolition of Indian slavery, however, did not stop the church from exploiting their labor on the missions of the hinterlands such as Amazonia, southern Brazil, and California. While small sectors of the church, led by the prophetic figure of Bartolomé de las Casas, had denounced the enslavement and exploitation of Native Americans, very few ecclesiastics raised their voice in protest of the oppression of Africans in the Americas. In fact, when religious orders, particularly the Jesuits, were not busy managing their own slaves, priests who lived on sugar plantations in the Caribbean and Brazil gave benediction to the slavocrats who exploited African labor to an almost unimaginable extreme.[2] Plantation priests were not about to denounce the *senhor de engenho* (plantation owner) (as he was called in Brazil), when it was he who paid their salaries. Thus, whether through loans or labor, the colonial church bolstered its influence over parishioners of all classes and ethnicities by making them economically dependent on the same institution that was charged with their spiritual salvation.

Ironically, these same mechanisms by which the Catholic Church secured its spiritual monopoly in colonial society served the needs of its demise in the twentieth century. During the period of Iberian rule, the religious monopolist naturally devoted a disproportionate amount of ecclesiastical resources to servicing the spiritual and temporal needs of financially privileged laypersons. Put differently, the church spent its greatest amount of religious capital on those with the most financial capital. In investing heavily in the elite of colonial society, the church could expect to be rewarded with generous bequests. Indeed, bequests from wealthy planters, hacienda owners, and merchants were one of the principal means by which the church amassed its fortunes. Institutionally, it simply made no sense to expend scarce ecclesial resources on the masses of impoverished laity who had no capital or real estate to donate to church coffers. And since there was no legal or organized religious competitor to lure African slaves, Indians, and the growing population of miscegenated Latin Americans away from the True Faith, the colonial church could afford to leave the financially impoverished masses to their own spiritual devices while it adopted a preferential option for the privileged. Had there been serious competitors for the souls of the colonial masses, the Catholic Church would have had to have directed substantial resources toward ensuring the loyalty of the popular classes. But since there was no real competition, the church did not have to concern itself after the initial mass evangelization of the Indians with the great majority of parishioners who had nothing to offer in terms of material assets.

With most ecclesiastics busy ministering to the elite of colonial society, the Indians, African slaves, and mestizos and mulattoes, who represented the great majority of the population, developed their own type of popular or folk Catholicism. Practiced beyond ecclesial walls, popular Catholicism syncretized the medieval folk religion of Iberian commoners with elements of either indigenous or African (or both) belief systems, depending on the region. In contrast to priest-centered orthodox Catholicism, the popular variety was practiced largely without sacerdotal mediation. Popular Catholics tended to ignore the three persons of the Trinity in favor of devotion to the Virgin Mary and myriad saints. Mirroring the clientelistic social and economic relations of colonial society, devotion to the Virgin and saints was based on a contractual relationship known as the *promessa* (in Portuguese), or promise. In return for a miracle or divine intervention, believers promise to "pay" for the supernatural aid by performing a ritual act of sacrifice, typically a procession or pilgrimage. Of course, if the Virgin of Guadalupe, for example, fails to perform a miracle, the supplicant has no obligation to "pay." Since popular religion in general focuses on healing poverty-related afflictions, the kinds of miracles requested by noninstitutional Catholics relate to everyday issues of material deprivation, especially health and illness.

Until urbanization began to erode this type of agrarian-based faith, popular Catholicism was the predominant form of Christianity practiced by the majority of Latin Americans. And it was in this vast sea of popular Catholics who were ignored by the institutional church that Pentecostalism would become a highly skilled fisher of Latin American souls.

National Monopolies

Independence from Spain and Portugal in the first quarter of the nineteenth century presented no immediate threat to the constitutional basis of the Catholic Church's monopoly but caused considerable damage to the ecclesiastical edifice. In general, the church's position on the wars for independence divided along the lines of ecclesiastical rank. The bishops tended to side with the royalists, while the clergy, especially in Argentina and Mexico, generally supported the cause of national liberation. As both the maximum representatives of the ecclesia and *peninsulares*, the bishops had strong incentives to back the efforts of the decadent Spanish crown to preserve its American empire. Since the bishops were employees of the colonial state and the church had prospered under the *patronato real*, the episcopacy naturally perceived ecclesial interests to lie in continued allegiance to the Spanish crown. That the overwhelming majority of the bishops serving in Latin America were Iberian-born only reinforced their royalist perspective. In Brazil, where the institutional church was weaker than in most parts of Spanish America, the bishops did not face the same degree of political strife and rupture in independence from Portugal as their hispanophone counterparts did in liberation from Spain. Because it was the Portuguese monarch Dom Pedro I who declared independence and initiated the hemisphere's only enduring monarchy, the heads of the Brazilian church found few reasons to oppose liberation from the imperial master. The degree of continuity with the colonial period in Brazilian church-state relations during most of the nineteenth century is unparalleled in Ibero-American history.

Back in Spanish America, priests, who were predominantly criollo, had a strong professional, if not institutional, interest in casting their lot with the *independencistas*. Like their American-born parishioners, the creole clergy had suffered from discriminatory policies, which reserved higher office, in this case the bishoprics, for the *gachupines* (a derogatory synonym for "people from the peninsula"). They logically expected independence from Spain to result in the creation of national churches, which would be run not by those who gave benediction to a decadent Old World empire but by the vigorous sons of America. Thus, as part of the educational elite of colonial society, thousands of priests from Mexico to Argentina, and especially in these two countries where the wars for independence were the bloodiest, lent their intellectual and organizational

San Simon, a syncretic Guatemalan saint

skills to the cause of national liberation. The most obvious examples are the aforementioned Mexican padres Hidalgo and Morelos, who in leading the struggle against Spanish oppression became the fathers of Mexican independence. One hundred fifty Mexican clerics followed Hidalgo and Morelos in taking up arms against the royalists (Mecham 51). At the opposite end of the Spanish-American empire, sixteen of the twenty-nine signers of the Argentine declaration of independence were priests. In addition, during the war for national liberation, many Argentine clerics would conclude mass by reading articles in support of independence to their parishioners (Mecham 50).

The victory of the Mexican Virgin, Guadalupe, over the Spanish Virgen de los Remedios meant that the church would initially be able to maintain its state-sanctioned monopoly in the new Latin American republics but without the leadership and institutional resources that the episcopal devotees of Remedios had provided during the colonial era.[3] Eager to exert the same control over the church that the Iberian crowns had, the fathers of Latin American independence replaced royal patronage with national patronage. That is, the fledgling nation-states, in exchange for legally guaranteeing the church's monopoly on religious production, claimed the same powers over the ecclesia as did the Spanish and Portuguese thrones. Claiming patronage over the church was especially important, given episcopal opposition to Latin American independence. Mexico's first constitution, adopted in 1824, typifies the general pattern in which the Catholic Church was reestablished as the official national religion. Article 4 states that "the religion of the Mexican nation is and shall be perpetually the Roman Catholic Apostolic. The nation will protect it by wise and just laws and prohibits the exercise of any other" (Mecham 343–344). The Brazilian Imperial Constitution of the same year declared Catholicism the religion of the empire but provided for a modicum of religious liberty in allowing other faiths to be practiced privately in "houses destined for that purpose without any exterior form like a Church" (Mecham 263).

While constituent assemblies guaranteed the church's continued religious hegemony in Latin American societies, the wars of independence severely debilitated what had been the largest and most influential institution during the late colonial era. Much of the church's atrophy was self-inflicted in that the ecclesiastical hierarchy, both the episcopate and the Vatican, had supported the losing side in the wars of independence. Some bishops opportunistically embraced the struggle for national liberation as it became clear that the *independencistas* would emerge victorious, but most, fearing for their lives, fled to their mother country, Spain. An ally of imperial Spain, the Vatican refused to recognize the newly independent Latin American nations until 1831, almost a decade after they had declared independence from Spain and Portugal. Pope Gregory, after two papal encyclicals against Latin American independence had been issued, finally moved to extend pontifical recognition to what had been a fait accompli for years. Diplomatic recognition from Rome was also slow in coming due to conflict over the issue of national patronage. The Vatican was naturally eager to reclaim the right to appoint bishops and generally exercise greater influence over the Latin American churches.

Papal and episcopal opposition to independence thus weakened the ecclesiastical edifice in the Americas. The episcopacies left vacant by the royalist bishops were not filled for almost a decade after independence. Mexico, for example, lived its first eight years of independence, until 1829, without a single bishop to head the church in Spain's largest former colony (Poblete 44). The absence of the episcopacy for more than two decades spanning the wars of independence and the first years of nationhood essentially resulted in an encephalic church in Latin America during the period in question.

Even though priests had tended to support the cause of liberation, their ranks were severely depleted by the disruption caused by the revolutionary wars and the constriction of the supply of new sacerdotal blood from Spain. In the aftermath of independence, seminaries were closed and the ranks of the clergy were depleted, as some priests had perished in battle while others fled to Spain or left the priesthood altogether. Mexico suffered a dramatic decline in clergy with the number of secular priests declining from 4,229 to 2,282 from 1810 to 1834, and regular padres dropping from 3,112 to 1,726 from 1810 to 1831 (Prien 383). With the exception of Colombia, the church to this day has never been able to successfully recruit priestly candidates among the sons of Latin America. In the course of conducting my research in Guatemala, I did not meet a single Guatemalan priest. Every padre I interviewed about the Charismatic Renewal turned out to be a Spaniard. Thus, while the church had successfully retained its three-century monopoly on religious production in the difficult transition to independence, the loss of its bishops and the depletion of its clergy left it significantly attenuated and therefore vulnerable to future attacks by the state and competition from Protestantism.

The first quarter-century of independence, 1825 to 1850, was generally the tranquil eye of the political storm for the Latin American church. It did suffer political attacks in several nations, especially Mexico, Argentina, and Chile, but these tended to be limited campaigns, unlike the systematic offensive that would commence at mid-century. The revolutionary force that brought the creole elite to political power damaged the ecclesiastical institution but did not demolish its constitutional foundation. During this period, the nascent republics were more interested in the urgent task of nation building than in investing in ecclesial relations. Having asserted the right of patronage over the church in their new constitutions, Latin American statesmen could move on to more pressing matters, such as taxation and national security. In addition, pro-church conservatives tended to have the political upper hand during this period and were able to maintain the privileged position of the One True Faith in their fledgling nations.

Disestablishment by the State

The ascent of liberal parties to the seat of political power at mid-century ended the hiatus of relative ecclesial tranquility and marked the beginning of a powerful continental force that would sweep away the legal foundations of the church's monopoly. In the 1850s, the liberal governments of Colombia and Mexico initiated a six-decade period in which the Latin American republics revoked Catholicism's three-century legal monopoly on religious production. While it would continue to enjoy extra-legal privileges in almost every nation and even legal ones in some countries, the Catholic Church was disestablished from its position as official state religion and could no longer look to the state for comprehensive protection from religious competition. It is true that the church would regain some of its lost privileges during the populist era of the second quarter of the twentieth century, but these were merely the death pangs of a moribund model of religious economy. Once the legal foundations for religious liberty had been established throughout the region by the 1920s and Pentecostalism had begun to win millions of converts at mid-century, the monopolistic type of religious economy that had prevailed for centuries faced certain extinction.

A confluence of economic, ideological, and political considerations drove the Latin American republics to disestablish the church. On the political front, by the time liberal governments took office during the mid-nineteenth century, the church had allied with the conservatives, who essentially sought to preserve the institutional pillars of colonial society, of which Catholicism was the largest and strongest. As the most powerful ally of the conservatives, the church was a natural target for liberal attack. An attenuated church meant weakened conservative parties. Just as the ecclesiastical institution had paid the price for backing the losing side in the struggle for independence, it would now be even more severely penalized for allying itself with the political forces of reaction, which would ultimately succumb to liberalism.

In addition to castigating the church for its alliance with the conservatives, the liberals had ideological reasons to legally disenfranchise the church. For many liberal intellectuals, especially those who embraced positivism, the Catholic Church represented one of the main obstacles in the path to progress. A pseudo-scientific philosophy of national development, positivism viewed organized religion as an obscurant force that could only impede the material development of the nation-state. Particularly baneful was the church's monopoly on education through which it inculcated impressionable young minds with its backward doctrines. And as the strongest and most prominent institutional link with the colonial order, the church was a potent force of reaction that kept Latin American societies firmly anchored in the past.

Probably more important than the ideological factors were the powerful economic incentives to disestablish the church. The Catholic Church's vast wealth, especially in real estate, that had been accumulated during the colonial era stood in stark contrast to the empty treasuries of the Latin American states. Moreover, the church's monopoly on cemeteries and marriages, for which it charged not insignificant fees to parishioners, also attracted the state's attention. Disestablishment gave liberal governments the opportunity to neutralize a powerful opponent, as well as the chance to nationalize ecclesiastical property, thereby expropriating the region's largest and most vulnerable source of wealth and income.

Another compelling reason to terminate Catholicism's monopoly of the Latin American religious economy and grant freedom of worship was the liberals' desire to expand trade with Western Europe, particularly Great Britain and the United States. Many leading liberals intelligently understood that a freer religious economy would be conducive to unfettered trade with the economic masters of the world, who happened to be predominantly Protestant, especially the British and North Americans. For example, allowing English merchants to worship in Anglican churches in Buenos Aires could only make for a more hospitable business climate and create good will toward the Argentine republic. And given the policy of certain Ibero-American nations, particularly those of the Southern Cone and Brazil, to attract western European immigrants (in an effort to "whiten the race"), a relatively free religious economy would make it more likely that Anglican merchants or German Lutheran farmers would decide to settle in southern Brazil, among other places (Bastian 321). In effect, the liberal desire to engage in free commercial intercourse with the economic hegemons of the world necessitated a relatively free religious economy. Liberals feared that religious intolerance would drive away Protestant-controlled trade and preclude immigration from non-Catholic areas of Europe.

Hence, for the aforementioned reasons, during the next half-century the nations of Latin America followed the Colombian and Mexican vanguard in stripping the Catholic Church of its status as official religion of the state. Without question, the Mexican republic's disestablishment of the church was the most radical. After defeating the conservatives in a three-year war, the liberal government of President Benito Juárez was able to implement "La Reforma" (the reform), a series of anticlerical laws that had been both incorporated into the 1857 constitution and passed subsequently. La Reforma disestablished the church, nationalized its property, suppressed religious orders, established free education, and even prohibited the public display of religiosity, such as wearing clerical habits and religious processions. However, the liberals found it politically advantageous not to enforce many of the restrictions against the church. Enforcing the reforms would have risked greater popular unrest and undermined their attempt to consolidate political power. Thus, liberal authorities chose to ignore many of the laws and in doing so actually won ecclesiastical support. The Mexican episcopacy served as one of the main pillars of support of the three-decade dictatorship of the liberal *caudillo* (strong man), Porfirio Díaz (Reich 9). Nevertheless, La Reforma set the legal stage for the end of the Catholic monopoly and the development of a competitive religious economy a century later.

Separation of church and state in most of Latin America was not as conflict-ridden as in Mexico. In Brazil, for example, the nascent republic disestablished the church with relative ease. Heavily influenced by positivist thought, the republicans who had terminated the region's only long-term experiment in monarchy separated the church from the state and established freedom of worship in early 1890. In sharp contrast to Mexican liberals, the provisional republican government in Brazil did not expropriate ecclesiastical property and even allowed for an additional year in which the clergy would continue to be subsidized by the state (Bruneau 30). In almost diametrical opposition to the Mexican episcopacy, who had threatened government officials with excommunication over La Reforma, the Brazilian church, to a certain degree, welcomed the divorce from the state. A collective episcopal letter issued in March 1890 spoke of newfound freedoms under the new arrangement and that the church had felt "suffocated" during the empire (Mecham 275). Neighboring Uruguay brought the seven-decade period of disestablishment to a close with the legal disenfranchisement of the church in 1917.[4] As the Mexican Revolution violently extirpated vestiges of the colonial past, liberal governments throughout the region had demolished the legal basis for a monopolistic religious economy. The constitutional framework for a free market in faith had been erected in Latin America by the end of the Mexican Revolution in 1920.

A Stateless Faith

The period from the late 1800s to the 1950s is one in which the church, having been disestablished by the state, struggled to preserve its religious hegemony and societal influence through a series of interrelated strategies. While each Latin American church exhibits its own national characteristics, sufficiently similar patterns emerge to be able to discern general regional tendencies. Indeed, this is especially the case due to the Romanization process, which began during

the second half of the nineteenth century and refashioned the Latin American
church now into more standardized and homogeneous institutions that operated
along Roman lines, as opposed to Iberian models. The roughly seven-decade
era of church history can be divided into two periods. The first half-century after
disestablishment is one of institution building and modus vivendi with the
state. After the trauma of losing its state-secured monopoly, the Catholic
Church focused on fortifying the weakened institutional edifice and continued
to lobby governments for support. Having successfully rebuilt the ecclesiastical
edifice and forged relatively harmonious relations with the state, the church in
several Ibero-American nations, starting in the 1930s, won partial reestablishment as the official state religion. Until the 1950s, the Argentine and Brazilian
churches, in particular, achieved such an impressive degree of reincorporation
with the state that the period has been christened one of neo-Christendom.

Freed from their moorings to the state, the Latin American churches initially
made no attempt to fashion a religious product that would appeal to popular religious consumers. Although the church had lost its legal monopoly, the absence of any serious religious competition until the 1950s meant that the bishops could continue the centuries-old pattern of ignoring the majority of their
parishioners, who had nothing, in material terms, to contribute to the ecclesia.
So instead of embracing its downtrodden flock, the episcopacy sought to preserve Catholic hegemony through a two-pronged approach of institution building and political lobbying. On the first score, the abrogation of the *patronato nacional* as part of disestablishment allowed the Latin American churches to
greatly strengthen their ties with the Vatican. The latter part of the nineteenth
century marked an era when the Roman church, in reaction to liberalism and
the forces of modernization in Europe, became increasingly reactionary and attempted to reimpose its authority over its churches overseas. This Vatican policy, known as *ultramontanism*, served to fortify and standardize the Latin American churches but also refashioned them along Roman models, which had little
relevance to Ibero-American societies and cultures.

Perhaps the greatest instrument for Romanizing the Latin American church
was the Colegio Pio Latino-Americano, founded in Rome under Pope Pius IX
in 1859 (Beozzo 130). The Pio Latino brought to Rome the most promising
Mexican, Brazilian, and Argentine seminarians, among others, for theological
training that would turn them into disciples of the Roman church, as opposed
to native sons of their respective national churches. Their studies completed,
these ecclesiastical elites returned to Ibero-America to head the region's seminaries and assume bishoprics. And as seminary rectors and bishops, these leaders of the Latin American churches began to build the ecclesiastical institution
by establishing new seminaries, recruiting new clergy, creating new dioceses,
and in some instances even revitalizing monasteries and convents.

In Mexico, the church prospered during the Porfiriato. The value of ecclesiastical property is estimated to have doubled during Porfirio Díaz's reign from 1874 to 1910. But property values were not the only church asset that doubled: in 1905 there were twice as many Catholic schools, 593, as in 1885 when just 276 educated the sons of elite Mexican parishioners. Misrepresented to political authorities as schools and charitable agencies, monasteries and convents were restored during the long Porfiriato. Finally, the Mexican bishops founded many new dioceses and added eight new bishoprics and five new archbishoprics (Mecham 377-378).

Concurrently, at the southern end of the region, Brazilian bishops labored hard to build an ecclesiastical institution that ranked as one of the weakest in Latin America at the end of the nineteenth century. On the eve of disestablishment by the new republic in 1889, the Brazilian church had only eleven dioceses; after three decades of institution building in 1920, the church boasted fifty-eight dioceses. Like their Mexican counterparts, the Brazilian episcopacy also greatly expanded the network of national seminaries. Between 1890 and 1927, the number of theological institutions more than doubled, from twenty to forty-five (Bruneau 33).

If the Latin American churches were not only able to recover from the shock of legal disenfranchisement by the state but also to grow and prosper, it was due in large measure to a more astute exercise of political relations with the state. Despite ecclesiastical antipathy toward liberalism, during this period the episcopacies came to realize that it was in the church's best interest to develop harmonious relations with whichever political faction of the Latin American elite, liberal or conservative, happened to hold political office. To the contrary, active opposition, especially to a liberal regime, could have meant the passage of additional anticlerical legislation or enforcement of the extant laws, which in some countries, such as Mexico, were sufficiently radical to have driven the institutional church to the edge of extinction. Hence, after more than a half-century of allying itself with the ultimately vanquished forces of reaction (the royalists and then the conservatives), the national churches began to enter into a relationship of modus vivendi with Latin American governments, regardless of their professed political ideology.

Probably nowhere was the policy of accommodation as successful as in Mexico under the Porfiriato. Mexican bishops were able to preclude enforcement of the reform laws through their strong support for the dictator, Díaz, who was a positivist and referred to his cabinet members as "scientists" (*científicos*) who practiced the "science" of economy and government. In a great demonstration of support for Díaz, Archbishop of Mexico Antonio Labastida y Dávalos instructed both clergy and laity to aid the government in its preparations for the international exposition of 1879. On a more mundane level, the episcopacy frequently urged the clergy to endorse the government and refrain from intervening in politics (Reich 9). In return Díaz ignored the laws of the reform, allowing the church to embark on a live-decade period of institution building. But the *caudillo* went even further and granted powerful state legitimation to the church through public affirmations of Catholicism. Contradicting his professed positivism, the dictator publicly declared himself to be a Catholic and also had many of his cabinet members attend the coronation of the Virgin of Guadalupe in 1895, a symbolic act that was intended to publicly declare the nation's rededication to Catholicism (Reich 10).

The real test of the Mexican bishops' political acumen, however, came with twentieth-century Latin America's first social revolution. While it initially opposed the revolution as inimical to ecclesiastical interests, the church, with the exception of the Cristero Rebellion in the late 1920s, continued its modus vivendi with the revolutionary state from the end of armed revolt in 1920 through the 1950s. Reflecting the pronounced anticlericalism of many revolutionary leaders, the Mexican Constitution of 1917 incorporated the most draconian provisions on religion in the history of Latin America. Article 130 stripped the church of its juridical status, limited the number of clergy who could serve in the country, proscribed foreign priests from Mexican soil, and denied suffrage to the clergy (Mecham 388). Other articles, inherited from the reform, banned public religious ceremonies and denied the church the right to own property and to run charitable agencies (Mecham 386; Reich 11).

However, in continuity with the Díaz regime, the first two revolutionary presidents, Venustiano Carranza (1917–1920) and Álvaro Obregón (1920–1924) largely ignored the anticlerical articles of the constitution. Focused on more pressing issues of political consolidation of the revolutionary government, the two heads of state essentially allowed the bishops to continue fortifying the ecclesiastical edifice. In fact, the Mexican church prospered, and Carranza and Obregón looked the other way as the church continued to run parochial schools and even create new dioceses (Mecham 390). Responding in kind, the episcopacy, while not offering benediction to the revolutionary government, refrained from direct criticism of the new political order. Overt opposition was left to lay associations, such as the Catholic Association of Mexican Youth (ACJM), which conveniently exerted pressure on the government from below (Reich 12).

A half-century of modus vivendi between the Mexican church and state came to an abrupt end during the administration of Plutarco Elías Calles (1924–1928). Without delving into the particulars of the well-documented conflict, suffice it to say that President Calles assumed office intent on enforcing anticlerical provisions of the constitution. Calles's opening salvo against the church was his support of the schismatic Mexican Catholic Apostolic Church, which carried out a hostile takeover of a Catholic parish in Mexico City. President Calles not only refused to return the house of prayer of La Soledad to the Catholic Church but also converted it into a public library (Reich 13). In response, the ACJM and the National League in Defense of Religious Liberty (a lay organization of Catholic professionals) started organizing "defense leagues."

As both state and church became increasingly intransigent, armed rebellion, led by the National League, broke out in late 1926. Known as the Cristero Rebellion, the guerrilla war against the Mexican state was fought predominantly in western Mexico between 1927 and 1929. Between federal soldiers and Cristeros, some 100 thousand Mexicans perished in the brief but bloody uprising. While it was Catholic laity who had taken up arms against the government, the Mexican episcopacy granted its tacit approval by refraining from denouncing the rebellion. Months of negotiations on the part of ecclesiastical and government moderates brought the conflict to an end in 1929. Without consulting the National League or ACJM, in 1929 the bishops signed an accord with the administration of Emilio Portes Gil (1928–1930) in which the church hierarchy committed to resuming suspended Masses and encouraging respect for the law in exchange for greater episcopal control over the registration of priests with the government.[5] The signing of the accord marked the resumption of the historical relationship of modus vivendi between church and state, an arrangement that would last at least until the 1950s.

The Last Hurrah

While Mexican bishops struggled to achieve a relationship of modus vivendi with Latin America's most anticlerical state, the Brazilian church, led by Cardinal Sebastiao Leme, was able to go much further and actually partially reestablish itself as the official religion of the Brazilian state. Dom Leme, who served as archbishop of Olinda-Recife (1916–1921), coadjutor in Rio de Janeiro (1921–1930), and finally as Rio's cardinal archbishop until 1942, was the master architect of engineering an era of neo-Christendom in which the Brazilian Catholic Church regained many of the perquisites and privileges that it had lost with disestablishment. In his first year as archbishop of Olinda-Recife, Dom Leme outlined his ideas on the future of the church in a pastoral letter addressed to the people of the archdiocese. In his missive the archbishop asked how the church could possibly have so little influence in society and the body politic in such a Catholic country. The answer, according to Leme, lay in religious ignorance. Since precious few Brazilian Catholics had been taught the fundamentals of the One True Faith, most were ignorant of church doctrine. And the most efficient manner of catechizing Brazilians was through Catholic instruction in the public schools, which had been forbidden by the republican constitution. Naturally, the reintroduction of Catholic curriculum in the public schools could only be achieved with the consent of the Brazilian state. Thus, Dom Leme, very much a product of the old school of ecclesiastical thought, saw access to state power as the primary means of realizing his goal of greatly expanding the church's influence in Brazilian society. In short, the cardinal sought to Catholicize Brazilian society by reestablishing the legal foundations of the church's monopoly on religious production.

During his tenure as coadjutor in the 1920s, Leme strengthened ecclesiastical ties with the state through critical support of and frequent communication with the Brazilian presidents. Dom Leme hoped his collaboration with President Artur Bernardes (1922–1926) would pay dividends during the modifications of the constitution of 1891 in 1925. But the constitutional amendment proposed by Leme, which would have recognized Catholicism as the official religion of Brazilian society and allowed for Catholic education in the public schools, was rejected largely due to presidential opposition (Bruneau 38). This was but a temporary obstacle, however, in the path to neo-Christendom. Dom Leme positioned the church to recapture many lost privileges by playing an instrumental role in the coup that brought Getulio Vargas to power in 1930. At the request of Vargas's military junta, which hoped to effect a relatively bloodless takeover, Dom Leme persuaded President Washington Luis to abdicate. Vargas, who would dominate the political landscape for the next quarter-century, was eternally grateful to Leme for his role in facilitating the coup with minimal violence (Bruneau 40).

While the relationship of modus vivendi in most Latin American nations continued until the 1950s, bishops in two nations were able to reclaim lost ecclesiastical privileges to the extent that this era is known as one of neo-Christendom. During this time, in Argentina and particularly Brazil, the church enjoyed a temporary return to its legal monopoly on religious production. In effect, this was the church's last hurrah as a religious monopolist. The disestablishment of the Latin American churches between the last half of the nineteenth century and the first quarter of the twentieth had initiated an inexorable, if not always linear, march toward religious pluralism. With the legal framework in place, it would be only a matter of time until other faiths attracted sufficient converts to be in a position to challenge Catholic hegemony. And by the 1950s, Pentecostalism had won enough converts to be able to bring a permanent end to the four-and-a-half-centuries of a monopolistic religious economy. But before turning to the new free-market economy, the rather anomalous era of neo-Christendom will shed light on how the Brazilian and Argentine churches were able to partially reestablish themselves and enjoy their final moments as hegemonic producers of religion.

Thanks to the indefatigable efforts of Dom Leme, Brazil is where neo-Christendom was first and most fully implemented. Having earned great political capital through negotiating President Luis's abdication, Cardinal Leme moved quickly to lobby the Vargas administration for reestablishment of the church as Brazil's official religion. Leme's three-pronged strategy—combining mass demonstrations, the creation of a Catholic political action committee, and lay movements—resulted in the church's reintegration with the state within a few years of Vargas's ascendance to power (Bruneau 40–41). In massive public displays of the church's capacity to mobilize the faithful, in 1931 Leme held two back-to-back weeklong religious celebrations of Our Lady of Aparecida, patroness of Brazil, and Christ the Redeemer, whose statue atop Corcorvado hill watches over Rio de Janeiro. Mobilizing the fifty bishops who participated in the latter event, Dom Leme led the national episcopacy in submitting a Catholic wish list to Vargas.

To increase the probability that the wish list would come true, Leme presided over the creation of the Catholic Electoral League (LEC) in 1932. Leme correctly believed, contrary to many of his assistants, that a political action committee would be more efficacious than a Catholic political party in realizing ecclesiastical goals in the political arena. Removing the church from the factiousness of partisan politics, the cardinal sought to organize the Catholic electorate in support of pro-church candidates, especially those who pledged to promote the church's agenda at the constituent assembly of 1933. The majority of candidates backed by the LEC were victorious in the elections to the assembly in mid-1933. Leme's brilliant strategy bore abundant fruit in the 1934 Constitution, which incorporated the LEC's platform, including financial aid for the church "in the collective interest," suffrage for members of religious orders, full recognition for religious marriage, and prohibition of divorce; most important, Catholic catechism was permitted in public schools, and parochial schools were eligible for government subsidies. The 1934 Constitution, in partially reestablishing Catholicism's religious monopoly in Brazil, marks the beginning of neo-Christendom in the world's largest Catholic country. The establishment of Vargas's dictatorial regime, the Estado Novo, in 1937 did not significantly alter church-state relations.

The third part of Leme's strategy for reestablishing his church and Catholicizing Brazilian society consisted of promoting lay movements. While several were founded during Leme's tenure, Catholic Action (AC) stands out as the largest and most influential in both Brazil and the rest of Latin America. Formed by the Vatican as part of a strategy to keep the European working classes from adhering to socialism, Catholic Action was exported to Latin America to combat both atheistic Marxism and burgeoning Protestantism. At the behest of Pope Pius XI, in the 1930s Latin American bishops established the movement throughout the region, and by the end of the decade it had become the largest and most dynamic ecclesial movement from Brazil to Mexico. With the exception of Chile, AC targeted the Latin American middle classes, including university students and professional workers. The Chilean AC was unique in focusing on the popular classes because both socialism and Protestantism had gained greater footholds there than in most other nations (A. Gill 128-129). Its function as a bulwark against Protestantism presaged the development of Base Christian Communities and the Catholic Charismatic Renewal, both of which were the church's answer to surging Pentecostalism, starting in the 1950s.

While neo-Christendom achieved its fullest expression in Brazil and endured until the 1950s, the anachronistic model of church and society also found temporary expression next door in Argentina. The Argentine episcopacy found itself in the odd position of supporting a populist presidential candidate, Juan Perón, in the 1945 elections. Of course, episcopal endorsement of Perón was not based on any great ideological affinity with populism but, rather, on gratitude for the 1943 decree that reestablished Catholic religious instruction in the public schools (Mecham 245). In addition, the main opposition party, the Union Democrática (UD), ran on a platform that was anathema to bishops. The UD advocated legalizing divorce and further separating church and state in the Argentine republic (A. Gill 157). After the decree was ratified by the congress in 1947, Cardinals Luis Copello and Antonio Caggiano paid Perón an official visit to express their gratitude in person (Mecham 245).

For little over a decade, the neo-Christendom model of church-state relations united the conservative Argentine episcopacy and Peronism. But by the mid-1950s, Perón had come to view Catholic dissidents as a threat to his rule, and he launched a frontal attack in a 1954 speech in which he accused the church of attempting to undermine the government. Supporting his verbal attack with action, Perón imprisoned several priests, shut down Catholic newspapers, suspended state aid to parochial schools, and rescinded compulsory Catholic catechism in the public schools (Mecham 249). The brief era of neo-Christendom in Argentina had come to an abrupt end.

The end of neo-Christendom in Brazil and Argentina marks the dissolution of the Catholic Church's four-and-a-half-century religious monopoly in Ibero-America. Although it would continue to enjoy certain privileges and advantages in many countries, by the mid-1950s it was no longer the official uncontested producer of religious goods. By the end of the 1950s, Pentecostalism, a religion (albeit a peripheral one) of the cultural, political, and economic hegemon of the region, the United States, had won enough converts to be in a position to offer a culturally appropriate religious alternative to the millions of impoverished Latin Americans who for centuries had been ignored by a monopolist church which had naturally adopted a preferential option for the privileged. Pentecostal proselytizers evangelizing in the swelling *ciudades perdidas* and *favelas* (slums) of mid-century Latin America encountered nominal Catholics who had little contact with the institutional church, yet whose profound religiosity had not been lost in migrating from the countryside to the burgeoning cities.

Data from a mid-1960s survey reveal that in Brazil the popular classes rarely attended Mass. In the northeastern city of Natal, 31 percent of middle-class Catholics attended Mass, while in the poor areas of the city, not more than 7 percent did. Figures for church attendance in another northeastern capital were similar: 2 to 6 percent for the poor, and 31 percent for the middle class. And in Riberão Prêto, in the heart of the relatively prosperous state of São Paulo, 50 percent of those attending Mass were literate, while just 12 percent could not read and write (Bruneau 48). Three decades later, a major survey of the religious landscape in Rio de Janeiro found the same pattern in which the popular classes generally avoided Mass and did not actively participate in Catholic Church life (Instituto Superior de Estudos da Religião).

Whereas such statistics did not concern the monopolist church, since religious alternatives were suppressed, they alarmed the Catholic Church, which for the first time in Latin American history would have to compete for parishioners. Suddenly, the bishops began to express concern for their long-neglected humble flock, millions of whom were converting to the Assemblies of God, Brazil for Christ, and Foursquare Gospel Church. Pentecostal preachers, promising to heal the poor of their earthly afflictions, had broken up one of the world's longest religious monopolies during the past five hundred years. It is to Pentecostalism, the main architect of the new religious economy, that we now turn.

Cornering the Market

An Anatomy of Pentecostal Success

A s the premier non-Catholic religion of Latin America, Pentecostalism has been the primary religious architect and developer of the region's new free market of faith. If the region's popular consumers are now free to choose to consume the religious goods that best satisfy their spiritual and material desires, it is largely due to the unparalleled growth of Pentecostal churches since the 1950s. This Charismatic branch of Protestantism single-handedly created religious and social space where Latin Americans from the popular classes are free not to be Catholic. Given Catholicism's historical role as one the constituent elements of Latin American national identities, Pentecostalism's construction of an alternative religious identity for those dissatisfied with their inherited faith is no minor achievement. For more than four centuries, to be Colombian or Mexican, for example, was to be Catholic. The tiny minorities who began to convert to historic Protestant denominations, such as Methodism and Presbyterianism, in the latter half of the nineteenth century and then to the faith missions around the turn of the century risked social ostracism and sometimes even violence at the hands of Catholics who viewed Protestant converts as traitorous to the One True Faith, if not the nation itself. Not surprisingly, during this period Protestant converts tended to be those Latin American men and women who had the least religious, social, political, and financial capital to lose in abandoning their native religion. Very rarely did members of the privileged classes shed their Catholic identities.

That as late as 1940 no more than 1 percent of Latin Americans identified themselves as Protestant is evidence of the failure of historic Protestantism and the numerous faith missions to attract a critical mass of converts. Since Pentecostal churches currently account for approximately 75 percent of all Latin American Protestants after almost a century of evangelization, the obvious conclusion is that Pentecostalism's predecessors did not offer attractive religious goods and services to popular religious consumers. If the social cost of renouncing Catholicism had been the only factor impeding conversion to Protestantism, the historic churches and faith missions would be thriving at present, now that there is much less social stigma attached to shedding one's Catholic identity. However, the only historic churches able to effectively compete with the Pentecostals are those that have embraced spirit-filled worship and become like them. In Brazil, these schismatic churches generally maintain their denominational title but distinguish themselves from their non-Charismatic brethren by adding the term "renewed" (*renovada*) to their name. The Presbiteriana Renovada and Batista Renovada are prime examples. Nevertheless, the lack of an appealing set of religious goods on the part of mainline Protestants and faith missions in no way diminishes their pioneering role in laying the historical infrastructure of the region's new religious economy. While the Presbyterians, Lutherans, and Methodists and the various faith missions did not attract substantial numbers of converts, they enterprisingly penetrated a monopolistic religious economy and pioneered in offering Ibero-Americans a bona fide alternative to the Catholic faith.[1] In providing a non-Catholic option (albeit not a popular one), the mainline Protestants and faith missions thus unintentionally set the stage upon which their Charismatic brethren, and not they, would act as the protagonists in remaking Latin America's religious landscape.

Recalling that the main objective of this study is to explore the elements of success in the region's free-market economy of faith, in this chapter I consider the religion that to date has thrived like no other in the popular spiritual marketplace. The roughly 50 million Latin American Pentecostals easily outnumber their chief competitors—the African diasporan groups and the Catholic Charismatic Renewal—combined. Through this examination of the elements that determine the success or failure of any religious organization competing in an unregulated religious economy, Pentecostalism's recipe for success will become clear. Analyses of the Pentecostal product, marketing, sales representatives, organizational structure, and consumers will illuminate the determining factors in this ecstatic religion's commanding position in the free religious market.

María Hernández, an Archetypical Consumer

Since it is the tastes and preferences of religious consumers that largely determine the fate of any given religious enterprise in a competitive economy, consideration of the large class of popular religious consumers who have purchased the Pentecostal product is imperative. In other words, who are these millions of Hondurans, Paraguayans, Bolivians, and Guatemalans, among others, who have converted to Pentecostalism since it first sank roots in Latin American soil in the initial decades of the twentieth century? Sufficient research on Ibero-American Pentecostalism has been conducted over the past decade to allow for a fairly accurate socioeconomic profile of believers.

The archetypical Latin American Pentecostal would be María Hernández, a poor, married woman of color in her thirties or forties living on the urban periphery. She works as a domestic servant in the home of a privileged compatriot and was a nominal Catholic before converting to the Assemblies of God during a time of personal crisis related to her experience of material deprivation. Of course, Charismatic Protestantism is so widespread and differentiated now that there are hundreds of thousands of believers who possess none of these constituent elements of the Pentecostal archetype. For example, many of the members of the neo-Pentecostal denominations in Guatemala (such as Shaddai and El Verbo) are upper-middle-class, professional men. Nonetheless, María Hernández personifies the most common socioeconomic traits found among the vast population of believers.

Most salient among the socioeconomic characteristics of Latin American *crentes* (or believers, as they are often called in Brazil) are poverty, a nominal Catholic background, and gender. Historically, the great majority of Pentecostal converts have been poor nonpracticing Catholics. Numerous studies, including my own in Brazil, have shown that not only are Latin American Pentecostals poor, but also they tend to have lower incomes and less education than the general population. The largest study ever conducted of Latin American Protestantism, the 1996 ISER (Instituto Superior de Estudos da Religião) survey of the Protestant population of Rio de Janeiro found *crentes* to be considerably more likely to live in poverty and have less schooling than the carioca population at large (ISER 12).[2] Although Pentecostalism has ascended the region's socioeconomic pyramid, particularly since the 1980s, it continues to be predominantly a religion of the popular classes.

In addition to social class, most Latin American Pentecostals share a common former religious identity: the majority of *creyentes* had been nominal or cultural Catholics before converting (Miguez; ISER; Chesnut). Most would have been baptized in the Catholic Church and perhaps had even taken first communion, but their contact with the institutional church was minimal. However, their weak or nonexistent ties to the ecclesia in no way meant that their worldview had become secularized or disenchanted. In times of both need and celebration, nominal Catholics, like their practicing coreligionists, would send prayers of supplication or thanksgiving to the Virgin or one of the myriad saints. Thus, due to their estrangement from the church and the perennial

A Penetcostal woman and her daughter in Mexico City

shortage of clergy, no priest or pastoral agent would likely be present at the time of their poverty-related crisis, which so often leads afflicted individuals to the doors of a Pentecostal temple. It is among this vast field of nominal Catholics, who compose the majority of the Ibero-American population, that Pentecostal evangelists have reaped such bountiful harvests of converts.

While the third salient characteristic of the Pentecostal consumer market, the great female majority among believers, is not peculiar to the faith, it merits discussion due to the religion's status as the most widely practiced faith among women of the popular classes. Pentecostalism holds extraordinary appeal among impoverished Latin American women. Hence, product development and marketing strategies naturally must take into account the fact that women believers outnumber men by a ratio of two to one. In one of Brazil's largest and fastest growing Pentecostal denominations, the Universal Church of the Kingdom of God (IURD), the ratio climbs to four to one (ISER 53). Male believers, of course, continue to monopolize the pastorate and high-ranking church offices, but Pentecostalism is largely sustained and spread by sisters in the faith.

Practical Products

The preceding profile of Pentecostal consumers allows for a better understanding of the religious products that believers are purchasing and consuming in *crente* churches and in their daily lives. Recalling that the religious product is defined as the doctrine and worship services of faith-based organizations, in this section I consider the spiritual goods and services that have resulted in Pentecostalism's unmatched success in the free market of faith. Thus, the task at hand is not to identify every single Pentecostal product but to examine those whose popularity among consumers has led to pneumacentric Protestantism's dramatic expansion in Latin America since the 1950s.

Before analyzing the major Pentecostal products, it should be noted that of the two Christian enterprises under consideration in this book, it is the Pentecostal firms that produce the most authentically popular goods. In other words, Pentecostalism was conceived among impoverished Angelinos in southern California and has flourished in Latin America among the poor. Much more than Charismatic Catholicism, which emerged among university students and professors (see chapter 4 in this volume), Pentecostal doctrine and worship reflect the Weltanschauung and aesthetics of the popular classes in Latin America. Here there are no seminary-trained priests who make a (self-)conscious decision to opt for the poor. Rather, there are mostly poor and uneducated Pentecostal preachers who minister easily to their impoverished brethren. Hence, the huge educational gap that often separates Catholic clergy from their humble parishioners rarely exists in Pentecostal churches. Therefore, since Pentecostal consumers and professional sales representatives (the pastorate) usually belong to the same social class, the latter quite naturally develop and market products that reflect the spiritual and material needs and preferences of the Latin American popular classes. The type of scenario in which liberationist Catholic priests emphasized social and political liberation over miracles is almost unimaginable in most Pentecostal denominations. Miraculous manifestations of the divine pervade popular religiosity, and only those with years of seminary training could view miracles such as divine healing as obstacles in the path to "liberation."

The utilitarian nature of popular religion means that the spiritual products offered to consumers of the divine must prove useful in their daily lives. Products that do not relate to believers' quotidian existence will find few purchasers in the popular religious marketplace. This does not mean that popular consumers are only religious instrumentalists, who evaluate spiritual products solely on the basis of their capacity to provide relief from the afflictions of everyday poverty. However, since the relation between religion and society is dialectical, spiritual products that hold little relevance to the social reality of impoverished believers will collect dust on the lower shelves of the market. If Pentecostalism is thriving in the Latin American marketplace, it is largely due to the utility of its products in consumers' everyday lives.

Since most Latin American religious consumers are much better acquainted with Catholic products, rival spiritual firms, in order to compete, must offer goods that are simultaneously familiar and novel. That is, the non-Catholic product must provide sufficient continuity with Catholic doctrine or worship to maintain the potential consumer's comfort level. At the same time, the product must offer novelty that piques consumer interest enough to draw them away from the Catholic product. Pentecostalism possesses exactly this type of product in its doctrine and practice of faith healing. More than any other of its line of products, it is the Pentecostal belief that Jesus and the Holy Spirit have the power to cure believers of their spiritual, somatic, and psychological ills that impels more Latin Americans to affiliate with *crente* churches. All Catholics, whether practicing or nominal, are familiar, if not experienced, with the healing powers of the saints and Virgin. In fact, it is their status as powerful agents of divine healing that has won such world renown for virgins such as Lourdes, Fátima, and Medugorje.

Pentecostal faith healing thus is really not a new product per se but a greatly improved one. With the great exception of the Charismatic Renewal, divine healing has existed on the fringes of the twentieth-century Ibero-American Catholic Church. The curing of all types of ailments through promises and petitions to the Virgin and saints has customarily taken place beyond the pale of the institutional church, and if any human mediators were involved at all, they were more likely to be *curanderas* (folk healers) than priests. In striking contrast, Pentecostal preachers, from the earliest days made *cura divina* a centerpiece of both doctrine and practice. Indeed, it was an act of faith healing in 1911 that led to the birth of the Western Hemisphere's largest Pentecostal denomination, the Brazilian Assemblies of God (Chesnut 27). Whereas Catholic Masses offered little liturgical space for the healing of believers' quotidian afflictions, Pentecostal worship services and revivals in which Jesus or the Holy Spirit would fail to operate through the congregation to cure worshipers of their illnesses are almost unimaginable. Of such importance is faith healing to the mission of the IURD of Brazil that two days of its weekly schedule of services are devoted to it. Hence, Latin American Pentecostalism took what had been a marginal product in institutional Catholicism and turned it into the sine qua non of its own religious production.

Recent research on Ibero-American Pentecostalism substantiates the role of faith healing as its most compelling product in attracting new customers to its brand of faith. In separate studies, Tennekes (34) and Wilson (123) in Chile and Argentina, respectively, found that a majority of converts had adhered to the faith in an attempt to cure an illness. Similarly, three-quarters of the Pentecostals surveyed by Conway (13) in Haiti had converted through illness, either their own or that of a relative. Conway, interestingly, points out that Haitian demand for faith healing is partly a function of Vodou whose *lwas* (spirits) typically express displeasure with believers by inflicting them with illness (8-9). Although the authors furnish no statistics, two recent studies in Guatemala, the nation with the largest relative Protestant population, found sickness (Pedrón-Colombani 173) and alcoholism (Canton 100), which can be considered a type of illness, to be primary factors in conversion to Pentecostalism.

In my own recent study of the Pentecostal boom in Brazil, home to the world's largest Charismatic Protestant population, I found that over one-half of my informants in the Amazonian city of Belem had come to the faith through sickness (53). And in accord with research in Guatemala, I also discovered that more than any other reason, it was the desire to stop abusing alcohol that led Belenense males to affiliate with the Assemblies of God or the Foursquare Gospel Church, among others (58). Finally, the largest survey ever conducted on Latin American Protestants, the 1996 ISER study, revealed that 55 percent of 921 carioca evangelicals had converted to the faith at the time of a "serious problem," of which physical illness was the predominant affliction. Sickness, together with alcohol abuse, accounted for nearly half (49 percent) of the majority of believers who had converted during a time of personal crisis (ISER 21).[3] That spiritual problems accounted for only 9 percent of those who converted through crisis provides compelling evidence of the dialectical relation between popular religion and society. Above all, religious consumers purchase Pentecostal products because of their relevance to the dramas of their everyday lives.

Recent research, particularly in Brazil, reveals that there are three main poverty-related afflictions that lead Latin Americans to join the Pentecostal enterprise through its paramount product of faith healing. It should be of little surprise that, in a region of the world in which affordable health care is a scarce commodity, physical illness leads poor Latin Americans to the doors of a Pentecostal house of worship more than any other factor. A serious illness can threaten the very existence of an impoverished household, particularly when the infirm happens to be a major breadwinner whose condition prevents him or her from working. Since members of the popular classes most often work in the informal economy or service sector where manual labor is common, a serious somatic malady can have disastrous consequences. To make matters worse, poor Latin Americans are often denied access to medical care because of their inability to pay, or they are told their condition is terminal or untreatable by physicians who often provide substandard care to impoverished patients.

It is in this social context that millions of Latin Americans turn to Pentecostalism as an alternative source of healing. The infirm and mothers seeking to remedy the illness of a family member come to Pentecostal worship services with the hope that Jesus, the Physician of physicians, can cure what medical doctors and perhaps other faith healers could not. Any improvement, however slight, in one's condition is often interpreted as a miracle, an act of faith healing, which demonstrates the power of the Pentecostal Jesus and frequently leads the individual to join an evangelical church.

After physical illness, it is domestic conflict that most commonly induces religious consumers to become members of the Pentecostal enterprise through its magnetic product of faith healing. Of the majority of carioca Protestants surveyed by ISER who had converted during a personal crisis, 25 percent cited family conflict as the main problem (21). Similarly in Belem, 29 percent of my Pentecostal informants "accepted Jesus" due to domestic strife (59). Family conflict obviously cuts across class lines, but the emotional stress caused by material deprivation exacerbates it among the popular classes of Ibero-America. The daily struggle to make financial ends meet can greatly sharpen and increase the conflicts that to some degree are a normal part of family life. Men, in particular, may feel enraged by socioeconomic conditions that do not allow them to earn enough to provide proper housing, food, clothing, and education for their families. A profound sense of powerlessness felt by many unemployed, underemployed, and underpaid men can lead them to express their rage in the only locus in which they hold any power—the home. Domestic abuse, expressed both verbally and physically, compels millions of both perpetrators and victims to embrace the Pentecostal Jesus as a potent source of mending the frayed fibers of family life. In addition, parental and spousal abandonment and philandering rank among the principal family problems that lead afflicted religious consumers to acquire Pentecostalism's foremost product.

Sickness and domestic strife are the main pathogens of poverty that compel millions of Latin American men and women to consume the Pentecostal product of faith healing. However, it is quite possible that for male converts, who account for approximately one-third of all believers, it is a third pathogen that most often sends them to *crente* services in search of divine healing. In Belém, a desire for sobriety brought more men off the streets and into the church than any other factor: 40 percent of my male interviewees had converted as a way to solve their drinking problem (58). Likewise, the ISER survey, which does not analyze believers by gender, found alcohol abuse to be the third most common serious problem suffered by Rio de Janeiro's Protestants at the time of conversion (21). Other researchers (including Mariz "Pentecostalismo"; Annis; Garrard-Burnett *Living in the New Jerusalem*; Canton) have emphasized the importance of alcoholism as a factor in conversion to the faith.

As is the case with somatic maladies and family conflict, alcoholism is certainly not peculiar to the popular classes. Abusers are found among all social strata, from the beachfront condominiums in Rio's Barra da Tijuca district to the slums of Tijuana and Ciudad Juarez on the U.S.-Mexican border. Nevertheless, there is no question that the liquor flows more freely in the slums, where men, in particular, seek to numb the pain of poverty through a bottle. That the most impoverished ethnic group in the United States, Native Americans, suffers the country's highest rates of alcoholism is strong evidence of the correlation between poverty and alcohol abuse.

It is especially in this aspect of the product of faith healing that Pentecostalism enjoys a major advantage over its rivals in the free market of faith. In marked contrast to Catholicism and African diasporan groups, Pentecostal doctrine demonizes alcohol consumption. Believers cannot claim to be fully converted until they have emptied their beer and rum bottles and become teetotalers. While Pentecostals believe hard drink to have been distilled by the devil, practitioners of Umbanda, for example, often receive certain liminal spirits with drink in hand. Catholic doctrine does not forbid drinking, and the fiestas of popular Catholicism most often associated with certain saints, such as São João (St. John) in Brazil, typically involve the free flow of distilled spirits. Thus, through its demonization of hard drink, Pentecostalism enjoys a major advantage over its religious rivals in recruiting millions of Latin Americans who suffer the consequences of one of the most virulent pathogens of poverty.

If the product of faith healing, more than any other, induces religious consumers to join the Pentecostal enterprise, it is another good that facilitates the recovery and maintenance of believers' health over the long term. The doctrine of conversion—in which joining a Pentecostal church is conceptualized as part of a process of spiritual rebirth—allows the believer to be born again into a healthy new environment where the demons of poverty can be neutralized. Conceived of as a "positive transformation of the nature and value of a person," religious conversion appeals most to those individuals and groups who have been stigmatized or negatively evaluated by society (Stark and Bainbridge 197). A conversionist religion, then, which offers the possibility of a new life far removed from

Assembly of God church, "The Beautiful," Lake Atitlan, Guatemala

the afflictions of the old, would be understandably popular among those millions of Latin Americans seeking to turn away from family conflict, alcoholism, and illness.

The doctrine and experience of conversion provides the type of rupture with secular society that many afflicted men and women are looking for. In accepting Jesus and receiving baptism by the Holy Spirit, neophytes are called on to abandon their worldly life for a holy one. What this implies on a practical level is a reorientation from the mundane pleasures and perils of the street to the godliness of church and family life. The theological dualism and asceticism of this conversionist religion present church and home, on the one hand, and the street, on the other, as polarities on a continuum of good and evil. The street is the devil's playground with its crime, prostitution, gambling, and substance abuse. In stark contrast, God is manifest in the fraternal worship of the church and harmonious family life. Converts thus learn to demonize the street and its devilish temptations and thereby renounce the very patterns of comportment that might have led them to convert to Pentecostalism in the first place.

Of such importance is this element of conversion that two-thirds of my male informants in Brazil mentioned the repudiation of "vice" as the most important change in their life since conversion. And not surprisingly, they cited worldly temptations as their second greatest problem after financial hardship (Chesnut 112). Since the streets of Latin America, especially on the urban margins, are

still largely a male domain, it follows that the rupture of conversion to Pentecostalism is greater for men. In short, the product of conversion allows believers
to reclaim and maintain their health through their rebirth into a salutary new
environment that is largely devoid of the demons of the street.

If believers find themselves assailed by such demons, their religion offers
them a specific brand of faith healing to exorcise them. Exorcism, usually referred to as liberation, *libertação* in Portuguese, has been practiced by Pentecostal preachers since the early days, but over the past two decades, neo-Pentecostal churches have brought it from the fringes of religious practice to center
stage. Indeed, in its weekly calendar of worship, the Universal Church devotes
Fridays to *cultos de libertação* (exorcism services). Far removed from the Assemblies of God preachers who used to prefer to keep the demons at bay, Universal
pastors actually invoke the evil spirits, inviting them to "manifest themselves" in
tormented worshipers. In scenes often reminiscent of the recently re-released
film, *The Exorcist*, or the staged wrestling matches that are so popular in Latin
America, pastors demonstrate their superior spiritual power by forcefully "tying
up" (*amarrando*) the demons, thus releasing their human victims from their
malevolent grip.

Pentecostalism's final salient product, ecstatic power, is one that it shares
with its main religious rivals but possesses in greater measure than diasporan
faiths and Charismatic Catholicism. Just as the dialectic between illness and
faith healing attracts millions of converts, a similar one between socioeconomic
impotence and spiritual power appeals to many impoverished Latin Americans.
With direct access to the Holy Spirit through baptism in the Spirit and through
charismata such as glossolalia and prophecy, economically impotent Pentecostals experience intense spiritual power. Filled with the power of the Holy
Spirit, poor believers are fortified to do battle with the demons of deprivation,
which can make life on the urban and rural margins seem hellish at times. The
often ecstatic nature of Pentecostalism's spiritual power in which believers enter
a dissociated state of consciousness allows them to temporarily transcend their
difficult earthly station and experience the rapture of communion with the Holy
Spirit. Since Pentecostalism prohibits popular mundane sources of ecstasy,
such as psychotropic drugs and casual sex, worship services and prayer groups
are the main loci in which believers can experience the sensation of being trans-
ported from their social place (ekstasis) to an extraordinary space of supernatural rapture.

Herein lies one of the principal reasons for Pentecostalism's greater spiritual
power. Unlike rival religious firms, *creyente* churches demonize many competing
mundane sources of ecstasy. Thus with beer and rum, extramarital sex, smoking, and even movies and television banned in some denominations, worship
services become the primary source of ecstasy for believers. In marked contrast,

African diasporan religions actually incorporate mundane sources of ecstasy into worship services with certain ribald spirits such as Pomba Gira, patroness of Brazilian prostitutes, manifesting themselves in their human hosts through erotic dancing punctuated by swigs of *cachaça*, a rum-like distilled spirit. In the middle is the Catholic Charismatic Renewal, which does not proscribe such mundane activities, with the great exception of extramarital sex, but frowns on excess. After spending much time with Brazilian Pentecostals, whom I never saw smoking, I was somewhat taken aback by the sight of Charismatics in Rio de Janeiro and Mexico City lighting up before and after Catholic prayer meetings. Smokers, drinkers, and "fornicators" looking to kick their habit are therefore more likely to find sufficient spiritual power to achieve their goal in a religious firm that prohibits, if not demonizes, their mundane pleasures.

A Faith in Marketing

As any business student knows, it is not sufficient for a firm to simply possess an appealing product. In modern consumer societies where prospective customers are presented with a dizzying array of goods and services, businesses must aggressively market their product, attempting to pierce the cacophony of omnipresent advertising and deliver their message to consumers. So important is marketing, particularly in affluent consumer societies such as the United States, that the way in which a particular product is packaged and advertised often has greater bearing on its sales than the actual qualities of the product itself. The Mexican brand of beer, Corona, is a striking example. In the 1980s, sales of this insipid light lager took off in the United States. At bars from San Diego to Boston, yuppies stuffed wedges of lime down the long graceful neck of clear bottles of Corona, this at a time when most beer was packaged in tinted glass bottles. Even more important than the novelties of a transparent bottle and citric acid to add some flavor to the mediocre *cerveza* were the brilliant television ads that convinced young North American professionals, and then some, that every time they downed a Corona they were not merely imbibing an alcoholic beverage but soaking up the image of a relaxing Mexican beach vacation, replete with white sand, palm trees, blue sea, and cloudless sky. In effect, Corona was marketed as a Cancun vacation in a bottle.

Admittedly, the science of marketing is not as developed in religious economies as commercial ones, but without a successful strategy of evangelization that offers doctrine and worship directly to prospective believers, spiritual firms operating in a free market of faith will find it hard to compete with their rivals who actively and creatively evangelize. And in the religious economies of twentieth-century Ibero-America, no religion evangelized as successfully as Pentecostalism. If pneumacentric Protestantism has been able to convert millions of nominal Catholics and claim at least three-quarters of the region's total Protestant population in less than a century. It is in no small measure due to Pentecostal marketing of the faith. This section, then, considers the ways in which the Assemblies of God, Foursquare Gospel Church, and other Pentecostal denominations have successfully delivered their religious products to spiritual consumers through advertising and packaging. What follows is examination of the methods of evangelization that have won myriad souls for Jesus.

Like their Pentecostal brethren in the United States, Latin American *crentes* are the most skilled marketers in the region's new religious economy. They have used diverse media to deliver the simple but potent message to prospective converts that affiliation with Pentecostalism will imbue them with sufficient supernatural strength to vanquish the demons of poverty. It is the dynamic and controversial IURD that has captured the essence of Pentecostal advertising in its evangelistic slogan, "stop suffering." The pithy phrase "pare de sofrer," typically printed in bright red letters, calls out to the afflicted poor of Brazil from the church walls, pamphlets, and newspapers of this innovative denomination. A combination of low- and high-tech media invite religious consumers, mainly nominal Catholics, to relieve their suffering by embracing Jesus and the Holy Spirit specifically within the walls of the particular church that is advertising its product.

One of the most effective means of marketing the Pentecostal product is the oldest method of *creyente* evangelization in Latin America: home visits. The founders of the Assemblies of God in Brazil, Swedish-American immigrants, Gunnar Vingren and Daniel Berg, proselytized in early twentieth-century Belem through visits to victims of a yellow fever epidemic and other maladies (Chesnut). Since then, hundreds of thousands of Pentecostal pastors and lay persons have knocked on flimsy doors throughout Latin America's urban periphery and countryside to spread the good news of healing to those suffering from poverty-related afflictions. In the Assemblies of God, lay women evangelists, called *visitadoras* (visitors) proselytize not only door to door but also in hospitals filled with those who are especially predisposed to accept a dose of divine healing. Until the Charismatic Renewal developed its own home visit campaign in the 1980s targeting nominal Catholics, Pentecostals and neo-Christians, such as Mormons and Jehovah's Witnesses, were the only groups who brought their products directly to Latin American spiritual consumers in their own homes.

Indeed, it is within the household that Pentecostalism recruits most of its converts. However, it is not the visit of a church evangelist that most often results in affiliation with a Pentecostal denomination but intimate contact with believers in the family. Almost one-half of my ninety Pentecostal informants in Belem had first come into contact with the faith through family members (Chesnut 76). In Guatemala, Pedrón-Colombani found a similar pattern with friends

"Stop Suffering," Universal Church of the Kingdom of God billboard in Barcarena, Brazil

and colleagues also figuring as agents of conversion (174). In the intimacy of the home, nonbelieving family members can observe the benefits that affiliation with the faith has brought to kin who have purchased the Pentecostal product. It is one thing to hear the conversion testimonial of a stranger, and quite another to actually witness firsthand the positive changes experienced by a family member as a result of her adherence to the faith. Despite the considerable investment in high-tech marketing, it is low-tech advertising in which family members, coworkers, and friends tout the advantages of Charismatic Protestantism among each other that has been the most efficient medium for attracting new religious consumers.

For those Ibero-Americans who do not come into contact with Pentecostalism through low-tech marketing, evangelists have made it hard to avoid exposure to their product through its advertisement in the mass media of radio, television, and even the Internet. Despite the rapid growth of Pentecostal televangelism in the region since the early 1980s, it is the oldest form of electronic media—radio—that continues to account for the bulk of *crente* broadcasting. Whereas even Pentecostal-owned television stations, such as the IURD's Rede Record, transmit mostly commercial programs, many radio stations broadcast nothing but Pentecostal preaching, music, and conversion testimonials twenty-four hours a day. By the mid-1980s, the Brazilian church, God Is

World headquarters of the Brazilian Pentecostal Church, "God Is Love,"
in São Paulo

Love (Deus é Amor) had assembled an impressive radio network through own-
ership of three regional stations in the south, transmission of its flagship program, *The Voice of Liberation* (*A Voz da Libertação*), on 573 stations throughout
the country, and claiming the majority of air time on São Paulo's powerful
Radio Tupi, which had belonged to the Catholic archdiocese until its concession was canceled (Assman 100). Likewise, radio has been instrumental in the
vertiginous expansion of the Universal Church. In the early 1990s, the
IURD's AM station, Radio Record (which broadcasts religious programming
exclusively), ranked number three in listenership in greater São Paulo, South
America's largest city. Often the first step taken by IURD pastors assigned to
found a new church is to evangelize on the radio and then invite listeners to
prayer meetings, which eventually form the nucleus of a new congregation
(Mariano 68-69).

Radio's advantage over television as a marketing tool for the Pentecostal
product is twofold. First and foremost, it is significantly cheaper than television.
Only the largest denominations, such as Assemblies of God, IURD, and
Foursquare Gospel Church can afford the high costs associated with propri-
etorship of a station or production of programs. In contrast, some smaller
churches that could never dream of appearing on television possess the funds to
purchase small amounts of air time, particularly on the AM band of the close to
one thousand stations in Latin America that carry Protestant programming

(Moreno 51). Second, while TV antennae have become a permanent fixture on the skyline of the urban periphery, radio is still more ubiquitous among the Latin American popular classes. A 1993 survey on mass media revealed radio to be the most frequently accessed medium in greater São Paulo, especially among the lowest income groups (Mariano 68 n. 38). In short, Pentecostal marketers reach a larger audience and deliver their product more cost effectively on radio.

Following in the footsteps of their North American brethren who dominate religious broadcasting in the United States, a few large Pentecostal denominations enjoy a commanding position in the transmission of spiritual programs. With the exception of the pioneering but short-lived programs of the nationalistic Brazil for Christ denomination in the 1960s and the Universal Church in the early 1980s, Latin American–owned and produced Pentecostal television did not take root until the late 1980s. Since the early part of the decade, U.S. televangelists, such as Assemblies of God members Jimmy Swaggart and Jim Bakker, had dominated Protestant broadcasting in Latin America. Given the superior resources of the North American televangelists, it was only natural that they would serve as the trailblazers in Latin American Pentecostal television.

However, by the end of the decade, a few major *crente* churches, particularly in Brazil—such as the Assemblies of God, Foursquare Gospel Church, IURD, and International Church of the Grace of God (Igreja Internacional da Graca de Deus)—were producing their own programs, and in the case of the IURD, purchasing its own station. In November 1989, the Universal Church made Latin American history in buying the Rede Record television and radio stations for US $45 million.

With Record owned by the IURD and Rede Globo, Latin America's largest broadcasting corporation, by the staunch Catholic impresario, Roberto Marinho, the battle for Christian market share has erupted onto the small screens of Brazil. Both networks have aired *novelas* (evening soap operas) that satirized and even demonized each other. And Padre Marcelo Rossi, the dashing young star of the Catholic Charismatic Renewal, has appeared on numerous occasions in the late 1990s on Rede Globo's variety and talk shows.

Interestingly, the majority of Record's programming is commercial. Record reserves only the early morning and late night hours for IURD programs. Its commercial programming differs little from that of its rivals, even to the point of advertising "sinful" products such as alcohol and tobacco (Mariano 67-68). The church's decision to favor commercial over religious content on Record must be seen in purely economic terms. Secular programs attract more viewers and are thus more profitable. For a church that aspires to be as "universal" as its Catholic rival, a steady cash flow from such a lucrative medium as television is of crucial importance to the operation and expansion of its neo-Pentecostal empire. The IURD's preference for profane programming notwithstanding, Brazil now ranks second after the United States as the largest producer of Pentecostal television in the world (Freston 87).

Ever seeking a novel way to sell their product, large Latin American Pentecostal churches have joined the revolution in information technology and have developed websites on the Internet.[4] The IURD website even has its own chatroom in which members and the curious can discuss matters of faith in "real time." The small but increasing minority of Latin American believers who have Internet access can take pride in the fact that their denominations have embraced the latest mass medium as a novel way to market their religious product to those in need of healing.

The Pentecostal product is most appealing when it is sold in the packages of testimonials, music, and exorcism. Whether on television or radio or at rallies in soccer stadiums, the conversion narrative of a Pentecostal convert is often a powerfully emotive account of how Jesus or the Holy Spirit restored the believer's health or saved her from one of the demons of deprivation. Listeners and viewers experiencing their own crisis hear and see how someone from the same or similar social class dramatically turned his life around through acceptance of Jesus and affiliation with the church broadcasting the program. Such advertising is ubiquitous among even nonreligious commercial firms, of course: for example, dramatic before and after photos, along with testimony, of consumers who supposedly used a particular diet product invite obese North Americans to remake themselves as slim and fit men and women.

Pentecostal sales representatives also package their product in the emotional form of music. Romantic ballads, pop songs, and regional rhythms all set to evangelical lyrics blare from Pentecostal radio and television stations, in addition to worship services. The most musical of all the major branches of Christianity, Pentecostalism rouses its believers and attracts new converts through its melodic electric guitars, drums, tambourines, and synthesizers. Whether it is background mood music or moving hymns, melodic rhythms constitute such an integral part of *crente* worship that in Brazil they are sung and played during at least two-thirds of the typically two-hour long service. Likewise, songs of praise occupy significant time on Pentecostal radio and television programs. The decision to purchase the Pentecostal product—that is, to convert—is usually a highly emotional one made in the midst of personal crisis, and sacred music playing on an evangelical radio program can put the afflicted individual in the right state of mind that allows her to surrender herself to Jesus.

Fully cognizant of the fact that most Latin Americans convert to Pentecostalism through its premier product of faith healing, Pentecostal pastors advertise and package the doctrine and practice of *cura divina* in a manner that directly addresses the poverty-related afflictions of the popular classes. As a brand of faith healing, exorcism not only delivers believers from the demons of quotidian poverty but also serves as a useful marketing tool in the battle with diasporan religions for the souls of religious consumers in the Caribbean and Brazil. In Trinidad, Brazil, Haiti, and Cuba, among other Caribbean nations, the demons that Pentecostal pastors triumphantly exorcise from possessed worshipers are no ordinary evil spirits. Rather, the demonic agents are the Exus, or liminal trickster spirits of Umbanda, Candomblé, Vodou, and Santería. Considered amoral spiritual entities by the mothers and fathers of the saints who preside over diasporan *terreiros* (houses of worship), the Exus, such as Seven Skulls (Sete Caveiras in Brazil), possess no such ambiguity among Pentecostals. For *creyentes*, they are nothing less than tangible manifestations of pure evil that sow only misery and destruction in believers' lives. In driving Seven Skulls back to his lair at the cemetery through exorcism, Pentecostal pastors demonstrate to religious consumers the superior spiritual power of their faith. The Exus simply cannot resist the omnipotence of the Pentecostal Holy Spirit, and time and again they are "tied up" and expelled to their stations at the crossroads and cemeteries of Brazil and the Caribbean. It would be difficult to find a more literal demonization of a religious rival than the one in the late 1980s, when the Universal Church initiated a small-scale holy war against Umbanda and Candomblé: zealous members actually invaded and desecrated *terreiros* and assaulted mothers and fathers of the saints. The overarching Pentecostal strategy, then, is to portray its dynamic diasporan competitors as satanic cults that offer nothing but greater misery to religious consumers.

In conclusion, at the beginning of this century, Pentecostal products are outselling those of their diasporan competitors. Latin American Pentecostals have proved themselves to be the region's most skillful marketers of the faith by effectively employing every form of media available to them to offer their product to religious consumers. From the low-tech method of home visits to the high-tech Internet, *creyente* marketers have packaged and sold their product in Latin America's new religious marketplace with unrivaled acumen.

Army of Amateurs

The successful marketing of a product depends in large part on the skill and zeal of a firm's sale representatives. Without a motivated corps of salespersons who believe in the goods and services they are selling, even the most appealing product, whether spiritual or temporal, will often prove a difficult sell. And it is here again that Pentecostalism has developed a great advantage over its religious competitors. *Creyente* sales specialists are not well educated like their Catholic and mainline Protestant rivals but have proven themselves to be the superior vendors of religious goods and services for several reasons.

Perhaps of greatest importance is that each believer, whether clergy or laity, is a potential sales representative for his or her church. Contrariwise, it is only with the development of the Charismatic Renewal in the 1980s that the Latin American Catholic Church started to send lay missionaries to evangelize nominal Catholics door to door. Until then, what little proselytizing took place was carried out by priests. Conversely, for most of the nearly a century that Pentecostalism has been operating in the region, it is zealous lay evangelists who have done most of the knocking on the doors of Latin American homes. And when not making home visits, lay members sell the Pentecostal product very successfully to their family members, coworkers, and friends. Indeed, as has previously been mentioned, the majority of converts first come into contact with the faith along such interpersonal networks. Thus it is probably the case that these amateur sales representatives, the laity, have sold more Pentecostal products than the professionals, the pastorate. Leaving aside the fact that Pentecostal pastors outnumber Catholic priests in the region, Charismatic Protestantism enjoys the enormous competitive advantage of possessing millions of amateur salespersons who are eager to sell the same product that improved their lives to sisters and brothers, daughters and sons, and friends and colleagues.

If it were not enough to be able to rely on a force of dedicated amateurs to do most of the selling, Pentecostalism also excels at marketing because of the entrepreneurial skills and evangelical zeal of its professional sales representatives, the pastorate. Besides outnumbering their mainline Protestant and Catholic cohorts, creyente pastors enjoy several distinct advantages over their religious rivals. First, as ironic as it may seem, Pentecostal pastors are more likely to share the common elements of nationality and social class with prospective converts than Catholic clergy do with theirs. Surprisingly, in a region that is putatively the most Catholic in the world, in most countries the majority of the priests are foreign. Leading the region is the most Pentecostal nation, Guatemala, where in the early 1980s, an astounding 87 percent of the clergy were foreign born, especially from Spain; Bolivia, Mexico, Honduras, and Venezuela follow as nations in which more than two-thirds of the priests were foreigners, and non–Latin American clergy also constituted the majority in Chile, Paraguay, and Peru. Indeed, only in Uruguay, Ecuador, and top-ranking Colombia did national priests significantly outnumber their foreign confreres (Barret 1982). In diametrical opposition, the great majority of the Pentecostal pastorate in every Latin American country is native born. Other factors being equal, religious consumers are more likely to purchase products sold by compatriots who speak their same language fluently and share their national culture. Paradoxically, a religion that less than a century ago was brought to the region by foreign missionaries is now more authentically Latin American, at least in terms of its clergy, than the faith that has had half a millennium to sink its roots into the area from Argentina to Mexico.

Compatriotism, however, is not the only competitive advantage possessed by professional Pentecostal sales representatives. That *crente* pastors normally belong to the same socioeconomic class as those they seek to convert also makes for easier sale of Pentecostal products. In contrast, both nationality and educational level distance the majority of Catholic clergy from prospective practitioners. Years of seminary training place priests among the educational elite of Latin America. Even if they came from humble origins, they have acquired considerable sacred and secular knowledge through higher education and no longer speak the language of the unlettered *pueblo*. Hence, the gap between the highly educated foreign priest and the potential parishioner with no more than an elementary school education makes for a harder sell of the Catholic product.

In contradistinction, the professional Pentecostal salesman is not only a fellow Mexican, for example, but also an individual who had to quit school in the sixth grade to work to help support his family. He makes his sales pitch in the same colorful and often ungrammatical Spanish spoken by his prospective consumers, who will recognize him as both a *paisano* (compatriot) and a *carnal* (a term employed by the Mexican popular classes that roughly translates into the U.S. slang of "blood" or "brother"). Marketed in the popular idiom of the Latin American pueblo, the Pentecostal product proves a much easier sell than religious goods and services offered in sophisticated and often foreign-accented Spanish and Portuguese.

The final major competitive advantage enjoyed by the professional Pentecostal sales force derives from the organizational structure of many *crente* churches. In almost all of the storefront churches in which one or two houses of worship constitute the extent of the "denomination," and even in many large churches, the local pastor's salary depends on the tithes and offerings of members. The more pesos or reais collected at worship services, the greater the pastoral remuneration. The logic of the organization thus motivates the professional sales representatives to sell their dynamic product to an ever-greater number of religious consumers who can augment the Pentecostal vendor's salary and prestige through their donations. Those pastors who recruit a critical mass of congregants can earn enough to be able to quit their day jobs as bus drivers, popcorn vendors, security guards, and other low-ranking positions in the service sector. The cold logic of the free religious market means that those pastors who are not able to attract a critical mass of members will either continue to work in the "world" or might even be forced to suspend their pastoral vocation and close the church.

Among the major Pentecostal denominations of the region, most of which are relatively bureaucratized, the IURD stands out as an extreme in its emphasis on collecting tithes and offerings from believers. That typically a full hour of the two-hour IURD worship service is devoted to preaching, soliciting, and collecting the tithe should come as little surprise in a denomination in which pastoral promotions are largely dependent on a preacher's ability to multiply his talents. Those with a talent for collecting "ten percent for Jesus" and who have demonstrated unswerving fealty to chief bishop Edir Macedo become likely candidates for promotion to the highest church office of bishop. Even in churches such as Latin America's oldest Assemblies of God in Belem, where local pastors receive only reimbursement for travel expenses and nothing more, professional advancement hinges to a great extent on the ability to develop a sizeable congregation and collect tithes from it (Chesnut).

Whereas the professional Pentecostal sales representative is a religious entrepreneur, his Catholic cohort, as scholar and former Maryknoll missionary, Phillip Berryman, points out, is more of a bureaucrat (185–186). Pentecostal competition has led to a novel emphasis on tithing in parishes throughout the region, but in no way does clerical advancement depend on a priest's skill at fundraising, although this may change in the not too distant future as levels of competition increase. Thus, in nine decades of selling their Pentecostal product in Ibero-America, *creyente* churches have outsold the competition by reliance on a huge army of amateur vendors (the laity) and dedicated professionals (the pastorate), who outnumber their Protestant and Catholic counterparts and share the elements of nationality and class with potential consumers whose contributions to church coffers largely determine their pastoral fate.

Organizational Charisma

The final contributing factor to Pentecostalism's unmatched success in Latin America's new religious economy is its organizational structure, or polity in the ecclesiastical idiom. In accord with the logic of the commercial economy, the ways in which religious firms organize their operations have a direct bearing on their fate in the free market of faith. In the popular religious marketplace where consumers and producers are strapped for resources, those spiritual organizations that have structured their operations in efficient, cost-effective ways will enjoy obvious advantages over their competitors. On a larger plane, Pentecostalism as a whole benefits from its unrivaled differentiation. That is, the hundreds, if not thousands of distinct Pentecostal denominations that crowd the popular marketplace allow for a high degree of specialization and niche marketing that targets specific sets of consumers. For example, believers who are looking for a liberal dose of exorcism in worship services will find the Universal Church of particular interest. Hence, this final section will consider how Pentecostal polities have contributed to making Charismatic Protestantism the most dynamic producer of religious goods and services in Latin America.

The great differentiation of Pentecostalism obviates discussion of a uniform polity found in all denominations and churches. Rather, the multiplicity of congregations has resulted in a wide range of organizational structures. Nevertheless, the larger denominations have sufficient common organizational features to allow for the identification of key elements. A brief examination of two of the region's largest denominations, which in many ways occupy opposite ends of the organizational continuum, will shed light on the key factors that unite these two in their impressive growth.

The largest and one of the oldest denominations in Latin America, the Assemblies of God has adopted one of the more democratic and participatory forms of church government in a religion that manifests strong authoritarian and hierarchical tendencies. Although this denomination is one of the most bureaucratized, with myriad ecclesial departments and professional administrators, Assemblies of God polity allows for high levels of lay participation in the daily operation of the churches, particularly local ones. Numerous church offices, such as deacon, presbyter, and even doorman, permit lay members to become actively involved in the administration of their own churches. At annual general assemblies at the regional, state, and national levels, delegates discuss and vote on matters of church policy. Few other *crente* denominations can compete with the Assemblies' extraordinarily high levels of lay participation in the operation of tens of thousands of houses of worship. The ISER survey of Protestantism in Rio de Janeiro found that close to half, 43 percent, of all *Assembleianos* had served as church officers (ISER 37). My own investigation in Belem, based on a much smaller sample, discovered that an astounding four-fifths, 80 percent, of *Assembleianos* in the Amazonian city had held church office (Chesnut 135).

Despite such high levels of lay participation and ostensibly democratic forms of decision-making, however, strong authoritarian currents flow through the church. In the Assemblies of God in Belem, Latin America's oldest, the chief pastor, the *pastor-presidente*, had led the church for a quarter of a century and had concentrated ecclesiastical power to such a degree that he merits the moniker of Pentecostal pontiff. The most important decisions on church policy were made by the head pastor, often in consultation with a cabal of loyal salaried pastors. The term *participatory authoritarianism* best captures the dialectical model of the organizational structure of the Assemblies of God.

Brazil's fastest growing denomination, the IURD, shares the Assemblies' authoritarianism but not its high levels of lay participation. In fact, of all the major churches surveyed in Rio de Janeiro, the Universal had the lowest rate of lay engagement: only 13 percent of IURD members had ever held church office (ISER 37). In great contrast to lay participation in Assemblies worship services in which ordinary members read Bible passages, give testimony, lead hymns, and make announcements, IURD services are notable for their complete control by pastors. Lay participation is limited to ushering duties and highly choreographed testimony. When I queried an IURD member in Belem as to why lay persons were never invited to the altar to read a Bible passage or lead a prayer, she explained that the altar is so holy that those who are not pastors risk defiling it.

The church's episcopal polity, rare among Pentecostals, makes for one of the most authoritarian and centralized denominations. Chief bishop Macedo, concentrating even more power than the Catholic pontiff, involves himself in all aspects of ecclesiastical policy. Yet, despite its extreme authoritarianism, the IURD has grown to become the second largest Brazilian Pentecostal church in less than three decades. How has a denomination that is reminiscent of pre-Vatican II Catholicism in its exclusion of laity been able to attract millions of religious consumers? The answer lies in both IURD polity itself and the larger organizational structure of Latin American Pentecostalism in general. Although it seems counterintuitive, there is obviously a demand for brands of Pentecostalism in which the laity is restricted to a relatively passive role in church life while autocratic pastors monopolize the production and administration of religious goods and services. Indeed, most Latin Americans belonging to the popular classes are accustomed to such relationships in the secular world and are not necessarily looking for egalitarianism in their religious lives. And those who are can choose from other Pentecostal churches, such as the Assemblies of God, that offer greater opportunities for lay engagement.

Herein lies the second component of the IURD's organizational success. The range and diversity of Latin American Pentecostalism has led to a high degree of specialization and niche marketing. Thus the IURD fits the bill for religious consumers who prefer the traditional division between laity and clergy, as well as those who are attracted to exorcism, prosperity theology, and aggressive combat against Umbanda and Candomblé. The Universal Church in Rio de Janeiro, for example, has the highest percentage of former practitioners of African-Brazilian religion among its ranks of any major Pentecostal denomination (ISER 18). Consumers looking for extreme asceticism and draconian moral and comportmental codes gravitate toward God Is Love or similar denominations.

In effect, there are so many varieties of Pentecostalism available in the religious marketplace that consumers can choose their brands according to preferences in gender, class, age, musical tastes, and so on. IURD membership, for example, is the most heavily female (81 percent in Rio) in a religion in which women typically outnumber men two to one (ISER 60). In class terms, the IURD attracts the poorest cariocas, while the "renewed" or breakaways from the mainline churches that have Pentecostalized, such as the Renewed Presbyterian

(Iglesia Presbiteriana Renovada) appeal to those with higher income levels (ISER 10). Of course, Catholicism is also offered in many varieties in the religious marketplace but not to the same extent found in the hundreds of different denominations of Pentecostalism.

The final element of Pentecostal polity that gives this branch of ecstatic Protestantism a competitive edge over its rivals is its preference for charisma to theological training for its professional sales representatives or pastors. While larger and older denominations, particularly the Assemblies of God, have institutionalized to the point that its salaried pastors are required to have several years of seminary training, Pentecostalism, as a popular religion, has historically emphasized spiritual gifts over theological education. That a male believer with not more than an elementary school education but a healthy dose of charisma can rise through the pastoral ranks of most denominations opens the ministry up to tens of thousands of impoverished male believers who would never qualify for the rigorous educational requirements of the Catholic priesthood or mainline Protestant ministry. The result has been a proliferation of Pentecostal pastors, who in Brazil, the largest Catholic nation on earth, now outnumber priests by two to one.

With a larger pastorate, there are more Pentecostal preachers available to evangelize Latin Americans door to door, as statistics from El Salvador dramatically reveal. In the late 1980s, some 77 percent of Salvadoran Protestants surveyed had been visited at home by a pastor, while only 28 percent of practicing Catholics and just 16 percent of nonpracticing or nominal Catholics had received a visit from a priest (Aguilar et al. 120). An additional advantage of Pentecostal and Protestant polity in general is its allowance for married clergy. Indeed, single pastors are often pressured to find a wife, lest they become objects of gossip or speculation about their sex lives. Given the lack of enthusiasm for celibacy on the part of Latin American men, Protestantism in general enjoys an enormous advantage over Catholicism in recruiting and retaining professional sales representatives.

If at the beginning of the twenty-first century, Latin American Christianity has Pentecostalized to the extent that the Catholic Church's most dynamic movement is its own version of Pentecostalism, it is because Charismatic Protestantism has developed superior religious products and marketed them in the free market of faith more successfully than its competitors have. Unlike Catholicism, which enjoyed a monopoly on religious production that lasted more than four centuries, Pentecostalism had to compete for religious consumers if it were to survive and grow in the region. Thus, from its arrival in the first decades of the twentieth century, Pentecostalism had to convince Catholics, predominantly nominal ones, that Pentecostal products are superior. And this it has done with such success that on this past Sunday (September 2000) there were more *crentes* worshiping in their churches than Catholics at Mass in Brazil the largest "Catholic nation" on earth.

Such is the situation because Pentecostal churches, responding to popular consumer demand, developed products that offer healing of the afflictions of poverty and positive personal transformation for those who have been rejected and stigmatized by societies that have the steepest socioeconomic pyramids in the world. Amateur and professional Pentecostal sales representatives have marketed the product to religious consumers with great zeal and acumen. Finally, the organizational structure of both Pentecostalism in general and specific denominations has helped propel this ecstatic religion to its current commanding position in Latin America's religious marketplace. It is to Pentecostalism's main Christian competitor, the Catholic Charismatic Renewal, that this study of the region's new religious economy now turns.

A Preferential Option for the Spirit

The Catholic Charismatic Renewal

While Base Christian Communities (CEBs) struggle to maintain a presence throughout Latin America, a contemporaneous Catholic movement easily fills soccer stadiums in the major cities of the region with tens of
thousands of fervent believers. At the beginning of the twenty-first century, the
Catholic Charismatic Renewal (CCR) stands as the largest and most dynamic
movement in the Latin American church. Even leaders of the liberationist
wing of the Catholic Church, who often view Charismatics as alienated middle-class reactionaries, admit that no other ecclesial movement has the CCR's
power to congregate and mobilize the faithful. In Brazil, the CCR's popular
appeal is not limited to the realm of the sacred. In 1999, the latest CD of
samba-inspired religious music sung by the young star of the Brazilian CCR,
Padre Marcelo Rossi, sold more copies than any other recording artist, including So Pra Contrariar (an immensely popular *pagode* band),[1] in Latin America's largest country.

At this point, many readers with some acquaintance with the Latin American religious landscape must be wondering why the region's most vibrant
Catholic lay movement has received precious little academic attention. If the
CCR's popular appeal has yet to register among students of Latin American religion, it is because liberation theology and CEBs have captured the hearts and
minds of many North American and Latin American social scientists during
the past quarter century. Adopting a "preferential option for the poor" and attempting to build the Kingdom of Heaven on Latin American soil through political and social transformation proved far more appealing to many scholars

than a socially disengaged movement dedicated to transforming individual lives through conversion to Jesus. Moreover, as Brazilian sociologist Maria das Dores Machado has pointed out, many scholars of Latin American religion have ties to the progressive sectors of the Catholic church or to the ecumenical movements in the region and are less interested in religious groups that tend to be sectarian and politically conservative.

Academic sympathies aside, however, the Charismatic Renewal demands scholarly attention because of its extraordinary appeal among Catholic laity and its unanimous approval by national episcopacies. If the perennial shortage of priests has eased somewhat in the last two decades, and if the Catholic church is finally employing mass media, especially television, as a tool for evangelization, it is due to the Charismatics, whose missionary zeal rivals their chief competitors in the religious marketplace, the Pentecostals. Thus in this chapter I focus on analyzing the reasons for the Renewal's rapid growth in Ibero-America among Catholic laity and its approval and promotion among the episcopacy. Since there are no academic histories of the CCR in the region, I also examine the major historical trends during the movement's three-decade existence.

Pentecostal Catholics

Although the CCR manifests diverse local and national characteristics, it is a Catholic lay movement that seeks to revitalize the church through the power of the third person of the Trinity, the Holy Spirit. That both U.S. and Latin American Charismatics initially called themselves Pentecostal Catholics is revealing. Catholic Charismatics share the same ecstatic spirituality with Protestant Pentecostals. Like Pentecostals, Catholic Charismatics are pneumacentrists—that is, the Holy Spirit occupies center stage in the religious praxis of believers. Through baptism in the Holy Spirit, individual Charismatics are endowed with gifts of the Spirit such as glossolalia (speaking in tongues) and faith healing. For both Charismatics and Pentecostals, these charismata are powerful and palpable proof of the presence of the Spirit in their lives. In addition to pneumacentrism, Charismatics tend to share, though to a lesser degree, the biblical fundamentalism and asceticism of their Pentecostal progenitors. Of course, what most distinguishes Charismatics from other Catholics is their special emphasis on the transformative power of the Holy Spirit. And separating Charismatics from Pentecostals, particularly in Latin America, are the formers' continued fealty to the pontiff and Virgin Mary. As the CCR has expanded in Latin America, the Virgin has moved from an initially peripheral position in the movement to the center, where she now constitutes, more than any other element, the dividing line that separates Charismatics from Pentecostals. During the past decade, the CCR not only has become the largest and most vibrant Catholic lay movement in Latin America but also is thriving in parts of Asia and Africa, unsurprisingly in the same regions where Pentecostalism has grown rapidly since the 1950s.

The most recent figures from the International Catholic Charismatic Renewal Services (ICCRS), the CCR's international headquarters at the Vatican, estimate that some 73 million Catholics belong to the movement in almost two hundred countries (www.iccrs.org/CCR%20worldwide.htm). Latin American Charismatics probably number between 22 and 25 million, accounting for approximately one-third of the global total (*Comunicado Mensal* 4/97). With a Charismatic community of between 8 and 10 million, Brazil constitutes the center of the Latin American CCR. Since fewer than 10 percent of Brazil's 122 million self-proclaimed Catholics actively participate in church life, it is very likely that at least one-half of all active Catholics in Brazil are Charismatics. The same appears to be the case in El Salvador, where other Catholic lay groups are dwarfed by the CCR with its approximately 400,000 members (Garrard-Burnett 2001). Hard data for other Latin American countries are lacking, but the CCR is the largest and most active Catholic lay movement in most nations.

Made in the U.S.A.

Like Pentecostalism, its Protestant forebear, the Catholic Charismatic Renewal is an imported religious product from the United States. In the late 1960s, the same Charismatic spirituality that had given birth to Pentecostalism in the first decade of the twentieth century and which in the 1950s and 1960s had led to the formation of Charismatic communities among mainline Protestants, such as Episcopalians and Presbyterians, finally penetrated the U.S. Catholic Church. The CCR specifically traces its genesis to the "Duquesne Weekend" in early 1967. During the weekend of February 17, some twenty-five students at Duquesne University (which appropriately was founded by members of the Congregation of the Holy Ghost) in Pittsburgh gathered for a spiritual retreat with two professors who had already experienced baptism in the Holy Spirit under the direction of Presbyterian Charismatics. In a weekend of intense prayer and fellowship, many of the students were baptized by the Holy Spirit and received charismata, marking the first event in which a group of Catholics experienced Pentecostal spirituality.

From Duquesne, the nascent movement spread rapidly to other college campuses, foremost of which were Notre Dame and Michigan State Universities. During the next decade, the Renewal grew rapidly, spawning Charismatic prayer groups and "covenant communities" in which members sought to develop their spiritual lives in a communal setting. By the mid 1970s, the CCR had expanded to the point where it could pack stadiums on its native soil with thousands of Charismatics. In 1974, approximately twenty-five thousand believers attended a CCR international conference at Notre Dame. Three years later in Kansas City, some fifty thousand Protestant and Catholic Charismatics participated in an ecumenical assembly, which drew extensive press coverage (Soneira 474).

These two events are not only significant for their size but also for two major themes that were underscored at the assemblies. At the Notre Dame convention, a mass healing ritual led by Dominican priest Francis MacNutt propelled the product of faith healing to the center of Charismatic religious praxis. Father MacNutt, who already was a pioneer in exporting the CCR to Ibero-America, consolidated his position as a leading proponent of faith healing in the movement with the publication of his book called *Healing* in 1974 (Bord and Faulkner 93). At the Kansas City gathering, the ecumenism of the assembly took center stage. From its inception, the CCR in the United States had been strongly ecumenical, particularly with mainline Protestant Charismatics (known as neo-Pentecostals or Neopentecostals). Many CCR prayer groups included Protestants, and even some covenant communities counted "separated brethren" among their ranks.[2] Although many, if not most, of the original CCR groups in Latin America were founded by ecumenical pastoral teams, faith healing has proven to be a much more attractive good than ecumenism south of the Rio Grande.

Mirroring the pattern of Pentecostal expansion to Latin America more than a half-century before, the CCR was brought to the region by professional sales representatives (or evangelists) only a few years after its birth in the city of steel. In this case, Catholic priests, mainly Dominican and Jesuit, exported the CCR to major cities throughout Latin America in the early 1970s. The same Dominican priest, Francis MacNutt, who emerged as a pioneer in faith healing played a pivotal role in establishing the CCR in several Latin American nations, including Mexico, Colombia, Peru, Chile, and others. True to the movement's ecumenism in the United States, MacNutt's pastoral team often included North American Protestant ministers (Cleary 215).

Typical of the CCR's pattern of expansion to Latin America is Guatemala, where the movement was invited to demonstrate its novel spiritual products by Cardinal Mario Casariego. After an aborted attempt by two U.S. religious to introduce the CCR to Guatemala in 1972, Fernando Mancilla, a prominent Guatemalan layman who had been active in the Cursillo and who had adhered to the CCR in Honduras, requested permission to start a Charismatic prayer group in Guatemala City.[3] The archdiocese instructed Mancilla to wait and then seized the initiative from lay hands at the end of 1973, when Cardinal Casariego invited Jesuit priest Harold Cohen of New Orleans to lead a Charismatic retreat in December for a select group of thirty priests. A few months later, Monseñor Ricardo Hamm, the head of apostolic movements in the archdiocese, led a similar retreat for religious and laity. In 1974, Father Rodolfo Mendoza founded the first Charismatic prayer group in the country in his parish of La Asunción in Guatemala City (Delgado 233–240; Hugo Estrada, personal communication, July 13, 1999). Already by mid-1974 the archdiocese had created a pastoral service team to supervise the CCR. It was originally headed by Auxiliary Bishop Monseñor José Pellecer (Estrada, personal communication).

According to Father Hugo Estrada, the CCR's current national advisor, the first prayer groups in Guatemala began among the same sectors in the church as in other Latin American countries. Reflecting the CCR's rarefied birthplace, a U.S. university, the first Catholics to join the movement in Guatemala, Mexico, Brazil, and many other Latin American countries tended to be middle- and upper-middle-class believers. Moreover, many of the original lay leaders had been active in the Cursillo movement (Estrada, personal communication). As in most other Latin American countries, in Guatemala the CCR initially embraced the ecumenism that formed an integral part of the U.S. movement, but within a few years it became clear that fraternal relations with Protestant Charismatics would not become a salient characteristic of the Renewal in the region.

Whereas in many Latin American nations, such as Mexico and Guatemala, leading bishops took the initiative to invite North American Charismatic priests to introduce the movement to their countries, the CCR was imported to Brazil without official episcopal invitation. Jesuit priest Edward Dougherty (also from New Orleans) and compatriot Father Harold Rahm were to serve as agents of the Renewal's expansion to Brazil. Having been baptized in the Holy Spirit at a Charismatic retreat at Michigan State University in early 1969, Father Dougherty felt moved to share the fruits of the CCR in Brazil, where he had already served as a missionary. In May he returned to the city of Campinas in the state of São Paulo and communicated his newfound spirituality to his Jesuit confrere, Father Rahm. Conversations with Dougherty, reinforced by the book *Aglow with the Spirit*, by Robert C. Frost impelled Rahm to embrace Charismatic spirituality, and within months he was organizing retreats for Catholics in Campinas, which he called Prayer Meetings in the Holy Spirit (Encontros de Oração no Espirito Santo).

After finishing a degree in theology in Toronto, Father Dougherty returned permanently to Brazil in 1972 and almost immediately, with the blessing of a free travel pass on Varig Airlines, began flying throughout the vast country to spread the CCR to all corners of the nation. Dougherty's typical course of action after arriving in a new city was to invite a select group of priests and religious to a retreat in which the fundamentals of the new movement were explained. Fervent prayer and fellowship created an intense spiritual climate so that some participants received baptism in the Holy Spirit. Once Dougherty had flown on to another city, the clerics and sisters who had adhered to the Renewal were to become the agents of its expansion in their respective parishes. In the beginning, the usual pattern of expansion was for Charismatic priests and religious to invite select lay persons to participate in retreats and prayer groups. As was the case in most other Ibero-American countries, the first Brazilian lay participants tended to be active middle-class Catholics, many having been members of the Cursillo (Dougherty, personal commication, July 16, 1998).

Yellow Caution Light from the Bishops

During the Renewal's formative years in the early and mid-1970s, the most common position adopted by the Latin American episcopacies was one of critical tolerance. Most individual bishops who took a public stand on the movement followed their U.S. counterparts and the pope, both of whom had given the Renewal a yellow light to proceed with caution. Meeting in 1969, U.S. bishops had concluded that the CCR should be permitted to develop, but with proper episcopal and sacerdotal supervision (McDonnell Vol. 1, 210). Pope Paul VI reaffirmed the U.S. church's stance when in 1975 he received a delegation of Charismatics in Rome during the celebration of the CCR's first international congress (Soneira 473).

The Panamanian episcopal conference's collective letter on the CCR, drafted in 1975, typifies the most prevalent attitude toward the CCR among the few national bishops' conferences that had considered the matter at the time. The Panamanian bishops called on Charismatics to accept clerical and episcopal authority, to participate in sacramental life, and to embrace the Virgin and saints. After their call for obedience to ecclesiastical authorities, the leaders of the Panamanian church concluded on a positive note, hoping that the "the CCR may be an efficacious means to make us more involved in the evangelization of our people" (McDonnell Vol. 2, 103).

Influencing the predominant "proceed with caution" attitude among Latin American bishops were not only the positions of the U.S. episcopacy and the Vatican but also the dynamics of the region's new religious economy and concern with potential threats to their own spiritual authority. On the first score, the CCR arrived in Latin America at a time when the Catholic Church was in a state of crisis. Although the Latin American church had suffered a perennial shortage of priests since the colonial era and extremely low rates of church attendance, this did not develop into an institutional crisis until significant religious competition emerged in the 1950s in the form of Pentecostalism. Until Pentecostal churches began reaping a bonanza harvest of nominal Catholic souls at mid-century, the Latin American church, enjoying a monopoly on religious production, could afford to ignore the paucity of clergy and masses of disengaged laity. Before the new religious products were offered by pastors of the Assemblies of God and Foursquare Gospel Church, among others, the poor Latin Americans (who constituted the majority of the population in most countries) had no other culturally appropriate Christian alternatives in which they could satisfy their religious needs.[4] Thus it was only when the Catholic Church faced serious religious competition for the first time in its four-and-a-half-centuries in Latin America that perennial institutional debilities reached the point of crisis.

During the CCR's first decade of development in Latin America, it was common knowledge among the national episcopal conferences that Pentecostalism was expanding at meteoric rates. Growing concern with the "sects" and the CCR's potential role in combating them was a major theme at the Second Meeting of the General Secretaries of the Latin American Episcopal Conferences, held in Rio de Janeiro in mid-January 1976. In establishing a working group on masonry and "sects," the bishops called for a general study of religion in Latin America that would illuminate the "phenomenon of the sects." Eschewing a "bellicose attitude" toward their new competitors, the episcopal leaders called for positive forms of evangelization and emphasized the importance of "dynamic communities" (*comunidades vivas*) and the facilitation of "authentic expressions of religiosity." After indicating Jehovah's Witnesses, Spiritists, and the Assemblies of God (Pentecostals) as "sects" of particular concern, the Latin American bishops identified the Charismatic Renewal as a movement that could stanch the flow of Catholics into Pentecostal churches. "In relation to the latter [Assemblies of God], we think that a correct and just appreciation of the Charismatic groups can establish a point of attraction which offers an alternative to the disquietude of our times" (*Comunicado Mensal* 1/76). In Curaçao, priests who were alarmed by the exodus of Catholics to Pentecostal churches put the bishops' ideas into practice by founding the first Charismatic prayer groups in the mid-1970s as a way to withstand Protestant competition (Boudewijnse 179).

Just a month after the Rio meeting, church representatives, gathering at the Meeting of Delegates of Ecumenism of the Latin American Episcopal Conferences in Bogotá, Colombia, also concluded that scientific and pastoral studies were needed of what they termed "free religious movements." Such studies, they urged, should specifically focus on the proselytism of Pentecostals, Seventh-day Adventists, Jehovah's Witnesses, and Mormons (*Comunicado Mensal* 2/76). Similarly, at the first general Latin American bishops' conference since the genesis of the CCR in the region, meeting in Puebla, Mexico, in 1979, the episcopate underscored the threat of the "sects" while making pastoral recommendations that converged perfectly with the action and mission of the CCR. In addition to mentioning the "invasion of the sects" as one of the important problems facing the Latin American church (Conferencia Episcopal Latinoamericana [CEL] 140), the bishops urged diligent study of the reasons for the rapid growth of "free religious movements." The aim of such study was to develop a pastoral plan of action that would respond to the needs of believers, which Pentecostals seemed to be addressing successfully. The needs identified by the bishops at Puebla—animated liturgy, a sense of fraternity, and active missionary participation—fit the CCR like a glove (CEL 310). The fulfillment of such religious needs constituted the very raison d'être of the Charismatic Renewal. In accord with the strategy of caution, however, ecclesiastical leaders at Puebla found it necessary to reiterate the need for pastoral discernment and guidance to prevent "dangerous deviations" (CEL 76).

Despite the Renewal's potential for revitalizing the Latin American Catholic Church in the face of fierce Pentecostal competition, the movement's pneumacentrism compelled the majority of bishops who made early pronouncements on the subject to urge great caution in the CCR's development. Chief among several major episcopal concerns during the Renewal's first decade was the movement's potential threat to the ecclesiastical authority of church fathers. Many bishops and priests feared that with direct access to the Holy Spirit, Charismatics would no longer feel the need for sacerdotal mediation. Why confess one's sins to an ecclesiastical agent of the Spirit when a direct channel to the Holy Ghost is offered through the Renewal? Thus, practically every episcopal statement, no matter how positive its content, demanded obedience and fealty to church authorities. For example, in one of the region's first episcopal statements on the CCR in 1975, Mexican bishops clearly stated that judgment about the authenticity and applications of charismata belonged to themselves. In claiming the omnipotent spiritual gift of discernment for itself, the Mexican episcopacy positioned itself as the CCR's final arbiter (McDonnell Vol.1, 100). Invested with the spiritual power to discern the direction of the movement, the bishops thus placed themselves in a position to prevent the CCR from becoming a parallel movement that would challenge institutional authority and operate on the periphery of church life.

While "proceed with caution" was the predominant episcopal dictum in the 1970s, a small minority of bishops opted either to embrace and promote the CCR or to proscribe it from their dioceses. Mexican bishop Carlos Talavera and his Colombian confrere Monseñor Diego Jaramillo were among the first of the Latin American episcopacy to adhere to the Renewal. Both bishops attended the first meeting of Latin American Catholic Charismatics (ECCLA I) held in Bogotá in February 1973 (Cleary 217). Under the direction of the Charismatic trailblazer, Father MacNutt, twenty-three priests from Colombia, Mexico, Puerto Rico, Venezuela, the Dominican Republic, and the United States assembled to discuss ways of propagating the CCR throughout the region (Uribe Jaramillo 29–30). Since ECCLA I, Bishop Jaramillo has published four books on various aspects of the Renewal, including the role of glossolalia and papal relations with the movement, and was appointed to the executive council of the ICCRS in 1987 (Soneira 476). Writing just six years after the CCR's import to Colombia, Jaramillo already perceived the new movement's importance to the Latin American church: "The Charismatic Renewal has become one of the most serious pastoral efforts of the church to attract the multitudes to the faith and conversion through the action of the Holy Spirit" (Jaramillo 124).

In diametric opposition to his Colombian coreligionist, the conservative Mexican Bishop Miguel García of Mazatlan saw not the action of the Holy Spirit in the CCR but the "smoke of Satan that has infiltrated the church" (Blancarte 359). For obvious reasons, Monseñor García banned the Renewal from his diocese. Fellow conservative Bishop Antonio López of Durango became one of the first Latin American church leaders to effectively ban the CCR in his diocese in 1977. Charging the CCR with elitism, fundamentalism, Protestant contamination, "charismania" (excessive emphasis on spiritual gifts), paraclericalism, and authoritarianism, the bishop ordered reforms that eviscerated the movement. His first commandment called for the CCR in Durango to change its name from the Movement of Christian Renewal in the Holy Spirit to the Prayer Group Movement. The bishop's prohibition of the fundamentals of CCR practice– clapping, "rhythmic movement," baptism in the Spirit, and all spiritual gifts—would strip the movement of its charisma, and thus its distinguishing characteristic (*Documentación e Información Católica* [DIC] 12/8/77, 681–687).

One of the most vociferous opponents among the Mexican episcopacy of the "invasion of the sects," Monseñor López belonged to a minority espiscopal current that viewed the CCR, because of its Pentecostal origins and influence, not as an effective pastoral response but as a dangerous gateway for even greater conversions of Catholics to Protestantism. In a major international document on the relation between the CCR and ecumenism, one of the movement's leading intellectuals, Kilian McDonnell, writing in 1978, responded to such critics of the Renewal by underscoring the fact that the Pentecostal boom was already well under way at the time of the CCR's arrival in Latin America (Vol. 3, 235). Nevertheless, bishops such as López could point to instances in which Catholic Charismatics had opted to continue practicing their pneumacentric brand of Christianity in Pentecostal churches. Scholar Barbara Boudewijnse reports in her 1985 study of the CCR in Curaçao that a local prayer group leader who was removed from her position because of her denigration of the Virgin left the church along with some one hundred fellow Charismatics and founded her own Pentecostal church (194 n. 9). Sociologist Silvia Fernandes recounts a similar incident in Bairro Mare on the urban periphery of Rio de Janeiro. After three years of tension with the local priest over issues of CCR autonomy, the local lay leader left the church for a neo-Pentecostal congregation in which he quickly became a pastor (S. Fernandes 111).

That no national episcopal conference in Ibero-America has, to date, proscribed the CCR is strong evidence of the relatively weak institutional position of those who would expel the movement from the region. Thus, among the great majority of bishops who either individually or collectively drafted positions on the CCR at the diocesan and national levels, "proceed with caution" was the watchword during the CCR's initial decade of operation. And among the majority of the Latin American episcopacy who took no public position on the Renewal in their diocese, tacit approval and indifference are the most common attitudes, positions that allowed Charismatic prayer groups to at least operate, if not multiply.

The CCR from Bottom to Top

Rarely facing active episcopal resistance, the CCR continued to expand and consolidate throughout the 1970s. At the structural base of the movement, Charismatic prayer groups introduced hundreds of thousands of Latin American Catholics to a new and dynamic way of practicing their faith, while at the top, CCR leaders formed executive committees from the diocesan to international levels. The sine qua non of the CCR, prayer groups are relatively small assemblies of Charismatics that meet on a weekly basis to deepen and renew their spiritual life through prayer and fellowship. The grupos de oración (their name in Spanish) range in size from ten to three hundred, but most probably average between twenty-five and thirty-five. Adding to their distinct identity are the colorful names, such as Light and Love and Come Lord Jesus, adopted by many groups. Others simply take the name of their local parish.

Meeting for two to three hours at their parish church, a CCR center, or a member's home, believers are led by lay leaders in diverse forms of prayer, including contemplative praise, silent petitions, spontaneous glossolalia, and hymns.[5] Of course, it is the emphasis on pneumacentric praise that distinguishes CCR prayer groups from traditional prayer and reflection groups. Prayer in which the believer feels the transformative power of the Holy Spirit is the essence of such groups. Spirited songs, speaking in tongues, faith healing, and testimonies of conversion provide Catholics with a novel way to practice their faith. Those seeking a more experiential and animated type of faith no longer have to seek out Pentecostal churches, such as the Universal Church of the Kingdom of God, for worship that includes both body and soul.

During the Renewal's first decade in Latin America, prayer groups constituted the principal port of entry into the movement. The predominant pattern of recruitment involved members inviting family and friends to experience a new way of being Catholic in the prayer groups. Since the first adherents to the CCR were disproportionately middle-class, practicing Catholic women, those who joined during the 1970s and well into the 1980s tended to have the commonalties of class, gender, and the active practice of their faith. Although the CCR is now expanding among the Latin American popular classes, the movement during most of its short history has been solidly middle class. In the early 1970s, in one of the first studies conducted on the CCR in Latin America, researcher Pedro Oliveira found that the majority of Brazilian Catholic Charismatics were middle and upper-middle class. More than one-half of the Charismatics surveyed had at least a secondary education, and only 1 percent was illiterate (Oliveira et al. 24). Even twenty years later, Brazilians averaged only five years of primary school education (UNDP). In Mexico, the Holy Ghost Missionaries, who took charge of introducing the CCR in Mexico City, had historically directed their pastoral activities toward the middle and upper classes. Indeed, Santa Cruz, their principal parish, is located in the Pedregal, one of the city's most exclusive residential districts (Díaz de la Serna 30).

After social class, gender was and continues to be one of the salient demographic characteristics of the Charismatic community in Latin America. Precise figures do not exist, but since the CCR's arrival in the region, women have comprised approximately two-thirds of the movement in Ibero-America. The study of Brazilian Charismatics in the mid-1970s reported women accounting for 71 percent of CCR membership (Oliveira et al. 24). A 1994 Brazilian survey found the gender ratio had remained constant at 70 percent female. Interestingly, the same poll found that while women also predominated in Base Christian Communities in Brazil, they did so at a significantly lower rate of 57 percent (Prandi 16). In Mexico, the archdiocesan coordinator of the Renewal in Latin America's largest city, layman Miguel Ramírez, estimated that the country's female Charismatics outnumber their male brothers in faith by a ratio of two to one. The predominance of women in the movement has greatly influenced Charismatic religious practice, but the CCR is no different from the region's other major religious traditions in which females represent the majority of active practitioners.

The third major commonality among Charismatics in the CCR's first decade is their prior status as active Catholics. In other words, the majority of those joining the Renewal in the 1970s were already active practitioners of their

Catholic faith; moreover, 80 percent had participated in other church lay groups, particularly the Cursillo (Oliveira et al. 27). Boudewijnse discovered the same pattern of expansion in Curaçao, where the CCR attracted its first followers among the ranks of practicing Catholics (179), and CCR lay leaders in Guatemala and Mexico reported the same recruitment strategy in those two countries (Sheny de Góngora, personal communication, July 8, 1999; Miguel Ramirez, personal communication, June 24, 1999). Thus, in its initial phase, the CCR was rarely attracting nominal Catholics, much less those who had converted to Pentecostalism. Rather, Pentecostal Catholicism drew from the ranks of active middle-class practitioners, predominantly female, who were seeking to renew and deepen their spiritual life.

Structured Charisma

While prayer groups expanded at the base of the CCR, executive committees created in the 1970s from the parish to international levels gave the movement a well-defined organizational structure and increasing legitimacy among the Latin American episcopacy. Within the first few years of its arrival in the region, many Latin American bishops moved to integrate the CCR into the national ecclesiastical bureaucracy through the creation of national service commissions or teams. By mid-1974, episcopal leaders in Brazil, Mexico, and Guatemala had established such commissions. The latter case provides a clear example of how bishops in some countries acted with uncharacteristic haste to attempt to seize control of the movement from lay hands.

Having been baptized in the Holy Spirit at a CCR encounter in Honduras, prominent Guatemalan lay leader Fernando Mancilla in February 1973 met with Bishop Ricardo Hamm, the head of apostolic movements in the archdiocese of Guatemala City, to discuss his desire of introducing the Renewal to the country. Monseñor Hamm told Mancilla to wait for episcopal instruction before taking any action, and by the end of the year the Guatemalan church's supreme leader, Cardinal Mario Casariego, had seized the initiative from Mancilla's lay hands by inviting the North American Charismatic priest Harold Cohen to conduct a retreat for a select group of his Guatemalan sacerdotal brethren. Shortly after the Cohen retreat, Bishop José Ramiro Pellecer held a similar one for religious and laity in early 1974. The first Charismatic prayer group in Guatemala was founded not by a lay leader, but by a priest who had adhered to the Renewal after the Cohen retreat. Father Rodolfo Mendoza, who had been baptized by the Holy Spirit at the Cohen retreat, started the pioneering prayer group in his parish located in Zone Two of the national capital. Greatly accelerating the wheels of the ecclesiastical bureaucracy, in June 1974 Cardinal Casariego estab-

lished a national Pastoral Service Team, headed by Monseñor Pellecer, to supervise the CCR. While lay leaders comprised the majority of the Pastoral Service
Team members, ultimate authority lay with Bishops Pellecer and Casariego (Delgado 234–240; Estrada, personal communication).

In Brazil it was not bishops but priests who took the initiative in establishing
a national-level executive committee. With approval from the local archbishop
in May 1973, CCR founding fathers Edward Dougherty and Harold Rahm created the National Service Commission in Campinas (*Comunicado Mensal*
9/73). A mixed group of twenty lay leaders, priests, and nuns formed the original national team (*Comunicado Mensal* 5/75). Currently headquartered in Ita-
juba, in the state of Minas Gerais, the national commission, like others in Latin
America, is charged with developing and coordinating countrywide events and
activities and defining and evaluating CCR goals and projects.

Concurrent with the establishment of national commissions, CCR sacerdotal and episcopal leaders in early 1973 founded a regional commission, the
Latin American Catholic Charismatic Council (CONCCLAT), at the first
ECCLA conference in Bogotá (Jaramillo 29–30). CONCCLAT, currently headquartered in Bogotá, exercises at the international level the same function as the
national commissions. One of the council's most visible achievements is the organization of biennial ECCLA conferences, which assemble not only Latin
American CCR leaders but also their hispanophone coreligionists from Spain
and the United States (Soneira 476). After international and national executive
commissions were created in the early part of the decade, similar coordinating
councils were established at diocesan and parochial levels as the movement expanded through the 1970s. Thus by the end of the CCR's first ten years in
Ibero-America, the movement had already begun to experience the institutionalization of charisma.

Separating from Protestant Brethren

As part of the institutionalization process and the intensification of religious
competition, the CCR had jettisoned its initial ecumenism by the end of the
1970s. At the beginning of the 1980s, an ecumenical Catholic Charismatic
would have been hard-pressed to find the type of early CCR prayer groups that
united Protestants and Catholics in worship. However, that the Latin American
movement's ecumenism was so short lived should be of little surprise, given the
rapidly shifting dynamics of the region's emerging religious marketplace. The
CCR's ecumenism developed in the United States where Catholicism is a minority church that had to compete with Protestantism for North American souls
but did not have to contend with a religious monopolist. In almost diametrical

opposition, the Latin American church was a religious hegemon whose monopoly was rapidly crumbling as a result of the "invasion of the sects"—that is, Pentecostalism. The ecumenical agenda emerging from Vatican II made little sense in Latin America where Pentecostalism was rapidly expanding at the expense of the Catholic Church.[6] To extend a fraternal embrace to the very same "separated brethren" who were raiding the Catholic flock could have only accelerated the exodus of Catholics to Pentecostal churches. Hence, from the outset, the ecumenism introduced to the region by North American Charismatic priests was destined to become an unviable import.

Early episcopal pronouncements on the CCR are replete with admonishments on the dangers of "false ecumenism." The Mexican bishop of Ciudad Juárez, for example, in his 1976 pastoral instruction on the CCR, wrote, "In fact, there have been Catholics who have lost the faith or left the Catholic Church after entering into contact with these ecumenical groups of reflection in the Holy Spirit" (DIC 1976). Three years later, Monseñor Ezequiel Perea, bishop of San Luis Potosí, prohibited CCR prayer groups from allowing Protestants to participate. Like his confrere on the Texas border, the bishop worried that ecumenical groups could lead to further Catholic losses:

> So the separated brothers and sisters, upon exchanging their reflections with those of Catholics, even without intending to, cause confusion among the faithful. They insinuate a false liberation from the Magisterium of the church, they devalue those Catholic truths that they don't admit and promote a loss of Catholic identity, which tends to sacrifice the truth in the name of ecumenical unity. And, in fact, there have been some Catholics who have followed this path away from the church, or who have become indifferent, believing themselves free from submission to the Magisterium of the church because of the doctrinal confusion caused by incautious contact with separated brothers and sisters. (DIC 7/5/79, 452)

On the opposite end of Latin America, a theological team convoked by the Argentine episcopacy to study the CCR instructed priests to guard Catholic tradition during the course of ecumenical exchanges and advised them that diocesan authorities must be informed of any interconfessional "paraliturgies" (McDonnell Vol. 2, 348). Interestingly, while many Latin American bishops were warning the CCR about the potential perils of ecumenism, one of the international movement's chief proponents, Belgian Cardinal Leon Joseph Suenens drafted a document in 1978 on the role of ecumenism in the CCR in which he presented the Renewal as a "special grace" for interconfessional relations (McDonnell Vol. 3, 82-174).[7] Hence, episcopal pressure to restrict contact with religious competitors and reinforce the Catholic identity of the movement forced the CCR to abandon its initial ecumenism. It is also probably the case that as leadership of the Renewal passed from U.S. to Latin American hands, the latter were simply much less interested in the cause of Christian unity, particularly with those who were often perceived as obnoxiously aggressive proselytizers. As the CCR entered the 1980s, it was in the midst of a radical metamorphosis from a movement on the vanguard of ecumenical relations with Latin American Protestants to one that would position itself on the front lines of the ecclesial battle to repel the "invasion of the sects."

Decade of the Renewal

As the Renewal continued to expand in the 1980s, three main trends would emerge during the movement's second decade of operation in Latin America. Most notably, the CCR experienced rapid growth and began to descend the social pyramid by recruiting among the region's popular classes. Second, the CCR won greater episcopal approval in the context of rapidly increasing ecclesiastical alarm, even panic in some cases, over the explosive growth of Pentecostalism and certain neo-Christian denominations such as Jehovah's Witnesses and Mormons. More bishops came to realize that in offering the same type of ecstatic spirituality as Pentecostal churches, the CCR functions more as a barrier than a bridge to further defections from the church. Interrelated to widening episcopal approval is the Renewal's development into the Latin American church's most dynamic force for evangelization. Mirroring their Pentecostal competition, Charismatics had moved to the vanguard of the church's battle by the end of the 1980s, not only to stanch the flow of nominal Catholics to Pentecostalism but also to "rescue" those who were baptized in the church but who did not actively practice their faith.[8]

While Pentecostal churches captured a greater share of Latin American Christians who were attracted to pneumatic spirituality in the 1980s, the CCR also greatly benefited from the Pentecostalization of Christianity in the region. Such was consumer demand for pneumatic spirituality that if religious specialists did not produce it, their churches faced stagnation and even decline. That in less than a century in Latin America Pentecostalism was able to claim approximately 75 percent of the region's Protestant population is dramatic evidence of the mass appeal of pneumatic spirituality from Tierra del Fuego to Matamoros. Mainline Protestants, such as Methodists and Presbyterians, who have traditionally relegated the Spirit to the margins in their more cerebral form of religious practice, simply cannot compete with more appealing Pentecostal products. And until the arrival of its own Charismatic import from the United States, the region's religious hegemon also struggled to contend with the rapid advance of God Is Love and the Assemblies of God, among other Pentecostal denominations.

Although statistics on CCR growth are nonexistent for many Latin American countries, those that are available point to extremely accelerated expansion during the movement's second decade. In Chile, the CCR's national office reported that prayer groups mushroomed from approximately eighty in 1975 to 426 in 1992; researcher Cármen Galilea estimates the latter figure to be closer to six hundred (34). In Brazil, the CCR expanded from no more than ten thousand members in 1976 (Carranza 32) to some 6 million in 1994 largely on the basis of exponential growth during the 1980s (Prandi 15).[9] In neighboring Argentina, sociologist Jorge Soneira reports "explosive growth" during the decade in question but unfortunately does not offer any figures (485). At the opposite end of the region, political scientist Philip Williams discovered "spectacular" growth in El Salvador (197), while both Mexican and Guatemalan CCR national leaders stated that rapid expansion began in their countries in the early 1980s (Ramirez, de Góngora, and Estrada, personal communications). On the regional level, an estimated total of 12 million Latin American Catholics had joined the CCR by 1992 (Hebrard *Os carismáticos* 24).

As an integral part of the larger process of the Pentecostalization of Latin American Christianity, the CCR multiplied exponentially for reasons similar to those that ignited the Pentecostal boom. Without rehashing the arguments developed in chapter 3, we recall that Pentecostal churches mushroomed in a field of poverty. More specifically, as Latin America sank into its worst economic depression in fifty years and lost a decade of growth in the 1980s, the Pentecostal message of divine healing of earthly afflictions resonated throughout the region but especially in the slums and shantytowns of the urban periphery. There in the *favelas* and *ciudades perdidas*, where the lost decade often meant slipping into extreme poverty, the Pentecostal product that promised healing of the pathogens of poverty—such as illness, alcoholism, and marital strife—proved exceptionally appealing.

Liberation of a Different Kind

A slight modification of the same dialectic between the product of faith healing and poverty-related affliction that propelled the Pentecostal boom illuminates the mass appeal of the Catholic Charismatic Renewal. While the thesis of affliction or illness is the same for both the Renewal and Pentecostalism, the higher social class position of the former translates into a less direct relationship between misfortune and poverty. In other words, the afflictions that impel middle-class Latin Americans to join the CCR are less directly the result of material deprivation and more often arise from psychological problems such as early childhood traumas. It follows, then, that the distinct origins of the Pentecostal and Charismatic dialectical thesis lead to variations on the same product (antithesis) of faith healing. Whereas the *cura divina* practiced in Pentecostal churches tends to focus on the healing of the physical illnesses that plague the Latin American poor, the *sanación* offered at Charismatic masses and assemblies in the 1980s more often involved the "inner healing" (*sanación interior*) of painful memories and past psychological traumas.

The centrality of inner healing in the CCR impressed me at a Charismatic prayer group meeting in downtown Rio de Janeiro in early August 1998. About halfway through the two-hour meeting, two lay leaders positioned themselves at the front of the packed assembly hall and began to "reveal" the afflictions of several of the some two hundred believers present. Taking the microphone from her male brother in faith, the diminutive middle-aged women in a surprisingly booming voice shouted, "I see that someone has a difficult court case." A well-dressed young woman quickly raised her hand. The lay leader continued. "I see that someone lost their personal documents." Another hand shot up. Her male partner then took the microphone and continued for another five minutes "revealing" similar middle-class problems. After a brief interlude in which a priest belonging to the Order of St. Vincent called on those present to practice charity and not to reject the poor "because Jesus is among them," the healing session resumed with several of those whose problems had been divulged walking to the front of the room to give testimony to thèir healing. The lost documents had been found, the court case was resolved, and vertigo no longer kept another believer from reaching to new heights.

Inner healing has been the predominant form of *sanación* practiced in the CCR, but there are two other types that complement the Charismatic typology of illness and healing. According to Charismatic etiology, illness has three causal types: emotional, physical, and spiritual. Physical illness arises from disease and accidents, while spiritual malaise results most often from personal sin and less frequently from demonic oppression. Corresponding methods of healing are straightforward for emotional and physical illnesses. Prayers for inner healing are directed toward the first, while petitions for physical curing are made for the second. Since spiritual afflictions have two distinct origins, personal sin and satanic oppression, there are two different methods of treatment: those spiritual problems diagnosed as originating in personal sin require prayers of repentance; affliction caused by the devil or his minions demands much stronger medicine—exorcism.

Since the late 1980s, competition with Pentecostalism has led to the formation of a cadre of priests who specialize in "liberation" (or exorcism) ministries. Such is current consumer demand for release from demonic possession that some priests, such as Brazilian Charismatic superstar Father Marcelo Rossi, even celebrate "liberation Masses" (*missas de libertação*) on a weekly basis ("Não sou artista").[10] Acknowledging his pastoral debt to Pentecostal leader Bishop Edir Macedo, whose Universal Church of the Kingdom of God brought exorcism to the fore of pneumacentric Christianity in Latin America, Padre Marcelo stated in a recent interview that "it was Bishop Edir Macedo who woke us up. He got us up" (Lima and Oyama 3).

Behind closed doors, CCR lay leaders also practice unofficial exorcism on believers who are manifesting symptoms of satanic influence. Many bishops feel such unsanctioned exorcisms are a threat to their ecclesiastical authority and have issued statements denouncing the practice. In its official statement of approval of the CCR in 1986, the Guatemalan Episcopal Conference referred to "irregularities" with exorcisms and reminded Charismatics that the rite can be performed only by priests with proper episcopal consent (Conferencia Episcopal de Guatemala [CEG] 415). The same year, the bishop of the Mexican industrial city of Toluca also informed the CCR of the need for episcopal authorization of any exorcism taking place in his diocese (DIC 10/16/86, 667). In one of the most extreme reactions to the practice of unauthorized exorcism, Archbishop Juan Sandoval of Guadalajara excommunicated several members of the Nueva Alianza (New Alliance) CCR covenant community for expelling demons without his approval and also on account of their "Protestant tendency," which led them, according to the bishop, to ignore the role of the Virgin (DIC 4/21/ 97, 287).[11]

In accord with the class basis of religious expression, as the CCR began to penetrate the Latin American popular classes and descend the social pyramid, demand for physical healing and exorcism became much greater than in the past. Like their Pentecostal counterparts, impoverished urban Catholics seek divine resolution of their poverty-related afflictions. Thus, popular Charismatics typically implore the Holy Spirit to empower them to overcome such afflictions as al--coholism, unemployment, physical illness, domestic strife, and demonic oppression, the latter of which in Brazil and much of the Caribbean often takes the form of possession by the Exus, or liminal trickster spirits, of Candomblé, Umbanda, and other African diasporan religions. In her comparative study of Pentecostals, Catholic Charismatics, and members of Catholic Base Christian Communities, Brazilian sociologist Cecilia Mariz observed no demonic possession or exorcism among middle-class Charismatics and few references to the devil ("Pentecostalismo" 35). In contrast, popular Charismatics, many of whom had attended Pentecostal churches before joining the CCR, were very focused on the role of the devil and, like Pentecostals, saw his hand in such "vices" as soap operas and drinking (Mariz "Pentecostalismo" 30). Exorcism in the CCR, however, has not developed to the point that it has in the IURD and other neo-Pentecostal denominations where the demons (in the form of Umbanda or Candomblé spirits) are actually invoked to then be expelled in dramatic fashion by combative pastors. As the CCR proceeds with its descent of the Latin American class scale, the specialized products of divine healing, exorcism, and physical healing will continue their trajectory from the margins of Charismatic practice to the center.

The scant research that has been conducted on the CCR in Latin America confirms the centrality of *sanación* in its various forms in attracting new members and retaining veterans. In Curaçao, the two most important charismata among Renewal members are reported to be healing and "freedom from the powers of evil," which, of course, is exorcism, one of the three types of faith healing (Lampe 430). More specifically, 80 percent of Charismatics surveyed on the island in the mid-1980s reported serious personal problems at the time of affiliation with the movement. Ill health was the leading affliction, followed by marital strife (Boudewijnse 183). Brazilian sociologist Reginaldo Prandi found a similar pattern among the CCR in his country. In his recent study of the Renewal, he found healing and glossolalia to be the salient gifts of the Spirit (Prandi 45). For Mexican *carismáticos*, there are two main entryways into the movement—"existential crisis" and the need for healing (Muñoz 108). In her recent thesis on the CCR in the state of Chihuahua, anthropologist Alma Muñoz punctuates the role of faith healing in the Latin American CCR with an extensive bibliography of titles on the topic written by leading Charismatic healers such as Robert De Grandis, Emiliano Tardiff, and Bishop Alfonso Uribe. Mexican CCR lay leader Miguel Ramírez confirmed Muñoz's findings and added that glossolalia is the second most popular charism (personal communication). Ramírez's Guatemalan counterpart, Sheny de Góngora, also affirmed that healing is the salient spiritual gift in the Central American nation (personal communication).

Research conducted on the CCR outside of the region indicates that the prominence of the product of faith healing is not peculiar to the Latin American movement. One of the main studies of the Renewal in its native land, the United States, discovered that 71 percent of North American Charismatics surveyed said they or someone close to them had been healed (Bord and Faulkner 93). And in Africa, where poverty-related illness finds fertile soil, faith healing is, unsurprisingly, the Renewal's premier charism (Hebrard *Les Charismatiques* 85).

Consumer demand for divine healing in its various forms increased sharply in Latin America in the 1980s among both the middle and popular classes as the region sank into deep economic depression.

Mass Appeal

By the end of the 1980s, in addition to proliferating on the basis of *sanación* in its second decade, the CCR was transforming itself from a middle-class to a multiclass movement. In contrast to its Protestant competitor, which was conceived among the Latin American poor and began to work its way up the social scale, the CCR started to descend from its rarified origins into the hotly contested religious marketplace of the popular classes. The Renewal's emphasis on divine healing during a decade of severe economic depression gave it great possibilities for expansion among the swelling ranks of the disprivileged, but it was only through skilled marketing (evangelization) that the CCR was able to realize its potential of becoming a mass movement. The CCR's entry into the popular religious market occurred simultaneously on two fronts. On the first, at the base, Charismatic lay leaders and priests began to organize prayer groups in the very same working-class districts, including the slums and shantytowns, where Pentecostal pastors were founding an average of one new church per day in such megalopolises as Rio de Janeiro (R. Fernandes 19). These pastoral agents at the vanguard of the CCR's expansion along the urban periphery originally hailed from the ranks of the middle class, but today, as the movement enters its fourth decade, a new generation of lay leaders is emerging from among the prayer groups of the popular classes.

On the second front of expansion, the Renewal climbed down the social pyramid by borrowing from the marketing playbook of their Pentecostal competition. By the mid-1980s, mass rallies, revivals, and healing marathons in which thousands of believers gathered in soccer stadiums and gymnasiums to receive the power of the Holy Spirit were no longer peculiar to Pentecostalism. Annual national CCR assemblies known as cenacles (*cenáculos*) filled soccer stadiums throughout the region.[12] The Mexican CCR packed the Estadio Azteca with some seventy thousand Charismatics several times in the middle and late 1980s (Hebrard *Les Charismatiques* 27), while the Brazilian Renewal attracted 150,000 at Pentecost in 1987 and then again in May 1991 (Benedetti 243). Renowned international CCR leaders, especially those who specialize in healing ministries, such as North American priest Robert DeGrandis and his recently deceased Canadian compere, Emiliano Tardiff, attract thousands of impoverished believers to rallies that are propelled by faith healing sessions and much upbeat music, which usually conforms to popular tastes.

Currently, no Charismatic luminary can fill Latin American soccer stadiums to capacity like Brazilian CCR superstar, Padre Marcelo. The former aerobic instructor's charisma, movie star looks, and song and dance routine to a samba and fado (the folkloric music of Portugal) beat, send Brazilian Charismatics, especially young women and girls, into a frenzied state. In November 1997, the then thirty-year-old priest drew seventy thousand people to a "megamass" at São Paulo's Morumbi Stadium (Lima and Oyama 4). In congregating thousands of believers in very public arenas, the CCR not only demonstrates its ability to branch out from its middle-class roots but also displays its strength as a movement of mass appeal to both ecclesiastical authorities and secular society. Since

1998, Padre Marcelo has appeared as a regular guest on the *Faustão* show, a very popular Sunday television program on the Rede Globo network that combines the talk-show format with musical entertainment and contests. And in 1998, Father Marcelo joined the Brazilian pantheon of celebrities by gracing the cover of *Veja*, the equivalent of *Time* or *Newsweek*, with a circulation of more than a million.

Invasion of the "Sects"

As the CCR multiplied and became a mass movement during Latin America's lost decade, the bishops of the region, both collectively and individually, began to grant official approval to the lay movement that many increasingly viewed as the church's most appealing product in the surging competition with Pentecostalism for religious consumers. While episcopal concern with the growth of Protestantism in Ibero-America had been evident since mid-century, the Pentecostal boom of the 1980s caused panic among wide sectors of the Latin American episcopacy by the middle of the decade. Throughout the region, from the diocesan to regional levels, bishops denounced the "invasion of the sects" and formed ecclesiastical committees and commissions to study the Pentecostal interlopers in order to formulate an effective pastoral response to stem the exodus of millions of their flock toward the Protestant competition.

On the regional level, the Latin American Episcopal Conference's (CELAM) alarm in the late 1970s over the rapid spread of the Pentecostal contagion developed into a sense of panic by the mid-1980s. A 1978 study sponsored by the CELAM Mission Department entitled "Latin American Missionary Panorama" warned that each day two thousand Latin American Catholics were leaving the church for the "sects." Pointing out that in many cities and dioceses there are dozens of Protestant houses of worship for each Catholic church, the authors of the study expressed their fear about the future of the Latin American ecclesia: "Some episcopacies ask themselves if the majority of the population in their countries will identify themselves as Catholic in twenty years from now. The impact of the sects constitutes a new missionary situation which we cannot minimize" (*Comunicado Mensal* 8/78). The document concludes that if urgent pastoral action is not taken, the "popular masses," particularly in the cities, will be lost to the "sects." In the fourth edition of *Las Sectas en America Latina* (Sects in Latin America) co-published by CELAM in 1986, the president of the Bogotá-based conference, Monseñor Antonio Quarracino, stresses the gravity of the Pentecostal boom: "This problem of the sects is undoubtedly one of the deepest concerns of the Latin American bishops" (Santagada et al. 5).

Episcopal consternation over their dynamic competitors reached the point that by the middle of the decade, CELAM's office on ecumenism was not focusing primarily on the cause of Christian unity but on the battle against the "sects." Meeting in Brasilia in late January 1985, CELAM representatives devoted their attention to the "great concern and alarm" caused by what they referred to as "free religious movements." Pentecostalism, of course, was the focus of attention because of its extraordinary growth. The three pastoral recommendations made for revitalizing the church in the face of aggressive Pentecostal proselytism were a prescription for remedial action led by the Charismatic Renewal. The first recommendation called for "revalorizing the sense of action of the Holy Spirit in all church life." More explicitly, point two recommended actively accompanying the CCR so that it would serve as testament to the value of the Spirit in the church and also as an "ecumenical bridge." The third prescriptive urged greater pastoral attention to the most vulnerable sectors (the urban poor, youth, migrants, and women) of the church through CEBs, renewed liturgy, embracing popular traditions, and social and health pastorals (*Comunicado Mensal* 1-2/85). Of course, at the time of the CELAM meeting, the CCR was at the ecclesial vanguard in liturgical innovation and its very raison d'être revolved around healing.

At the national level, episcopal preoccupation with mushrooming Pentecostalism tended to be even more intense. In some countries, the struggle to preserve Catholic hegemony was even conceived of as a holy war. Nowhere was this more the case than in Guatemala where Latin America's first Pentecostal head of state, General Efrain Rios Montt, viewed his murderous offensive against the leftist guerrillas as a holy war against communist evil. In the midst of Rios Montt's abbreviated reign of terror in 1982 and 1983, the Guatemalan episcopacy drafted a collective pastoral letter entitled "Confirmed in Faith," which denounced governmental violence, human rights abuses, and actions against the church. In addressing the state of the Guatemalan church in the second section of the epistle, the bishops wrote on the "grave danger" that the "aggressive escalade of numerous Protestant sects" presented to Guatemalan national unity. The episcopacy warned, "But we cannot accept that often for nonreligious reasons, our faithful are pressured to abandon their native religion, and under the pretext of religious liberty, our communities are divided and confront each other in a struggle that could easily lead to a religious war of incalculable consequences" (CEG 337). Alarmed by Pentecostalism's extraordinary success in Central America's most populous nation, Pope John Paul II encouraged the bishops to embrace television and radio as effective media for "resisting the pernicious influence of proselytizing activities of groups that have very little authentically religious content and sow so much confusion among

Catholics" (CEG 867). Two years later, in 1985, Guatemalan bishops repeated their charge against the Pentecostal competition in a statement on the return to civilian rule after three decades of military dictatorship. Under the section labeled "corruption," the episcopacy denounced its religious rival for assaulting national cultural identity: "We cannot help but point to the enormous damage that the innumerable fundamentalist sects do in depredating the cultural elements of our indigenous peoples" (CEG 391).

To the north, in Mexico, even though Pentecostal growth rates were not nearly as high, the episcopacy expressed similar alarm over their dynamic competitors. The episcopacy's biennial plan for pastoral action from 1983 to 1985 called for concrete pastoral programs "as an answer to the alarming invasion of sects that make an attempt against Christian life and the cultural values of our peoples" (*DIC* 4/11-15/83). Like their Guatemalan counterparts, the Mexican bishops perceive Catholicism to be an integral part of national identity. Thus the Pentecostal boom threatens not only the church but also the very soul of Latin American national identities.

By the end of the decade, the Mexican episcopacy had become so disturbed by the proliferation of the "sects" that in 1987 they appointed the national church's most vociferous opponent of Protestantism, Padre Flaviano Amatulli, to head the newly created Department of Faith in the Face of Sectarian Proselytism. The author of such books as *Las sectas: Un problema pastoral* (Sects: A pastoral problem), *La iglesia y las sectas: Pesadilla o reto?* (The church and sects: Nightmare or challenge?), and *Cuidado con las sectas* (Careful with the sects), the Italian priest realized the magnitude of the Pentecostal problem during his missionary work among Oaxacan Indians in the 1970s. As executive secretary of the new department within the Episcopal Commission for the Doctrine of the Faith, Father Amatulli organized summer courses throughout the nation on "evangelization in regard to the invasion of the sects." Mexican clergy and laity alike could actually earn diplomas in "Protestantism." Borrowing from the playbook of his Protestant opponents, Amatulli emphasized the importance of home visits in administering a "general vaccination against the sectarian virus" (Amatulli 4). That Amatulli's students, as well as Chilean Charismatics (Galilea 26), were often mistaken for Protestants during their pastoral visits to Catholic homes reveals the novelty of such mission work in the Latin American church. And as in Chile, it has been the CCR that has blazed pastoral trails in evangelizing among nominal Catholics through home visits.

Returning to Mexico, consternation over the threat to Catholic religious hegemony reached an unprecedented level when in 1988 the main theme of the Mexican Episcopal Conference's annual meeting was "the church with regard to the new religious groups." The bishop of Nezahualcoyotl, a sprawling working-class district in Mexico City, introduced the theme of the conference by portraying his church as a victim of Protestant "persecution"; "The active presence and proselytism of so many religious groups constitutes a form of persecution against the unity of the church and its doctrinal integrity" (*DIC* 4/28/88, 315). The Mexican bishops' pastoral recommendations for responding to the Pentecostal contagion are essentially a prescription for the CCR. Among the salient pastoral recommendations are to intensify, streamline, and personalize evangelization (understood as conversion); revitalize liturgy; and cultivate small ecclesial communities that offer a feeling of shared closeness and fraternity. One of the underlying objectives of such mission work, according to the bishops, should be greater emphasis on mysticism and asceticism, key elements that the CCR imported from Pentecostalism.

At the other end of the Americas, in Brazil, after a decade of studies of "autonomous religious groups," the national episcopacy also made pastoral recommendations that pointed to the pivotal role of the CCR in shoring up the besieged ecclesiastical fortress. Following the lead of their Mexican counterparts, in 1989 the Brazilian bishops established a permanent working group on "the grave problems of the sects" within the department of ecumenism. The group's main function is to offer practical advice to clergy on strategies for countering the religious competition (*Comunicado Mensal* 11/89). The following year, Latin America's largest episcopacy demonstrated the same consternation as their Mexican cohorts over the proliferation of Pentecostalism. The main theme at the annual episcopal assembly of 1990 was "autonomous religious groups." After engaging in a round of self-criticism in which they cited their church's excessive rationalism and lack of spontaneity, opportunities for a more personal religious experience, and a well-defined behavioral ethic, the ecclesiastical heads recommended pastoral action that dovetails perfectly with the CCR's mission. The bishops called for pastoral work that emphasizes rediscovery of the spiritual realm, the value of subjective and personal religious experiences, and the importance of an immediate experience of God and the Holy Spirit. While the CNBB (Brazilian Bishops' Conference) did not specifically mention the Renewal, it cited "middle-class movements," as well as Base Christian Communities, for their "good work" (*Comunicado Mensal* 4/90). Since the CCR was the largest and most dynamic middle-class movement within the church at the time, the CNBB obviously had the Renewal in mind in its laudatory comments.

With the great exception of the Brazilians, the majority of those episcopacies who made official pronouncements of ecclesiastical approval of the CCR did so between the late 1970s and mid-1980s, just as panic over the Pentecostal "invasion" was reaching fever pitch. And it is no coincidence that the national bishops' conferences that extended official recognition during the period in question are those that were facing the most intense competition from Pentecostals for the loyalty of popular religious consumers. Beginning with the Panamanian bishops in 1975, the episcopacies of Chile, Puerto Rico, Costa Rica, Honduras, and Guatemala extended ecclesiastical recognition to the CCR over the period of a decade.[13] In addition to Brazil, the aforementioned countries have led the region in Pentecostal growth rates.[14]

While all the national episcopacies have embraced the CCR as a strategy to compete with surging Pentecostalism, nowhere is the link as explicit as in the document drafted by the Costa Rican Bishops' Conference in 1979. The episcopal letter is a two-part document that simultaneously addresses both the CCR and the Pentecostal boom. The first part endorses the Renewal with what are subsequently to become standard caveats, such as caution with charismata and instruction not to deemphasize the Eucharist. Most important, the bishops warn of the danger incorporating elements from "separated churches," or Protestantism (McDonnell Vol. 2, 505). The second part, called "Protestant Proselytizing," makes a series of pastoral recommendations "in face of the extraordinary intensification of Protestant recruitment, especially by sects who are fanatic, proselytizing and aggressive toward the Catholic church" (McDonnell Vol. 2, 505). The pastoral recommendations converge perfectly with the mission of the CCR. Bible courses, more attractive and participatory liturgy, better use of mass media for evangelization efforts, and greater catechism are the major pastoral directives. The Costa Rican bishops also naively insist that their "separated brothers cease all aggressive and proselytizing activities" (McDonnell Vol. 2, 506).

Although faced with the stiffest Pentecostal competition in Latin America, the Guatemalan episcopacy extended ecclesiastical recognition somewhat reluctantly to the CCR. The Guatemalan pastoral instruction on the Renewal merits some exploration because it neatly captures the ambivalence with which many episcopacies have given the green light to the CCR. During the 1980s and even today, most Latin American bishops are not Charismatics, and many have little affinity for its pneumatic spirituality. Nevertheless, despite reports of groups of Renewal members defecting to Pentecostal churches, most national bishops' conferences in the region have come to view the CCR not as a bridge to the Assemblies of God, for example, but as a barrier to further losses of the Catholic flock. In welcoming the CCR into the ecclesial fold, the bishops can offer the same pneumatic product as their Protestant rivals. Catholics no longer have to forsake the Virgin and pope in their quest for more spirited religion.

Perhaps the ambivalence of the Guatemalan bishops is best captured by the amount of ink devoted to the "fruits" of the CCR on one hand and the "risks" on the other. Although they are enumerated first, the positive points total only one-half as many as the potential dangers: eleven to twenty-one. The episcopal instruction recognizes the CCR's evangelistic work and focus on the Holy Spirit and Jesus as the movement's ripest fruits. Salient among the twenty-one potentially rotten fruits are risks relating to two major and often interrelated themes, faith healing and episcopal authority. Nearly one-half of the potential dangers relate directly to faith healing. Risk number eighteen captures the interrelation between the two main episcopal concerns and reveals the threat that faith healing poses to the bishops' Charismatic authority:

> In Charismatic Renewal groups massive assemblies are often organized at which the sick are prayed for in a special way. These assemblies must be under the responsibility of a priest, authorized for such an event by the bishop, so that everything develops according to the spirit of our Catholic tradition for the greater glory of God and for the good of the infirm who with faith come to receive the healing power of Jesus in his Church. (CEG 415)

The principal pastoral recommendations are aimed at increasing ecclesiastical control over the CCR. Priests and religious are urged to become involved in the movement to prevent it from straying and creating "parallel structures" (CEG 417).

The Virgin at the Vanguard

Further evidence of the bishops' ambivalence about approving a Pentecostal type of ecclesial movement is their emphasis on the Virgin as defender of the faith and guardian of Catholic orthodoxy. For a movement rooted in Pentecostal spirituality, which in Latin America has historically been radically anti-Catholic, what better way to preserve the Catholicness of the Renewal than through emphasis on the element that most distinguishes the Catholic Church from its Protestant competitors? Thus, over the past decade and a half, the Virgin in her myriad national and local incarnations has come to constitute the dividing line that separates Catholic Charismatics from Pentecostals. Episcopal emphasis on the importance of the Virgin of Guadalupe and Our Lady of the Immaculate Conception, among others, is a clear example of the marginal differentiation of a standardized religious product.[15] That is, in the figure of the Virgin, the church's chief religious producers offer an appealing variant of the pneumatic spirituality shared by both Catholic Charismatics and Pentecostals. Without the Mother of God to differentiate their brand of Charismatic spirituality from that of their Protestant rivals, only the pontiff is left to guard the bridge leading to Pentecostalism.

Thus, in their episcopal recognition of the Guatemalan CCR, the bishops attempted to place the Virgin at the center of the movement. Even before mentioning the positive and negative aspects of the Renewal, the episcopacy devoted an entire section of the instruction to the Virgin's role in the movement.

In their opening statement, the bishops reminded Charismatics that Pope John Paul II wants Mary to be at the heart of the Renewal since she is the one best equipped to guide and direct it (CEG 410). This point is then reiterated in the section on pastoral recommendations in which the Virgin is presented as the "guarantee of orthodoxy . . . in face of the danger of the certain influence of non-Catholic currents" (CEG 418–419). Finally, the bishops concluded their pastoral instruction on the Renewal by imploring the Mother of God to ensure faithfulness to the Holy Spirit and the church: "And may Mary, full of grace, help us all to be truly faithful to the Holy Spirit and to support her inspiration for a renewal of our church" (CEG 420). Even more explicitly than their Guatemalan colleagues, the Honduran bishops in their approval of the CCR stated that "devotion to the Virgin and the saints should be an element that distinguishes the CCR from Protestants and that gives a certain guarantee of orthodoxy to the simple faithful" (Conferencia Episcopal de Honduras [CEH] 20).

If both national episcopacies and individual bishops frequently exhort the Renewal in Latin America to embrace the Virgin, it is also because during its first decade and a half, roughly until the mid-1980s, the CCR kept Mary at the margins of the movement. *Jesus Vive e é o Senhor* (Jesus lives and is Lord), one of the two main monthly journals of the Brazilian CCR, reflects the Virgin's early peripheral role. From the journal's founding by Father Cipriano Chagas in May 1977 until 1983 there were no major articles on the Mother of Jesus. Rather, the journal's primary focus during its first six years was faith healing, conversion testimonials, and the role of the Holy Spirit in believers' lives. However, starting in 1984, Mary began to command more attention, and within a couple years major articles on her role in the CCR had become a regular feature of *Jesus Vive e é o Senhor*. And the Virgin currently has her own regular section called "Our Mother" ("Nossa Mãe") in the other major Charismatic journal in Brazil, *Brasil Cristão* (Christian Brazil), which was launched in 1997 by one of the two North American fathers of the Brazilian CCR, Padre Edward Dougherty.

The Virgin's migration from the sidelines of the Renewal to center stage is clearly the result of episcopal pressure to ensure the Catholicness of a movement that inherited its pneumacentrism from Pentecostalism. Mary played only a bit part during the first half of the Renewal's three decades in Ibero-America because of Protestant influences in the movement. But as the CCR rapidly expanded and sought episcopal approval, it increasingly became necessary to bolster its Catholic identity. And, of course, the Virgin, particularly Guadalupe (the "Queen of Mexico"), is the most potent and visible symbol of Catholic identity in Latin America. Thus by embracing her, the Renewal has fortified its Catholicness in the eyes of incredulous bishops and developed a differentiated religious product that clearly distinguishes itself among spiritual consumers from

Image of the Virgin of Guadalupe on the back of a devotee
in Cuernavaca, Mexico

its Pentecostal competitors. Latin American Christians seeking a more pneumatic type of faith can now choose between virgophilic and virgophobic brands of the same Charismatic religious product.

No single incident more clearly illustrates the pivotal role of the Virgin in differentiating the Charismatic product from the Pentecostal than the infamous "kicking of the saint" incident in which on Brazilian national television on October 12, 1995 (the holy day of the Virgin of Aparecida [Our Lady of the Apparition], the country's patron saint), Bishop Sergio von Helde of the Universal Church of the Kingdom of God kicked and punched a statue of the saint. Pastor von Helde's desecration of the Brazilian patroness, as offensive as it was to millions of Catholics, was more than a violent and irrational act of iconoclasm. Rather, his desecration of Aparecida was a strategic attack on the main element that differentiates the Charismatic product from the Pentecostal. Bishop von Helde and many of his Pentecostal brethren correctly perceive much stiffer Catholic competition in the form of the CCR. Pentecostal leaders must now contend with a Catholic church that offers the same spiritual power of the Holy Spirit that is found in their own temples. Therefore, in the context of an unregulated religious marketplace that offers a standardized product (pneumatic spirituality), successful spiritual entrepreneurs can be expected to attempt to attract new consumers of the divine through attacks on the features that differentiate a rival brand's product from their own. Put simply, many Latin American Pentecostal leaders understand that it is above all the Virgin Mary who keeps millions of Catholics, especially Charismatics, from abandoning their native faith. They logically worry that the Virgin's more central role in the CCR could reduce the flow of Catholic converts to Pentecostalism.

Thus having embraced the Virgin and won widespread episcopal approval, the CCR began its third decade in Latin America as the largest and most vital Catholic lay movement in the region. Even in Brazil where Base Christian Communities had found more fertile soil than in any other nation, CEB members in the early 1990s found themselves outnumbered by their Charismatic coreligionists at a ratio of two to one (Prandi 14). Given the continuing expansion of the CCR and the declining stock of CEBs, the former probably claims four times as many members as the latter at the beginning of the new century.

Waging War on the Wolves

In addition to continued rapid expansion during the 1990s, the most important pattern of development during the decade was the completion of the CCR's transformation from a loosely structured, ecumenically oriented movement to a bureaucratized ecclesial group at the vanguard of the church's competition with Pentecostalism for larger shares of the popular religious market. Long gone are the early days when Charismatics and Pentecostals worshiped together at ecumenical prayer groups. Today, CCR leaders, such as those gathered at the 1997 national congress in Brazil, are more likely to pray "to break the strength of the evangelicals" (Carranza 226). At the same congress, held in Guaratingueta, São Paulo, Padre Alberto Gambarini, a specialist in demonology and "sects," exhorted fellow Charismatics to invest in television and radio "In order to vanquish Satan and the enemy sects that are penetrating every home in the country" (Carranza 226).

During the 1990s, the panic over the "invasion of the sects" that had erupted in the mid-1980s only intensified. In Brazil, the president of the CNBB, Monseñor Luciano Mendes, in a 1991 speech cited the proselytism of the expanding "sects" as the greatest obstacle to pastoral action (*Comunicado Mensal* 3/91). Following suit, Mendes's successor, President Lucas Neves, stated in 1995 that the "sects" would be the CNBB's main adversary for the rest of the decade and that the bishops were considering joining forces with mainline Protestant churches in a holy war against "fundamentalist sects" (Oro 93). Alarm over burgeoning Pentecostalism reached the pinnacle of the international church in 1992 at the Fourth General Conference of Latin American Bishops in Santo Domingo, with Pope John Paul II denouncing Latin American Protestants as "rapacious wolves" raiding the vulnerable Catholic flock (Hennelly 48).

In direct response to surging Pentecostal competition, the pontiff and bishops developed New Evangelization as the main theme of the episcopal conference. The New Evangelization essentially seeks to revitalize the Latin American church through pastoral action aimed at members of the Catholic flock deemed most vulnerable to Pentecostal predators. In his opening address at the conference, the pope identified families, youth, and the infirm as the easiest prey for the Pentecostal competition (Hennelly 48), while the bishops in their conclusion singled out migrants, people unattended by priests, "religious ignorants," "simple people," the poor, and those with family problems as sectors of the Catholic population that are vulnerable to the "advance of the sects" (Hennelly 112). Collectively, the episcopal and pontifical definition of vulnerable sectors is so comprehensive that the great majority of Latin Americans would be included in it.

Despite the lack of specificity, the New Evangelization has made a preferential option for nominal Catholics among the popular classes of urban Latin America. Within this preferential populational group, those who are sick, adolescents and young adults, and families in crisis receive special attention. Numerous episcopally commissioned studies of the Pentecostal boom have identified these sectors as the most frequent converts to the Protestant competition. Cognizant of the supreme importance of faith healing in the extraordinary success of Pentecostalism in the region, the pope in his opening address called for special pastoral attention to the sick, "bearing in mind the evangelizing power of suffering" (Hennelly 58).

The type of pastoral action called for by the New Evangelization at Santo Domingo is essentially a prescription for the CCR. Although not mentioned by name, the CCR is lauded by the bishops as a movement that has "produced much fruit in our churches" (Hennelly 102). The episcopal leaders had the CCR in mind when they stated that "these movements give priority to the word of God and praying together, and they are particularly attentive to the action of the Spirit" (Hennelly 102). More important, the specific pastoral action recommended by the pontiff and the heads of the Latin American church represents the same missionary activity the Renewal had been carrying out for more than a decade. The pope's clamor for evangelization that focuses on a personal relationship with God, active liturgy and lay participation, and Marian devotion is an unequivocal endorsement of the mission of the CCR (Hennelly 48). Further endorsement comes from the bishops who stated that it is the task of the New Evangelization to "arouse a personal acceptance of Jesus Christ," with the Holy Spirit providing the "creative breath" of the New Evangelization (Hennelly 82). Moreover, the bishops specifically pointed to pastoral directions that the CCR, more than any other Latin American ecclesial group, had already been following. Besides personal acceptance of Jesus, the episcopal leaders recommended greater lay participation in church life, increased devotion to the Virgin and pope, welcoming the Spirit at moments of crisis, animated and participatory liturgy, and home visits to nominal Catholic families (Hennelly 113).

Although already at the forefront of church missionary activities, the CCR in Latin America responded to the call made at Santo Domingo for New Evangelization by intensifying its proselytizing activities. The Renewal took specific pastoral measures to win new adherents. At the grassroots level, Charismatics copied the Pentecostal competition by marketing their products through home visits.[16] The "visitation ministry," as it is called in Brazil, sends lay missionaries, who are mostly Charismatics, to the homes of the target population of vulnerable nominal Catholics to invite them to attend a prayer group or some other church function. Unaccustomed to Catholic missionary agents knocking on their doors, many mistake the visitors for Pentecostals, Mormons, or Jehovah's Witnesses who pioneered door-to-door evangelization in Latin America.

CCR versus IURD on TV

While individual Charismatics evangelize through personal contact, the CCR has also emulated its Pentecostal rivals in embracing mass media, particularly television and radio, as a potent marketing tool for spreading the Charismatic gospel. In fact, such is the Renewal's dominance of Catholic radio and television in many Latin American countries that there would be precious little church programming without it. In Brazil, the majority of the programming on the country's 181 Catholic radio stations is produced by CCR members ("Não sou milagreiro" 100), while in Guatemala, the Renewal almost single-handedly answered the papal call to the episcopacy in 1983 to take to the airwaves to "counteract the pernicious influence of the proselytizing activities of groups with little authentically religious content that create confusion among Catholics" (CEG 867). Six of the seven Catholic radio stations in Guatemala are run by the CCR (de Góngora and Estrada, personal communications). Padre Hugo Estrada's Charismatic Mass is broadcast on Guatemalan cable television twice a week. And in the strategic area of televangelism, it is the Brazilian CCR that has established the greatest presence on the small screens of Latin America.

The Brazilian Renewal has moved far beyond the simple broadcast of Charismatic Masses to the production of religious dramas akin to the country's wildly popular *novelas* or soap operas.[17] It is no coincidence that Charismatic television is strongest in the Latin American nation that has the greatest degree of Pentecostal programming. The Universal Church of the Kingdom of God, in fact, runs its own station, Rede Record. More than any other factor, it was Pentecostalism's dominance of religious broadcasting that compelled the Brazilian CCR to embrace television as a powerful medium for realizing their own evangelical mission. Father Edward Dougherty has made CCR history by importing the movement to Brazil and by pioneering in Catholic TV. In 1983, his Charismatic association, Associação do Senhor Jesus (Association of Lord Jesus), aired the country's first CCR program, *We Announce Jesus* (*Anunciamos Jesús*), which is currently the longest running weekly Charismatic program.

That a North American priest, hailing from a nation with the world's most competitive religious and television markets, should be the one to put the Brazilian CCR on TV is not surprising. Having come of age in a religious landscape thoroughly dominated by their own church, Dougherty's Brazilian coreligionist peers knew next to nothing about competing for spiritual consumers in a free market of faith. Emphasizing the importance of intelligent marketing of the Charismatic product, the North American Jesuit explained in a 1998 interview how market research to determine the tastes and preferences of spiritual consumers allows him to "satisfy the customers." During the past decade, Padre Eduardo has expanded his operation to include control of a large television production center, O Centro de Produção Século XXI (Century 21 Production Center). Century 21, located in the small city of Valinhos, São Paulo, comprises three large studios, which employ the latest technology in video production and a spacious auditorium for hosting studio audiences. Its programs are shown on national television covering 85 percent of Brazilian territory, and recently Century 21 has started to export its product to other Latin American nations, the United States and Europe (Carranza 198, 201).

Also a skilled fundraiser, Father Dougherty finances his enterprise through a combination of contributions from the seventy thousand members of his Association of Lord Jesus; sales of television programs and religious articles; and occasional donations from wealthy Brazilian, North American, and European Charismatics. Salient among the latter is the Breninkmeyer family who owns C&A, the international chain of department stores with a strong presence in Brazil (Carranza 198–199). In contrast to his initial efforts, which were spurned by the CNBB under the influence of progressive bishops, over the past decade Padre Eduardo has won widespread episcopal support for his starring role in bringing the Brazilian church into the homes of millions of TV viewers. Commenting on both Century 21 and the inauguration of Redevida (the church's answer to the IURD-owned Rede Record), Dougherty's local bishop, Monseñor Geraldo Azevedo of Campinas, said, "the Catholic church went for a long time without investing in communication . . . that's why we need an offensive to counterbalance the presence of Pentecostal churches in the mass media" (Carranza 203).

Undoubtedly, the church's most potent weapon in the battlefield of television is its newest creation, Redevida (the Life Network). Inaugurated in May of 1995, Redevida is Brazil's first Catholic television station. While the station is not technically an organ of the church, 80 percent of its programming is religious, and its creation was a joint project of the Catholic media impresario João Filho and the CNBB, who in 1989 won the concession for the station from the Sarney government. "The Christian family channel," as it is known in the church, is not directly controlled by the CCR, but the fact that Charismatics are its target audience and most of its programs (such as Seculo XXI) are produced by CCR producers translates into profound Renewal influence. Currently broadcasting eighteen hours a day, Redevida is transmitted throughout the nation via satellite and is financed through the sale of advertising space and donations (Carranza 210). In accord with its mission to the "Christian family," Redevida does not accept advertising of alcohol, tobacco, or other products that are deemed offensive to Catholic family life. The proscription of "sinful" advertising from Redevida largely reflects CCR influence on the station. Charismatics, especially from the popular classes, tend to adopt a Pentecostal-type ascetic code of conduct, which allows them to externalize their conversion to a life in the Spirit. Finally, beyond the world of Catholic television, the CCR has greatly benefited from increasing exposure on secular TV, especially on Latin America's largest network, Rede Globo. As mentioned previously, since 1998 Padre Marcelo has appeared as a regular guest on the *Faustão* show, one of Globo's most popular programs, and his carioca confrere, Father Zeca, a young Charismatic priest idolized by CCR youth in Rio de Janeiro, has also received widespread secular media coverage.

A Tardy Episcopal Embrace

Redevida went on the air less than a year after the Brazilian bishops finally granted official ecclesiastical approval to the CCR. That the CNBB recognized the movement more than a decade later than many of its Latin American counterparts requires an explanation. While the Brazilian church was facing some of the stiffest Pentecostal competition in the region, and many moderate and conservative bishops already viewed the CCR as an attractive product for Catholic consumers, the strength of the progressive wing of the episcopacy delayed ecclesiastical approval. Common among progressive bishops and clergy is the view that the CCR is part of a conservative restoration project that is designed to curtail the influence of liberation theology and the Base Christian Communities that subscribe to liberationist ideologies. Typical of this viewpoint is the CNBB department of communication, which in 1984 refused Father Dougherty's request for funding of his program *Anunciamos Jesús*.

Dominated by progressives, the episcopal department viewed *Anunciamos Jesús* as an obstacle in the ecclesial path toward liberation. In rejecting funding for the program, the department described *Anunciamos Jesus* as following a "line that is incorporeal, Pentecostal, spiritualist, authoritarian, hierarchical, and contrary to the pastoral path of the CNBB" (Carranza 185). Such "progressive" views forced Padre Eduardo to go abroad, particularly back to his native United States, in search of funding. The Brazilian bishops, of course, like their counterparts throughout Latin America, were also very concerned about the CCR's potential for developing into a parallel ecclesial movement and the threat to their own authority posed by a group that seemed to claim a direct channel to the Holy Spirit. However, the unparalleled strength of the progressive sector in the CNBB during the 1970s and much of the 1980s meant that Base Christian Communities and not the CCR would receive preferential CNBB support. It is only with the ascendancy of moderates and conservatives and ever-expanding Pentecostalism at the beginning of the 1990s that a critical mass of bishops came to view the CCR as one of the most effective means of revitalizing the Catholic Church in the face of relentless Protestant competition.

Also contributing to the episcopal green light was a new CCR program that was designed to promote further growth and confront the Pentecostals head on. Launched in 1993, a year before the episcopacy recognized the Renewal, the National Offensive (Ofensiva Nacional) set the ambitious goals of establishing at least one prayer group in every Brazilian parish, expanding at least 1 percent faster than the general population, augmenting the number of seminarians by 10 percent per year, promoting identical gender participation, and mobilizing at least one million Charismatics for a day of Marian prayer every October 12.

Under the slogan, "with renewed missionary ardor," the National Offensive also put together a more structured national office divided into twelve departments. One of the salient departments is Project Lumen, which coordinates the movement's evangelization work through mass media (Ofensiva Nacional; Lima and Oyama 7). In seven years, the offensive has already realized several of its goals. Most important, the CCR now has prayer groups in all Brazilian parishes. Thus, launching the offensive allowed the CCR to flex its ecclesial muscles and demonstrate to the bishops that more than any other church movement, it had the strength to turn back the tide of nominal Catholics rolling into Pentecostal churches.

The Politics of Charisma

The religious market is not the only place where the CCR competes with its Pentecostal rivals. After spending its first two decades on the political sidelines in most countries, the CCR, particularly in Brazil, has taken a page from the Pentecostal playbook and has sent some of its own players to the arena of electoral politics. In Brazil, the CCR's first step into the political arena occurred in the late 1970s with the election of its national president, Osmar Pereira, to the office of federal deputy representing the state of Minas Gerais (Carranza 122). A decade later, at the local level, Father Dougherty mobilized Charismatics in Campinas to elect one of their own, Salvador Filho, as alderman on the city council in 1988 and again in 1994 (Carranza 122). Reflecting its increasing interest in politics, the Brazilian CCR at its 1995 national congress created an additional department, Matias, which coordinates the movement's political strategy (Carranza 123). Not to be outdone by the Protestant *bancada evangelica* (a bloc of evangelical, predominantly Pentecostal, national legislators elected in the late 1980s), CCR members founded their own political party, the National Solidarity Party (PSN), which seeks to elect Charismatics to political office at all levels. In the late 1990s, the Brazilian CCR could claim two federal deputies, two state deputies (in São Paulo and Minas Gerais), and some five hundred mayors and city council members throughout the country (Carranza 125).

While CCR political activity in Brazil tends to confirm the suspicions of Catholic liberationists that the movement is a conservative force, other experiences in Latin America demonstrate that the Renewal is capable of engaging in a range of political behavior. At the federal level in Brazil, Charismatic legislators have adhered to a political agenda that very much resembles that of their evangelical counterparts. Not only have they opposed legislation to recognize same-sex unions and abortion, but also Deputy Filho headed a petition with twenty thousand signatures demanding that the proposal to legalize unions unions not even be brought to the legislative floor. He denounced the proposal as nefarious and abominable, which made him enemy number one of the Brazilian Association of Gays, Lesbians, and Transvestites (Carranza 128). Filho also led the national campaign against the legalization of abortion, which was launched on the Charismatic television program *Let's Praise the Lord* (*Louvemos ao Senhor*) on the Redevida channel in August 1997. In accord with Catholic doctrine, Filho opposes abortion even in the cases of rape and risk of mortality to the mother (Carranza 128).

Confirming the conservative political orientation of the Brazilian CCR, a poll of electoral patterns found Charismatics voting for conservative presidential candidate Fernando Henrique Cardoso at a higher rate than any other religion surveyed, including Pentecostals. Some 46 percent of Charismatics surveyed voted for Cardoso, while only 22 percent cast their ballot for the leftist candidate of the Workers' Party (PT), current president Luiz Inácio Lula da Silva. Charismatics, in fact, rejected Lula at a rate that was second only to Pentecostals. Perhaps even more notable, however, is the fact that Base Christian Community members, much to the chagrin of their liberationist leaders, preferred Cardoso over Lula, who has been the political darling of the progressive church. Cardoso won 40 percent of the CEB vote, while Lula garnered only 31 percent (Prandi 176). In contrast to the Brazilian CCR, Charismatics in a popular district of Curaçao joined a progressive political movement in support of agrarian reform in 1987 (Lampe 434).

While studies of Charismatic political activity in Latin America are lacking, it is probably the case that the Brazilian experience is quite typical. Some may predict that as the movement continues its expansion among the popular classes, the potential for progressive political action will grow. However, the predominantly conservative orientation of Pentecostal political action in the region should dispel the myth that the popular classes have any natural affinity for progressive politics. That more Brazilian CEB members voted for Cardoso than for Lula is dramatic evidence of the lack of such an affinity. One would expect that a candidate such as Lula, a former factory worker without a high school degree whose party claims to represent the interests of the Brazilian popular classes, would be the natural candidate of Catholics belonging to ecclesial communities that are conceived as the pastoral expression of liberation theology's "preferential option for the poor." Yet an astonishingly high proportion, more than two-thirds, of CEB members did not vote for Lula in the 1994 presidential contest (Prandi 176). The most likely scenario is for the CCR to continue following a moderately conservative political agenda as it expands on the urban peripheries of Latin America.

Free-Market Salvation

Thus in the space of just three decades, the Charismatic Renewal has developed into the largest and most animated Catholic lay movement in Latin America. Base Christian Community members watch from the sidelines as the CCR fills soccer stadiums throughout the region with spirited believers and dominates Catholic broadcasting with its own message of liberation, which calls not for freedom from political and economic oppression but for deliverance from demonic oppression. That the type of liberation promised by the Charismatic Renewal has proved far more appealing to popular religious consumers than the kind offered by many CEBs is powerful proof of the vitality of Latin America's new religious marketplace in which consumer demand (or lack thereof) determines the fate of spiritual enterprises. Thus, the CCR has prospered in the unregulated market of faith because it produces the standardized products—faith healing and pneumatic spirituality—that popular consumers in Latin America demand. In contrast, organizations such as the CEBs that offer neither supernatural healing nor direct contact with the Holy Spirit or spirits have failed to thrive in the popular religious marketplace.

If the dynamics of Latin America's new religious economy have facilitated the CCR's success in recruiting millions of Catholics to the movement, it is also the free market that has impelled the bishops to endorse the Charismatic product. Strong consumer preference for pneumatic spirituality has meant that, in the context of an unregulated religious market, if the bishops did not offer a product that facilitated direct contact with the Holy Spirit, their church would continue to lose members to the denominations that focus on the third person of the Trinity. Although many bishops themselves have no taste for Charismatic Christianity, and some actually perceive it as threatening or heretical, the meteoric rise of the Pentecostal competition has impelled them to accept, if not promote, a Catholic brand of Pentecostalism. In the face of surging Charismatic Protestantism, which recruits primarily in the vast field of nominal Catholics, episcopacies, regardless of their own spiritual preferences, in the interest of their own ecclesiastical institution have had to offer a religious product that can effectively compete with their evangelical rivals. In all likelihood, an episcopal red light given to the CCR would have resulted in even greater Catholic attrition, as those seeking ecstatic spirituality continued to flock to the Assemblies of God and Church of the Word, among others.

Thus, facing up to the stark reality of the logic of a free-market religious economy, the bishops not only incorporated the Charismatic product into their ecclesial firm but also intelligently insisted on differentiating it from that of their main competitors. To avoid confusion with the standardized pneumatic product of the Pentecostal competition, the chief Catholic producers have developed a virgophilic brand of Charismatic Christianity. This most potent of all symbols of Latin American Catholic identity joins the Holy Spirit in making the CCR the church's most appealing product in the new religious marketplace. Ironically, it is the competition of the free-market religious economy, which the church so steadfastly resisted until recently, that has led to the current Catholic renewal in Latin America.

Entrepreneurial Spirits

Religions of the African Diaspora

Joining Pentecostalism and Charismatic Catholicism in dominating Latin America's new spiritual marketplace is the region's third major pneumacentric religious tradition, the faiths of the African diaspora. Over the past half-century, the religions that African slaves brought over to the Americas as part of their cultural baggage have been thriving in Brazil and much of the Caribbean. In Brazil, Umbanda and Candomblé, the two principal African-derived religions, successfully compete with pneumacentric Christianity for the loyalty of urban spiritual consumers. In the Caribbean, Vodou forms an integral part of the Haitian cultural fabric, much as Catholicism has done historically in Ibero-America.[1] Indeed, it was Vodou that inspired and sustained the slave revolt that culminated in Haitian independence and the world's first black republic in 1804. Santería did not play the same revolutionary role in Cuba, but it has allowed African-Cubans to maintain their African cultural roots and derive spiritual succor and power from West African *orishas*, or spirits. Accompanying their human devotees, the *orishas* of Santería have followed Cuban *santeros* to their diasporan communities in Miami and New York, among other U.S. cities.

While the diasporan faiths exhibit diversity in their belief systems and practices, core elements of ritual and creed unite them sufficiently to permit some general comments. Origins in West and Central Africa, spirit possession, polytheism, animal sacrifice, syncretism with Catholicism, and a history of slavery and racism stand out as the salient elements that unite Candomblé, Santería, Umbanda, Vodou, and other smaller regional groups in doctrine and worship. Some general introductory remarks on each aspect will lead into a full examination of the four factors that have determined the success of diasporan religions, and indeed are determinative of the fate of any spiritual firm operating in a free-market economy. Just as analysis of the product, marketing, sales representatives, and organization of Pentecostalism and Charismatic Catholicism revealed their keys to success, it will also shed light on the impressive growth of African diasporan religions since the middle of the twentieth century.

Out of Africa

African-Latin religions have their roots in the great diaspora of Africans from the western and central part of the continent to the Americas between the sixteenth and nineteenth centuries. As major players in the Atlantic slave trade, the Iberians and Ibero-Americans imported approximately 5.2 million Africans to work on the sugar and tobacco plantations and in the gold and silver mines of Spanish and Portuguese America. Most hailed from the eastern part of West Africa, but the center and center-south were also well represented. Among the hundreds of African ethnicities who came forcibly to Latin America, a few stand out as the most important contributors to the development of diasporan faiths.

Of primary importance are the Yoruba of present-day Nigeria, Togo, and Benin. Brazilian Candomblé and Cuban Santería are sororal religions in that both are Yoruba religion syncretized with Catholicism, to varying degrees, and adapted to their respective national and regional cultures. After the Yoruba, the Ewe of Togo, Ghana, and Benin probably contributed the most to the development of diasporan religions in Latin America. Ewe slaves clandestinely practicing their beliefs in Haiti and Brazil were among the main architects of Vodou and Tambor de Minas, the regional diasporan religion of the northeastern Brazilian state of Maranhão. Also in Brazil and Haiti, the Bantu from the Congo and Angola played a leading role in the development of Macumba—the main diasporan group in Rio de Janeiro and São Paulo until the creation of Umbanda in the 1920s—and contributed their emphasis on ancestor worship, among other elements, to Vodou.

In addition to common origins in West and Central Africa, the diasporan religions share a history of slavery and persecution. As the state religion of Ibero-America, Catholicism enjoyed a monopoly on religious production, and its clergy viewed all other faiths as heretical. African faiths, however, were not even considered religions but superstition at best and witchcraft at worst. That the Catholic church was never very interested in the salvation of the souls of African slaves allowed for the surreptitious practice of the Yoruba, Bantu, and Ewe religion on the plantations of the Caribbean and Brazil. Since its practice was outlawed and practitioners summoned the *orishas* under the threat of persecution, diasporan religion during the Latin American colonial era functioned in a disorganized and atomized fashion. Persecution of African-Brazilian faiths by the state and by the Catholic Church lasted until the early 1960s when in Rio de Janeiro they were finally removed from the jurisdiction of the municipal vice squad. A new round of persecution commenced, however, in the 1980s. This time it was neither the Catholic Church nor the Brazilian state that demonized Umbanda and Candomblé but certain Pentecostal churches, led by the Universal Church of the Kingdom of God. Locked in a fierce struggle for the same popular religious market share, neo-Pentecostals, in particular, denounced diasporan religion as satanic and even raided and desecrated Umbanda and Candomblé *terreiros*.

Persecution at the hands of the Iberian church and state led to a process of syncretism and symbiosis in which diasporan religions incorporated elements of Catholicism into their worship and symbology in order to camouflage their continuing devotion to African *lwas* and *orixas*. The most obvious example is the association of Catholic saints with African spirits. Practitioners of Vodou, for example, associate the great *lwa*, Danbala, who is represented as a gargantuan serpent, with St. Patrick, the Catholic holy man who according to legend drove the snakes out of Ireland. Likewise, devotees of Candomblé associate Yemenja, queen of the ocean, with the Virgin Mary, particularly with Our Lady of the Immaculate Conception. Catholic confraternities, or lay brotherhoods (organized along ethnic and racial lines, among other divisions, during the colonial period), ironically served as one of the main vehicles of the preservation of African religion. In addition to their important functions as mutual aid societies and social clubs, the confraternities unwittingly allowed African slaves to continue their devotion to the *orixas*.

Over time, the Catholic symbols and rituals, which had initially only served to mask African religious practice, became incorporated into worship ceremonies, eventually forming an integral part of the diasporan faiths. In the more Afrocentric religions of Candomblé and Vodou, the association with Catholic elements is best conceived of as a relation of symbiosis in which the two belief systems are mutually interdependent but do not actually merge (Desmangles). On the other end of the spectrum, Umbanda is a clear case of syncretism in which discrete religious traditions—Catholicism, Macumba, and Spiritism— merged and coalesced to form a new religion. Macumba, however, remains the greatest contributor, at least in the Umbanda *terreiros* on the urban peripheries of Brazil. Santería, while clearly not syncretic to the degree of Umbanda, goes beyond the symbiosis of Vodou and Candomblé in its integration of Catholic elements. Of the four main diasporan religions, it is the only one that does not have an African name. Santería, or way of the saints, derives from the Spanish word, *santo*, or saint.

The symbiosis and syncretism with Catholicism was partly facilitated by the commonality of polytheism. With its primary focus on the myriad saints and virgins, popular Catholicism in Latin America often has been practiced more as a polytheistic than as a monotheistic faith. For the great majority of popular Catholics, God is a remote figure who rarely receives the kind of intimate prayers and petitions that are directed to the saints and virgins. Such is the case with the diasporan religions, which acknowledge an omnipotent creator, such as Oludamare in Santería and Candomblé, but whose ritual practice centers on the multiple spirits that manifest themselves through possession of their human mediums. While hundreds, if not thousands, of distinct spirits inhabit the pantheons of diasporan religions, it is usually not more than twenty or so that most often manifest themselves through the rhythmic dancing of their human mediums. In three of the four principal religions, the spirits are distinctly African and have retained their original names, such as Xango, Exu, Ogun, and others. Umbanda is the exception in that its *guias*, spirits, are thoroughly Brazilian and typically have Portuguese names. Preto-velhos (old Black slaves), Caboclos (Amazonian Indians), and Exus (liminal trickster spirits often manifested as Brazilian gangsters and hustlers) are the primary *guias* of the Umbanda pantheon and could not be more Brazilian in their roles as archetypes of national identity. Thus, whereas Umbandistas sacralize elements of Brazilian culture in their *terreiros*, practitioners of Vodou, Santería, and Candomblé recreate a piece of Africa on Caribbean and Brazilian soil through the presence of the *orixas* and *lwas*.

The commonality of polytheism shared by diasporan religions and popular Catholicism ceases at the former's leading product of spirit possession. Perhaps no single practice unites all African-derived faiths as much as the ritual possession of human mediums (called "horses" in the diasporan idiom) by the *orixas*, *lwas*, and *guias*. Trained mediums offer their mind and body to the spirits, who use them as vessels to both heal and cause affliction, as well as to impart wisdom and to entertain. The spirits most clearly manifest themselves in the ritual dances and consultations with clients, which form the experiential core of diasporan religions. And it is here in its pneumacentrism that African-derived religion most closely approximates its two vibrant, Christian competitors, Pentecostalism and Charismatic Catholicism. Spirit possession is explored here in depth in the discussion of diasporan religious products.

The final salient element that unites the disasporan faiths and distinguishes them from their Christian rivals is blood sacrifice. As in other Latin American popular religions, the relationship between human believer and the spirits is one of reciprocity, or exchange. The *orixas* and *lwas* do not work for free, and as part of their payment they often demand the blood of animals as rich nourishment. It is specifically the blood, and not the meat, that is offered to the spirits because it is the red fluid that is believed to contain the *ashe* (*axe* in Portuguese), or life force that sustains both humans and spirits. Diasporan priestesses and priests, known as mothers and fathers-of-the-saints (*maes-de-santos* and *pais-de-santos*) customarily pour the blood of sacrificial roosters, hens, and goats on the sacred symbols of the spirits, often stones, and have the animals dressed and cooked for consumption by the community of believers. Once again, Umbanda differs somewhat from the other three major diasporan religions. Influenced by Catholicism and Spiritism, middle-class Umbanda centers tend to reject blood sacrifice as "African primitivism." In the slums and shantytowns of Brazil, however, Umbandistas continue to sacrifice blood to the *guias*, particularly the amoral Exus, but probably more surreptitiously than do the devotees of Vodou, Candomblé, and Santería.

The Diasporan Market

Perhaps the most striking aspect of the consumer profile of diasporan religions over the past fifty years is its similarity to that of Pentecostalism. With slight variations, Charismatic Protestantism and African-derived groups have competed for religious consumers among the same populations. Although data on the growth of diasporan religions are incomplete, sufficient research has been conducted, especially in Brazil, to show that they have experienced accelerated growth contemporaneously with the Pentecostal boom, which began in the 1950s. In São Paulo, Latin America's second largest city, the number of registered Umbanda and Candomblé centers soared from just 85 in 1940 to 19,500 in 1980 (Mariz *Coping with Poverty* 165 n.16). The northeastern metropolis of Recife followed suit, with the number of registered Umbanda, Xangô, and Jurema centers estimated to have increased from 120 in 1951 to six thousand in 1975 (Mariz *Coping with Poverty* 165 n.16).[2] Further up the Atlantic coast in Belem, the number of registered Umbanda centers shot up by 150 percent for those houses of worship that ban drumming and an astonishing 473 percent for those that receive the spirits to the beat of the percussion (di Paolo 99).[3] Moving to the Caribbean, more than two-thirds of the shrines of Trinidad's Orisha religion surveyed by scholar James Houk were founded since the 1970s (188).

After five decades of accelerated growth, it is estimated that half of all Brazilians have visited an Umbanda center at least once. Local research in Belem and Rio de Janeiro corroborates this figure (Burdick; di Paolo). Similarly, one of the leading experts on Santería calculates that most Cubans have consulted with a *santero* or *santera* (Murphy *Working the Spirit* 85), as undoubtedly have the great majority of Haitians with a *manbo* or *ougan*, the priestess and priest, respectively, of Vodou. It should be noted, however, that most of these frequenters are occasional and sporadic clients who seek out the *orixas* and *lwas* in times of personal crisis.

Determining the numbers of regular participants is more difficult largely be cause so many practitioners of diasporan religions also consider themselves Catholics and because the enduring, though diminished, stigma attached to African-derived faiths leads many to identify themselves as Catholic to census takers. For example, 1990 census figures in Brazil reveal that only 1.5 percent of the population claim to belong to African-Brazilian religions. Even in Rio de Janeiro, the birthplace of Umbanda and the unofficial capital of African-Brazilian religions, along with Salvador da Bahia, just 5 percent of cariocas claimed affiliation with Umbanda or Candomblé (Prandi 20). Census data diverge widely from figures cited by academics who have studied African-Brazilian religions. One-fifth of anthropologist John Burdick's 140 informants on the urban periphery of Rio de Janeiro were regular participants in Umbanda (14), while nearly one-third (31 percent) of two thousand people surveyed in Belem claimed to be (di Paolo 117). Researchers Fernando Brumana and Elda Gonzalez estimated almost one-quarter of all Brazilians to be Umbandistas in 1990 (30). Given the stigma attached to African-Brazilian religions and the distrust of the federal government by large sectors of society, combined with the fact that researchers tend to concur on an Umbanda population of 20 to 30 percent, it is probable that estimates by academics are much closer to the mark than census figures are. Keeping in mind that the more conservative figure of 20 percent is for Umbanda alone, with the addition of Candomblé, Xangô, and other regional groups, it is not unreasonable to estimate the regular practitioners of African-Brazilian religions at between 15 and 20 percent of the national population. In all likelihood, the African-Brazilian religions can claim roughly the same number of followers, 30 million, as Protestantism. Figures for Vodou and Santería are harder to come by, but Barrett's generally reliable *World Christian Encyclopedia* estimates that roughly the same percentage of Cubans, 18 percent, practices Santería as Brazilians participate in diasporan religions (225). At 39 percent of the population, only Catholicism claims more faithful followers than Santería (225). Statistics for Haiti, the most impoverished nation in the hemisphere, are indubitably the most difficult to obtain. However, one credible source estimates the number of Vodou practitioners at 44 percent, close to one-half the Haitian population ("Vodoun" www.adherents.com).

María da Silva, an Archtypical Devotee

Diasporan religions mirror Pentecostalism not only in their period of rapid growth and numbers of practitioners but also in their demographic makeup. Devotees of African-derived faiths share with *crentes* the commonalities of gender, class, geography, and religious background. Indeed, with a few slight modifications, María Hernández, the archetypical Latin American Pentecostal in chapter 3, becomes María da Silva, the personification of the typical follower of diasporan religion. Like María Hernández, María da Silva is a poor, married woman of color in her thirties or forties and living on the urban margins. She had been a nominal Catholic before becoming an adherent of Umbanda and continues to identify herself as such. And like María Hernández, the Pentecostal, María da Silva first came to her religion searching for a resolution to her poverty-related personal crisis. Diasporan religions, of course, are not the exclusive province of poor Latin Americans of color, but María da Silva personifies the most common socioeconomic characteristics found among the millions of Brazilian and Caribbean devotees.

Diasporan religions parallel their two Christian competitors in their gender composition but differ significantly in the roles that woman play. Women in African-derived faiths, as in Pentecostalism and the CCR, outnumber men by an approximate ratio of two to one. Santería expert Joseph Murphy writes of an *ile* (worship house) in New York, where the gender ratio climbs to four to one (Santería 52). As mentioned in previous chapters, the predominance of female practitioners is the norm across the board in Latin American religion. Where diasporan religions depart from the norm, however, is their granting of the priesthood to women. As priestesses of their respective religions, the *maes-de-santos* of Umbanda, the *santeras* of Santería, the *iyalorixas* of Candomblé, and the *manbos* of Vodou possess far more ritual power than Catholic and Pentecostal women, who are prohibited from becoming clergy.[4] For a Latin American woman from the popular classes seeking to run her own religious organization, there is no greater opportunity than in the faiths of the *lwas* and *orixás*.

Like Pentecostalism, the diasporan faiths claim a majority of their followers among the Latin American popular classes. More specific studies are needed on the demographics of African-derived religion, but sufficient research has been conducted to show that most Umbandistas and Vodouists, among others, belong to the popular classes. In fact, as faiths developed by African slaves, the diasporan religions historically have been those of the poorest of the poor. Pentecostals and diasporan groups, and more recently the CCR, undoubtedly recruit among the same socioeconomic sectors of Brazilian and Caribbean populations. Having said this, it does appear that diasporan groups attract a larger portion of devotees who are doubly subaltern because of their social class and either sexual orientation or economic activity. On the first score, some scholars have noted a significant presence of male homosexuals in diasporan religions. In Belem, for example, Leacock and Leacock asserted that close to one-third (14 of 46) of their male informants in Batuque (the local diasporan faith) were gay (104). The sexuality of spirit possession would largely explain why the pattern evident in Batuque most likely holds for diasporan religion in general. In African-derived faiths, the spirits "mount" and "ride" the human mediums,

An Umbandista and her daughter in Belem, Brazil

and sexual norms in Latin America dictate that it is much more socially accept-able for heterosexual men to mount and ride than to be mounted and ridden. Indeed, the act of allowing oneself to be mounted is strongly associated with ho-mosexual behavior. The Leacocks even posited that this is the primary factor that discourages heterosexual men from becoming mediums (104).

Gender is another aspect of spirit possession that appeals to some gays, par-ticularly transvestites and transsexuals. Male mediums are free to be possessed by female spirits and manifest all of the traits associated with them. In the so-cial context of discrimination and violence faced by Latin American homosex-uals, diasporan religions serve as sanctuaries where gay men have greater lib-erty of self-expression. That Pentecostalism and Catholicism condemn homosexuality as immoral makes diasporan faiths even more attractive to gay spiritual consumers who are interested in maintaining and not transforming their sexual orientation.

The relative amorality of diasporan religions also holds a special appeal to those Caribbeans and Brazilians whose illicit economic activities, such as pros-titution, smuggling, and drug trafficking, are condemned by Christian denomi-nations as sinful. While Christian churches, especially Pentecostals, demand that converts repent and abandon their sinful activities, Candomblé, Santería, Umbanda, and Vodou actually offer spiritual protection to prostitutes, pimps, smugglers, traffickers, and others whose work takes them beyond the pale of the law. Such is the case that two of the most popular Umbanda *guias* are ze Pilantra and Pomba Gira, the former being the spirit of a carioca trickster or hustler, and the latter the unofficial patroness spirit of Brazilian prostitutes. Both belong to the Exú family of liminal spirits that have been associated with the devil by Brazilian Christians.

African-derived faiths not only allow believers to engage in illicit economic activities but also offer supernatural protection from the omnipresent danger that threatens prostitutes, drug dealers, con artists, smugglers, and others. For those seeking to escape a life of crime, Pentecostalism is the obvious religious choice, but for others who are looking for divine protection rather than a clean new life, diasporan faiths are more appropriate. Not surprisingly, then, researchers such as the Leacocks have noted a significant presence of those who are doubly subaltern due to their illicit economic activities. Prostitutes and smugglers were well represented in Belem's Batuques, and competition was stiff among mothers and fathers of the saints to secure brothels as clients (267).

In addition to gender and class, adherents of African-Latin faiths are united by their religious background. Like Pentecostal converts, the great majority were raised as nominal Catholics. However, unlike *crentes*, Candomblecistas, Santeros, Umbandistas, and Vodouists tend to maintain their Catholic identity. Of course, the syncretism and symbiosis with Catholicism has facilitated this. With the exception of the new generation of Afrocentric Candomblecistas who seek to purge the faith of its Catholic elements, most followers of diasporan religions see no contradiction between the two belief systems. In fact, recent research indicates that practitioners of African-derived religions see their diasporan faith and Catholicism as two parts of a single religious system. Some 60 percent of Umbandistas surveyed by Diana Brown held this view (135), as did most queried by other researchers (Brumana and Martinez; Burdick; di Paolo; Negrão). Thus, devotees can receive the spirits without shedding their Catholic identity. In stark contrast, conversion to Pentecostalism demands such rupture with one's Catholic past that neophytes often smash their statuettes (in a literal act of iconoclasm) of saints and virgins upon affiliation with a *creyente* church.

Historically, ethnicity has also been a salient characteristic of consumers of diasporan religions. In fact, until the 1960s, all diasporan faiths, to varying degrees, were essentially ethnic religions of African-Brazilians and African-Caribbeans. But with increasing religious liberty and social acceptance of African cultural roots, Candomblé, Santería, and Umbanda began to attract greater numbers of white, mestizo, and mulatto adherents. Today, these three are universal religions, with blacks still disproportionately represented, especially in Candomblé, but constituting a minority of believers. For example, according to census figures, blacks comprise 8 percent of the Brazilian population but represent 18 percent of practitioners of African-Brazilian faiths (Prandi 21). Pentecostalism actually claims a greater percentage of believers of color (black

A Pomba Gira in Recife, Brazil

and brown categories employed by the census) than Umbanda. Unlike the other three main diasporan faiths, Vodou remains an ethnic faith since more than 90 percent of Haitians are black. Hence, diasporan religions continue to hold a special appeal for African–Latin Americans, but as multiracial faiths, three of the four major groups can no longer be defined by a predominantly black clientele.

Nor can urbanism be identified as a defining characteristic of diasporan devotees. Like Pentecostals, they live in cities at rates similar to the general population, 73 percent of whom are urbanites. In comparison, 69 percent of Umbandistas and 74 percent of Candomblecistas are city dwellers. Having fleshed out the defining characteristics of María da Silva, the composite practitioner of diasporan religion, the focus shifts to the salient religious products that led María to become and remain an Umbandista, for instance.

Products of Healing and Harm

Again, the task here is not to examine all diasporan products but only those that are most responsible for the success of African-derived faiths among Latin American religious consumers over the past five decades. Diasporan religions join their pneumacentric Christian rivals in offering supernatural healing as their premier product. More than any other product, *cura* is what first attracts spiritual consumers to Santería and Umbanda and the others and what most keeps them coming back. That healing through faith is the leading product in the three religious traditions under consideration should come of little surprise in a region where poverty-related afflictions abound and health care is inadequate, at best.

Since divine healing and pneumacentrism are inextricably intertwined, spirit possession logically serves as another prized product of diasporan religions. When an afflicted client consults with an Umbanda medium, for example, it is not the latter who dispenses sage advice and proposes solutions but the *guia* who possesses the medium. Without the presence of the spirits, genuine healing cannot occur. If these two salient products approximate diasporan religions to their two Christian rivals, the third radically separates them. Diasporan doctrine, unlike Christian, is not dualistic.

The stark polarities of heaven-hell, sinner-saint, God-devil, and good-evil are largely absent from African-derived faiths. In contrast, diasporan doctrine presents a cosmos of moral shades of gray in which the black and white absolutes of good and evil are greatly obscured. This means that clients and regular practitioners can ask the diasporan spirits for things that Christians would find immoral or sinful. Thus, African-derived religions enjoy a competitive advantage over their Christian rivals in the form of a unique product that offers supernatural aid to religious consumers for petitions and acts condemned as immoral or even satanic by Pentecostalism and the CCR.

The paramountcy of the product of supernatural healing in diasporan religions cannot be overstated. The sine qua non of Vodou, Umbanda, Santería, and Candomblé—that is, the spiritual curing of poverty-related pathogens—is the product that first impels religious consumers to the door of a Candomblé *terreiro* and leads them to become regular practitioners or occasional clients. So central is healing to diasporan religions that Umbanda, like the Brazilian Assemblies of God, was founded through an act of ᴄ... in which ... Zélio de Moraes was healed of paralysis by a *guia* in Rio de Janeiro, in 1920, after conventional medical treatment failed (Brown 39). Indeed, even the term, Umbanda, itself is thought to derive from the Bantu family of languages in which it means the art of curing (Brown 50).

Both sociological surveys and ethnographies of diasporan religions confirm the primacy of the dialectic between illness and supernatural healing in attracting clients and regular customers. In one of the largest surveys of over four hundred Umbandistas, Brown found that 62 percent of her informants first came to their center for help in resolving a problem, and by far the most common problem was health, which comprised 64 percent of problems brought to their center since their initial contact (94–96). These figures are even more impressive in light of the fact that most of Brown's informants were middle class. Likewise, illness impelled 45 percent of Negrão's 570 informants and 53 percent of Trinidad's to become Umbandistas (Negrão 105). Rich ethnographies corroborate the centrality of divine healing in the other diasporan faiths (Murphy, *Santería* and *Working the Spirit*, Leacock and Leacock).

With one possible exception, the pathogens of poverty brought to diasporan centers are the same that impel the afflicted to the doors of a Pentecostal church. As is the case in Pentecostalism, somatic maladies are the most common affliction. Since so many members of the Latin American popular classes are engaged in manual labor, physical incapacity can threaten their livelihood if not their very existence. Thus the divine healing of dysfunctional bodies can be seen as the raison d'être of diasporan religions. Following physical illness, familial, marital, and financial problems are the afflictions most likely to attract a new religious consumer and to retain her as a regular client. The instrumentality of diasporan religions is underscored by the fact that fewer than 6 percent of Brown's respondents had gone to Umbanda *terreiros* seeking help for *spiritual* problems (97).

The one affliction that religious consumers do not seem to bring very often to diasporan centers is alcohol abuse. This, of course, differentiates diasporan faiths from Pentecostalism, which functions as a spiritual detox center for hundreds of thousands of Latin American men (Chesnut). In Diana Brown's survey of problems brought to Umbanda centers, drinking was included as part of a miscellaneous category that accounted for only 3 percent of all problems (97). In Belém's Batuque, wives and girlfriends afflicted by their husbands and boyfriends' hard drinking sought relief from their suffering, while the drinkers themselves apparently rarely sought out mothers and fathers of the saints for help. Further research on this intriguing subject is needed, but the fact that alcohol consumption (often in large quantities) plays an important role in diasporan healing rituals precludes African-derived religions from offering effective remedies for alcoholism. One can imagine that spirits who frequently manifest themselves intoxicated, such as Umbanda's Ze Pilantra, Pomba Gira, and *marinheiros* (sailors) do not exactly serve as models of sobriety for those who are unable to control their drinking.

Although there are important ritual differences among the diasporan religions, the mechanics of divine healing in Umbanda do not differ substantially from the others. The *consulta* (consultation) between the client and the spirit-possessed medium constitutes the ritual core of most Umbanda ceremonies. Having failed to resolve her problem through secular channels (home remedies, pharmaceuticals, and physicians) or other religions, an afflicted individual will attend an Umbanda session with the specific purpose of consulting with the *guias* via a medium. At larger sessions, clients are assigned numbers and wait their turn to speak with a medium. When her number is called, the client proceeds to meet face to face with the medium and recounts the problem to the *guia* that has possessed the medium. The *guia* then diagnoses the affliction and prescribes a course of treatment.

More often then not, the problem is diagnosed as spiritual and thus calls for remedies of the spirits, such as herbal baths and incenses, offerings of food and drink to a particular *guia*, or even the development of one's potential as an Umbanda medium. If the *guia* identifies the affliction as material or secular, however, it will recommend that the client consult with the appropriate secular authority, such as a physician, lawyer, or government official. In exchange for the opportunity to consult with a *guia*, clients typically pay a set fee or give gifts to the mediums for services rendered. If the treatment proves successful and the affliction is healed, clients often return to the medium with additional gifts of gratitude. Between the consultations and the mediums, who are often dressed in white nurses' uniforms, Umbanda sessions, like Pentecostal services, resemble the very medical clinics that failed to heal many of the clients in attendance. As is the case in a hospital, Umbanda clients, in pragmatic fashion, often leave the session after their own *consulta*, preferring not to stay for the more communal parts of the ceremony.

While they have been separated for analytical purposes, the two major products of diasporan religions are inextricably intertwined. Supernatural healing is unimaginable without spirit possession, and vice versa. The primary purpose of the diasporan spirits is to heal the poverty-related afflictions of their human devotees. In the consultations described, it is not the human medium but the spirit using the medium as a vessel that diagnoses the clients' problems and prescribes their treatment. For clients, the experience of consulting directly with a supernatural being renders the prescribed treatment more potent. Keeping in mind that many clients have already experienced unsuccessful remedies at the hands of human authorities, such as physicians, they have come to believe that only supernatural intervention can solve their problem. And the multiplicity of spirits in diasporan religions allows for a degree of specialization that is impossible in Pentecostalism and the CCR in which the Holy Spirit serves more as a general practitioner. For example, a medium may call on the *guia* Pomba Gira, an expert in sexual and romantic affairs, to aid a client whose husband is having an affair.

For the medium, the experience of spirit possession is even more powerful, as it is her body and consciousness that are taken over by the *guia*. Possessed by a spirit, the medium enters into a dissociated state of consciousness in which she manifests the particular personality traits of the *lwa* or *orixa* in question. For example, while possessed by a preto velho (old black slave) spirit, the medium will express the humility, compassion, and sagacity associated with this key member of the Umbanda spirit pantheon. Dance is one of the primary ways that diasporan spirits manifest themselves, and that of the preto velho is a slow, measured step reflecting the advanced age of the *guia*. The old black slave's preferred accessory is a corncob pipe, which he puffs while dancing and consulting with clients. His calm demeanor is as far removed as one could imagine from the frenzied and hysterical possessions shown in Hollywood films on "Voodoo." Such violent possession does occur in diasporan religion but is the mark of novice mediums who have yet to learn how to control their possession.

The product of spirit possession offers the primary benefit of inversive power to mediums of diasporan religion. The phenomenon of possession is similar to that of baptism by the Holy Spirit in the CCR and Pentecostalism, but especially the latter. As members of the Caribbean and Brazilian popular classes, most mediums in their secular lives experience a profound sense of impotence as they struggle to make ends meet for their families and themselves. And as women of color, many mediums are triply oppressed by class, gender, and race. They reside at the very bottom of the steep social pyramid that elite Latin Americans have constructed. However, when possessed by an *orixa* or *lwa*, they temporarily transcend their difficult material conditions while their bodies, which are exploited by manual labor, become vessels for powerful spirits. In a powerful inversion of their secular roles, the mediums are transformed from social marginals to spiritual protagonists.

The inversion of secular identities not only allows mediums to access spiritual power but also permits them to assume roles that provide rupture with their cultural and economic positions in Caribbean and Brazilian societies. Thus, a monogamous teetotaling mother possessed by Umbanda's Pomba Gira is transformed into a wine-guzzling lady of the night who dances erotically and flirts with the men in attendance. Likewise, a shy, soft-spoken night watchman becomes a proud, aggressive, and outspoken Indian chief while possessed by a Caboclo *guia*, such as Sete Flechas (Seven Arrows). And in one of the more dramatic instances of inversion, the young construction worker inverts his gender and becomes Yemanja, queen of the ocean.

Diasporan religions' third salient product is their most unique one and that which most differentiates them from their Christian competitors. While African-derived faiths are ones of inversion, they, in sharp contrast to Pentecostalism and, to a lesser extent, the CCR, are definitely not religions of *conversion*. Renouncing one's sinful past for a saintly new life is an alien concept to diasporan religion. For example, there is no doctrinal reason that a prostitute would have to look for new work upon becoming an Umbandista. To the contrary, in Umbanda, the streetwalker can find spiritual protection under Pomba Gira, patroness of prostitutes. Thus, the *garota de progama* (hooker) looking to leave her difficult trade would be more attracted to the Pentecostal or Charismatic product, while the one simply seeking spiritual aid or protection would find Umbanda the more appropriate choice.

Relatively amoral diasporan doctrine provides spiritual assistance and protection for purposes and acts considered morally dubious at best and evil at worst by its Christian rivals and prevailing social mores. Hence, African-derived groups enjoy the competitive advantage of being the only major religious tradition in Latin America to offer an amoral product that can be used against personal rivals and enemies. Indeed, the act of calling on a spirit to inflict injury on one's nemesis has a name in diasporan religions. In Umbanda, the *coisa feita* involves offerings of food and drink to an Exu in exchange for his or her assistance in "tying up" (*amarrando*) or blocking the path (*trancando a rua*) of a rival or enemy. Among the more common *coisa feitas* in Brazil are those intended to harm romantic rivals. A married woman, for example, who suspects an acquaintance of having an affair with her husband might ask Pomba Gira to harm the other woman so that she is no longer the object of her husband's affection.

In extreme cases, Umbanda clients have even contracted with an Exú, such as Seven Skulls (Sête Caveiras) to kill an enemy. In his study of Candomblé in Bahia, Jim Wafer tells of a medium who, possessed by the spirit ze Pilantra, sings a song about murdering his entire family (43). Similary in Belem, Leacock and Leacock cite a prominent *pai-de-santo* who was said to have had his wife murdered through a *coisa feita* so he could freely pursue another woman (272). Naturally, the great majority of diasporan mediums deny practicing sorcery or "black magic," but there is no question that many, if not most, do, since to refuse work with the Exús would probably result in a loss of clintele. This point is highlighted by Negrão's study of Umbanda in São Paulo in which she found the Exús, including the female variety of Pomba Gira, to be the most commonly manifested *guias* at the sessions (204). There is obviously significant consumer demand for sorcery in Brazil and the Caribbean, and diasporan religion's

The Exu, Tranca Rua, in Recife, Brazil

unique amoral product gives it a distinct competitive advantage over Christian rivals who produce no such goods.

More than any other element, it is the existence of the Exús in diasporan religions that allows for amoral practices and sorcery. As liminal trickster spirits, Exús are not seen as intrinsically evil but as unevolved spiritual beings who are willing to work with clients for the right price. In effect, they serve as amoral spiritual mercenaries who are ignorant of absolute standards of good and evil and ready to work for the highest bidder. If they have become associated with the Christian devil and his minions in popular culture, it is because the Catholic and Protestant churches alike have no room for amoral figures and have demonized the Exús. Interestingly, to a certain extent, practitioners of diasporan faith appear to be making the same association, as several Exús of Candomblé and Umbanda are commonly represented as statuettes of red devils, complete with horns and hooves. Thus, in a religious marketplace in which supernatural healing and pneumacentrism are standard products among the prosperous spiritual firms, the amoral goods and services of diasporan religions give them a unique product that has proven popular among Caribbean and Brazilian consumers.

Marketing the Familiar

Like the appealing products of its Christian competitors, those of diasporan religions are also sold to religious consumers through marketing of the faith. Here it is tempting to highlight the comparative disadvantages of Candomblé, Santería, Umbanda, and Vodou marketing in relation to the CCR and Pentecostalism, but to do so would obscure the overall success they have had in selling their religious products. There is little doubt, however, that since they are not proselytory religions, such as Christianity and Islam, the diasporan faiths generally do not engage in systematic evangelization as a way to win converts. The type of door-to-door proselytization conducted by Pentecostals and Catholic Charismatics is alien to African-derived faiths. Since diasporan groups are much less concerned with the salvation of souls and life in the hereafter, the apocalyptic urgency that compels evangelical Christians to win as many souls for Jesus as possible before the Second Coming is a foreign concept. The lack of such evangelical zeal in a free market of faith indubitably creates a distinct disadvantage for non-Christian groups. Another disadvantage derives from the lack of institutional organization and unity, which precludes any kind of systematic marketing strategy. Nevertheless, despite these inherent disadvantages in advertising their religious products, African-derived faiths have marketed well enough to rank among the three most prosperous religious traditions in Latin America today.

Diasporan religions join their main Christian competitors in utilizing preexisting social networks as the most efficacious manner of recruiting new clients and devotees to their centers. Family members, friends, and colleagues, who themselves have been healed or have had a problem resolved at a particular Umbanda *terreiro* or a Santería *ile*, are the primary media for marketing the faith. Some 82 percent of Brown's informants had been introduced to their Umbanda centers through members of their social network, most important of which are kin (109). Moreover, her respondents cited being brought by someone as the second most common reason, after health, for first attending an Umbanda session (95). There is no more powerful marketing device than a family member whose health has been restored by the spirits at a particular diasporan center.

The primacy of word of mouth among family members, friends, and coworkers does not mean that diasporan religions never use mass media as a tool for recruitment. Elite centers and federations, particularly in Umbanda, run radio programs, websites, and occasional television programs and publish journals. In Brazil, the presses print hundreds of books on Umbanda and Candomblé each year. However, disaporan presence in Latin American mass media pales in comparison to Pentecostalism and the CCR. While mass media might become a more important tool of diasporan marketing in the future, it has not been a significant factor in recruiting new clients and devotees during the past five decades.

Once the neophyte has made it to a diasporan service for the first time, there are a number of ways in which the mothers and fathers of the saints market the faith to encourage potential clients and adherents to consume their religious products. Of chief importance is the drama of spirit possession. In addition to functioning as one of diasporan religion's principal products, the manifestation of the *lwas* and *orixás* in their human mediums demonstrates the power and palpability of the spirits. Having typically failed to resolve their poverty-related crisis through secular channels, afflicted neophytes are looking for "strong medicine," the spiritual equivalent of the myriad injections that pharmacists throughout Brazil administer for every imaginable ailment from the common cold to dizzyness. Through the rhythmic dancing and singing of their mediums, the spirits not only prove their existence but also demonstrate their supernatural power. Thus the uniniated are more likely to believe that the *lwas* are capable of resolving their problem.

On a lighter note, spirit possession also makes for great drama, with animated dancing, syncopated drumming, smoking, drinking, colorful costumes, and gunpowder ignited with the arrival and departure of the Exús. Without question, of the three religious traditions under consideration, it is the diasporan faiths that offer the most entertaining ceremonies. The Umbanda and Xangô sessions that I have attended in Brazil could always count on a sizeable contingent of curious spectators who seemed to find the ceremonies highly entertaining. Only the Brazilian neo-Pentecostal denomination, the Universal Church of the Kingdom of God, approximates the spiritual pyrotechnics of diasporan religions.

As most priestesses and priests cannot afford to rent a locale for worship sessions, the *terreiro* (literally piece of earth) and *ile* (which quite appropriately means house in the Yoruba language) are typically a room or backyard in the *manbo*'s or *pai-de-santo*'s house. Chances are that the house resembles those of many in attendance and thus creates a familiar ritual space in which neophytes nervous about their first visit can feel more "at home." Therefore, the familiarity of both the ritual space and diasporan iconography puts newcomers, the majority of whom are nominal Catholics, at ease and encourages them to purchase the religious products.

Beside the ritual space, the inconography of the African-derived faiths reinforces the familiar. The symbiosis and syncretism of the religions present new-

Umbanda paraphenalia shop in São Luiz, Brazil

ⁱⁱⁱⁱⁱⁱⁱ ⁱⁱⁱⁱⁱ ⁱ ⁱⁱⁱⁱ ⁱⁱ ᵇᵒᵘᵗ ᵒᶠ Catholic saints and virgins, some of whose images might even populate the neophyte's home altar or niche. St. Barbara, St. George, and the Virgin of Aparecida, among others, provide great iconographic and ritual continuity for the large percentage of nominal Catholics that constitute diasporan religions' large clientele. The statues and pictures of non-Catholic *guias* and *orixas*, while not as familiar as the saints and virgins, are known to almost every Brazilian and Caribbean. *Botánicas* (as they are called in Santería), shops that sell all kinds of Catholic and diasporan paraphenalia, are part of the urban landscape in Brazil and the Caribbean—as well as in Los Angeles, Houston, Miami, and New York, for that matter. Caboclo *guias* depicted as fierce Apaches or Sioux and preto velhos stooped over on a stool with corncob pipe in hand watch passersby through the windows of the shops.

The final element of diasporan marketing involves the consulations between clients and the spirit-possessed mediums. On the part of the client, participation in a consultation involves no renunciation of one's religious background, whether nominal Catholic or even Pentecostal. *Consultas* are open to all, no matter one's past or current religious affiliation. This, of course, could not be more diametrically opposed to Pentecostalism, which demands renunciation and conversion in order for faith healing to occur. Recalling that many newcomers at diasporan services are not seeking conversion but curing and supernatural protection, the extreme accessibility and openness of the consultation with the spirits is very appealing.

The diagnosis of affliction, particularly physical illness, during the *consulta* also serves an an effective tool for marketing the faith. The *lwas* and *guias* diagnose a significant portion of clients' cases to be the result of undeveloped potential as a medium. In other words, the client's sickness is interpreted as a call from the spirits or a particular *orixá* to become a Santero or Umbandista and a human servant of the spirits. Given that most diasporan priestesses and priests initially became mediums as a result of a serious personal crisis, the diagnosis of affliction as a message from the spirits to develop one's potential as a medium is an efficacious way of converting occasional clients into regular pariticipants.

Spiritual Businesswomen

At first glance, one would surmise that the sales representatives or clergy of diasporan faiths would be at a great disadvantage with their Christian competitors. Diasporan mothers and fathers of the saints lack both the proselytory zeal of Pentecostals and Catholic Charismatics and the material resources that larger denominations enjoy. A closer inspection of those who sell the products of African-derived religions, however, reveals several aspects of the clergy that allow them to compete effectively with their proselytory rivals. The salient characteristic of the diasporan sales force probably constitutes its greatest competitive advantage. Of the three religious traditions under consideration, the African-derived are the only ones in which women are the majority of the clergy. Thus, in addition to the commonalities of class, compatriotism, and educational levels, diasporan sales representatives usually have the element of gender in common with their clients.

A second important component of diasporan sales representatives is their entrepreneurship. Even more than Pentecostal pastors, the heads of Umbanda and Vodou centers are religious entrepreneurs whose spiritual business depends on the fees and contributions paid by ritual clients. The larger the clientele, the greater the income and prestige for the *manbo* or *pai-de-santo*. Thus the mediums of diasporan religions have a strong incentive to aid the spirits in their role as problem-solvers of human misfortune. Those mediums who develop reputations for summoning efficacious *guias*, for example, will be more likely to have a larger clientele than their less talented competitors.

Diasporan sales representatives also enjoy a competitive advantage in the amount of personal attention they invest in religious consumers. In a consultation with a spirit medium, the client receives the undivided personal attention of the spirits and their human medium. Pentecostal pastors are also known for their investment in personal relations, but they do not make individual counseling sessions the core of Pentecostal worship services. And with the great paucity of clergy, Catholic priests can only dream about offering such personal attention to the majority of their flock. Finally, diasporan priests and priestesses distinguish themselves from their Christian counterparts through their status as expert herbalists. Home remedies throughout Latin America draw heavily on herbs, plants, and roots, so the spiritual medicine sold by diasporan vendors is made more potent by its reliance on natural products, which are familiar to many clients.

With the exception of the Pentecostal denomination the Foursquare Gospel Church, diasporan relgions stand alone in allowing women to enter the priesthood. The majority of mediums who receive the spirits from Brazil to Cuba are female. In Brazil, female heads of Umbanda *terreiros* appear to outnumber their male counterparts by a ratio of at least two to one (Leacock and Leacock 108; Negrão 175), and the figure is probably at least as high for Candomblé. Interestingly, women are also the preferred spiritual vessels of the Holy Spirit in the CCR and Pentecostalism, but with the aforementioned exception they are prohibited from becoming members of the clergy.

While gender sets diasporan sales representatives apart from their two main competitors, the entrepreneurship of diasporan clergy unites them with Pentecostal pastors, whose professional development also depends on the size and contributions of their clientele. Although they lack the evangelical zeal of Pentecostal sales representatives, diasporan clerics operate within the same economic parameters. Unlike Catholic churches or parishes, diasporan worship centers are independent entities, which typically are only nominally affiliated with the various Umbanda or Candomblé federations.

The size and prestige of a *terreiro*, as well as its income, are direct correlations of the head's ability to attract a sizeable paying clientele. Mothers and fathers of saints who have developed a considerable regular clientele over the years can often support themselves on the fees and contributions collected from spiritual consumers. And in the economy of scarcity that envelops most diasporan clergy, the supplemental income earned from *consultas* can mean an extra portion of rice and beans at dinner, if not more. Thus, heads of diasporan centers are small business owners whose entrepreneurial acumen largely determines the fate of their enterprise. In Brazil and the Caribbean, *iles*, *ounfos*, and *terreiros* afford poor women of color the rare opportunity of owning and running their own business, albeit ones based on spiritual rather than material goods and services.

That the consultations with clients are diasporan sales representatives' most important religious source of income means that mediums have a natural incentive to offer *consultas* that are efficacious and personalized. As the spiritual consultations are the raison d'être of African-derived religions, Vodou, Umbanda, Santería, and Candomblé enjoy a competitive edge over their Christian rivals in the amount of personal attention given to religious consumers. Neither the CCR nor Pentecostal worship service provides worshipers with the opportunity to engage in an extended tête-à-tête with the priest or pastor. *Crente* pastors provide extraliturgical counseling, but the therapy sessions that are Pentecostal worship services are collective rather than individual.

The Umbanda *consulta*, for example, gives the client direct and immediate access to the *guias* (via the medium), whose diagnosis and prescription are based on the specific personal problem of the individual in question. Keeping in mind that members of the Latin American popular classes are routinely treated as anonymous masses by government, medical, and even religious institutions, the personal attention received from the spirits and their human mediums makes the *consulta* extremely appealing. In relating their misfortune to the spirits via the medium, clients assert their individuality and are made to feel that the *lwa* or *orixá* has made a diagnosis and prescription solely on the basis of their own personal problem. In reality, of course, the affliction brought to the spirits is generally not unique or peculiar to any one client but, rather, a pathogen related to the individual's position at the base of the region's tall so-

A Santera in the streets of Havana

cioeconomic pyramid. The crucial point, however, is that the nature of the spiritual consultation makes the client feel that her problem is unique and that she has been treated as an individual as opposed to a faceless "popular."

Small Business

Without the type of rationalized ecclesiastical structures of their Christian rivals, diasporan religions would appear to be at a major disadvantage in competing for Latin American religious consumers. The lack of centralization and coordination means that African-derived groups could never organize and execute the type of systematic proselytization campaigns that their Christian rivals conduct on a regular basis. However, the organizational model of diasporan religions offers other advantages that allow them to compete effectively with the CCR and Pentecostalism. First, diasporan houses of worship, even more so than Pentecostal churches, are entirely self-supporting. In effect, they are small religious businesses whose profitability depends on the number of clients and fees that the mother or father of the saints generates. Second, the familial model of relations on which individual *ounfos* and *terreiros* are organized provides continuity and comfort to both members of the priesthood and ritual clients, who are made to feel at home by fathers and mothers, sisters, and sons and daughters of the saints. That the *terreiro* or *ile* is frequently the home of a *mae-* or *pai-de-santo* only reinforces the familial model. Finally, the loose organizational structure at the level of both individual worship centers and the few regional and national federations that exist makes for a striking variety in ritual and a high level of specialization. Umbanda centers, for example, range from those that draw heavily on Kardecist Spiritism to those that specialize in Quimbanda, or sorcery.[5]

Whatever the brand of diasporan religion in which a particular ritual head specializes, the fate of her *ile* or *ounfo* depends almost entirely on her talent as a religious entrepreneur. Since client fees and donations in exchange for consultations constitute the bulk of a center's income, the *manbo* and the *mae-de-santo* have a natural incentive to recruit a sizeable clientele. Some of those who attract a substantial following are able to quit their day jobs and make a living as diasporan clerics. Given the structure of the Latin American labor market, with high levels of unemployment and physically demanding jobs for unskilled workers, the possibility of earning a living from working with spirits appeals to many diasporan clerics. The ultimate ambition of many mediums is to eventually administer their own diasporan center. While most fail to realize this dream, the fact that they earn the great majority of their ritual income through *consultas* gives them a natural incentive to augment their clientele. Thus, the organization of diasporan temples into tens of thousands of independent religious enterprises without significant ties to a central administrative unit makes the fathers of the saints paradoxically more entrepreneurial than their Christian competitors.

A mirror image of Brazilian and Caribbean societies, individual *ounfos* and *iles* are organized along primary kinship relations. The father (*pai* in Umbanda) or mother (*manbo* in Vodou) heads the house of worship, and in larger temples is often assisted by an "elder sister" (*ebomim* in Candomblé). Not all mediums are affiliated with diasporan centers, but those who are known as children of the saints (*filhos-de-santos* in Umbanda) are members of particular houses of worship. In the larger centers, there is a greater degree of ritual specialization, with different categories of mediums, drummers, and assistants, but the aforementioned ones, particularly the father and mother, and sisters, and sons and daughters, are indispensable.

The reflection of secular social organization is clearest in the role of the mother of the saints. Households headed by single women are common, if not the norm, among the popular classes of the Caribbean and Brazil. Thus, in the *iles* and *terreiros*, which are predominantly headed by women, clients find a mirror image of their own familial organization in which the mother runs the household. This, combined with the fact that the house of worship is typically the priestess's own house, makes the client literally feel at home. Perhaps the continuity of diasporan organization with Brazilian and Caribbean family structures counterbalances the social rupture that is often associated with spirit possession. A hard-drinking, foul-mouthed Baiano spirit of Umbanda, for example, might be perceived less threatening within the confines of the home of a spiritual family than if encountered in the streets.

For those clients who would prefer to avoid such uncouth spirits as Baianos, numerous Umbanda *terreiros* exist that allow only more elevated *guias* to descend. The extreme decentralization of diasporan religions makes for a kaleidoscope of individual *iles*, *terreiros*, and *ounfos* that can vary widely in doctrine and practice. In none of the four major African-Latin faiths is there a national federation that can regulate religious doctrine and practice. There are national-level Umbanda federations in Brazil, but most centers pay little attention to them and join them only to receive legal authorization to operate. This, of course, precludes African-derived faiths from conducting planned and systematic campaigns to recruit new clients.

However, the lack of bureaucratic rationalization has resulted in highly differentiated diasporan products, often reflecting the tastes and preferences of an individual *padrino* or *manbo*. For example, clients who believe Caboclo spirits to be the most powerful healers can go to an Umbanda *terreiro* specializing in Indian *guias*, while those who seek the help of the Exús in defeating romantic rivals can frequent a center known for its work with Pomba Gira. Middle-class clients who cannot stomach the presence of less "enlightened" spirits at sessions may attend ones at centers that are heavily influenced by Kardecist Spiritism, while others preferring the raw power of Exús and other liminal *guias* can head to centers specializing in lesser "evolved" spirits. Hence, diasporan religions probably offer the most differentiated products to Latin American religious consumers due to the lack of any national or regional federations that can impose uniformity and standardization on individual centers.

In conclusion, in this chapter we see the tools of religious economy have proven to be especially powerful. With their emphasis on salvation and conversion, the success of the CCR and Pentecostalism among the popular classes is more readily apparent than is the prosperity of diasporan religion. Only a systematic analysis of the four components that determine the fate of any religious enterprise in an unregualted spiritual economy could discover the reasons for the significant growth of Candomblé, Santería, Umbanda, and Vodou since the mid-twentieth century. Such analysis, for example, reveals the relative amorality of diasporan religion to actually be an appealing product to millions of Caribbean and Brazilian religious consumers. And without careful examination of diasporan sales representatives and organizational structure, the importance of enterpreneurship would have been difficult to perceive. In short, religious economy has explained how the non-proselytory and decentralized diasporan religions have competed effectively with the evangelical zeal of their main Christian rivals over the past half-century.

Practical Consumers

The Success of Pneumacentric Religion
among Women

Since women constitute the great majority of religious practitioners in Latin America, any spiritual firm interested in prospering must develop and market products that appeal to the particular tastes and preferences of female consumers. This is not say that all Latin American women share a gendered religiosity. Gender identities can vary according to social class, ethnicity, nationality, region, and individual differences. Nevertheless, if the diasporan religions and Charismatic Christianity are thriving in the region, it is in large measure due to the popularity of their products among women from the popular classes. In this chapter I consider the reasons for the extraordinary success of these three religious groups among poor Latin American women.

Barely Visible

There is a surprising dearth of literature on the subject. Given the preponderance of women in Latin American faiths, one would expect a well-developed academic bibliography on women and religion in Latin America. Such is not the case, however, for several reasons. First, historically, most researchers have been men, who have been more likely to ignore or overlook the importance of women in religious enterprises. Second, studies of religion in Latin American have tended to focus on the ecclesiastical elite, primarily the clergy and, secondarily, on high-ranking lay leaders, who are often men.

In the past decade and a half, the roles of women have become more visible as a small group of predominantly women scholars have turned their attention to the subject, particularly in studies of Base Christian Communities and Pentecostalism.[1] The main question that has emerged centers on whether active participation in these religious organizations reinforces traditional patriarchal norms, or if it empowers and liberates CEB and Pentecostal women. Most analyses have discovered the coexistence of liberating and patriarchal elements, but on balance they see both Pentecostalism and the CEBs as positive forces for women's empowerment.

Elizabeth Brusco's pioneering study on evangelical women in Colombia found such liberating elements in their Protestant faith that she regarded it as the more progressive of Maxine Molyneux's two types of women's collective action movements. The first type is based on women's practical interests and struggles against some challenge to their ability to fulfill traditional obligations, but such movements tend to have a relatively narrow scope. Going beyond mere practical interests, the second type is based on women's strategic interests and seeks to change the hegemonic gender system. The result is a more comprehensive form of collective action that resembles Western feminism (Brusco 147). In contradistinction to Brusco, I regard all three pneumacentric groups as fitting squarely within the parameters of Molyneux's first type of women's collective action movement. The appeal of Pentecostalism, the CCR, and diasporan groups is firmly rooted in the crises and affliction that results from the inability of women to realize their practical interests, such as health and family, in the face of grinding poverty.

Marquee Products: Pneumacentrism and Divine Healing

In the preceding chapters in this volume I have demonstrated that, despite their significant differences, Pentecostalism, the CCR, and diasporan groups are united by two enormously popular products: pneumacentrism and supernatural healing in their diverse forms are the biggest sellers for all three of these prosperous religions. Not only are spirit-centered religiosity and *cura divina* the two products that initially attract the neophyte, they are also the ones whose long-term consumption keeps religious consumers coming back for more. Above all, it is the production and marketing of these two marquee products that propel Pentecostalism, the CCR, and diasporan groups to the top of religious charts. Given that at least two-thirds of believers who regularly consume these popular products are women, analysis of their particular appeal to those who constitute the great majority of the religious clientele (if not unofficial producers) in Latin America is imperative.

Gendered Spirit(s)

Pneumacentrism, while not an exclusively female product, is so successful because it fulfills the particular needs and desires of women from the popular classes. In part, this derives from the cultural realm in which, throughout Latin America, traditional (if not hegemonic) notions of gender view women as more receptive to matters of the spirit and the "heart." Most Brazilians and Mexicans, both men and women, would think it perfectly "natural" that the spirits and Holy Spirit manifest themselves more often in female believers.

Another cultural factor relates to the phenomenology of spirit possession. Traditional Latin American gender roles conceive sexual intercourse as an act in which the man possesses and penetrates the women, filling her with his presence. Diasporan religion conceives of spirit possession in a similar fashion. The *lwas* and *orixas* "mount" and "ride" their human "horses" or mediums to the extent that the body and consciousness of the mother of the saints are completely possessed by the spirit. While it is totally acceptable if not "natural" for women to be ridden and mounted by diasporan spirits, it is not so acceptable for Brazilian and Caribbean men to do so, and they do it at the risk of being perceived as homosexual.

Possession by the Holy Spirit in Pentecostalism and the CCR is apparently not associated with homosexuality, but usually it is conceived by both men and women as an act of penetration and possession. The third person of the Trinity, a masculine figure, takes and fills the believer with his spiritual power. For women used to being possessed by their husbands or partners, the concept of being taken by the Holy Spirit is natural and logical. Thus, most Latin American women are culturally predisposed to be more receptive to matters of the spirit(s).

If gender roles prime women's receptivity to the spirit(s), the ecstatic power offered by pneumacentric religion maintains their loyalty to the product. The ecstatic component of this supernatural power typically occurs during the moment of spiritual possession in which the believer enters into a dissociated state of consciousness. The original Greek meaning of the word *ecstasy*, "being taken out of place," neatly captures the sense of transport or flight felt by those being possessed by the Spirit or spirits. For many Charismatic and Pentecostal women, baptism in the Holy Spirit and the manifestation of charismata, such as glossolalia, are charged with eroticism. In fact, female narratives of such experiences often sound like accounts of an extraordinary encounter with an ideal lover.

Since poor women of color are relegated to the least desirable social and physical spaces in Latin America on account of their sex, class, and skin color, it should be of little surprise that they enthusiastically embrace the opportunity to be carried away by a supernatural power from a mundane place of poverty and crime to a heavenly state of bliss. The bliss that is frequently suffused with

A spirit-possessed Umbandista in Recife, Brazil

eroticism by Charismatic and Pentecostal women can be understood as spiritual compensation for hegemonic sexual norms that focus on male gratification to the detriment of female pleasure. Thus, the Holy Spirit becomes a kind of super husband or partner, demonstrating love and affection toward women whose worldly mates neglect or abuse them.

The supernatural power received during spirit possession fortifies and energizes believers well beyond the moment of communion with the *guias*, *orixás*, or Holy Spirit. The spiritual force remains with practitioners of pneumacentric religion well after the relatively brief moment of possession has ended. Outside the walls of the temple and *terreiro*, believers draw on this divine power to confront the tenacious demons of deprivation, such as substandard housing, crime, domestic abuse, and illness. These poverty-related afflictions often seem so overwhelming and intractable that millions of poor Latin Americans believe the only way to cope with them is through divine assistance.

While the experience of personal empowerment through spiritual possession also appeals to millions of men in the region, it is especially attractive to poor women of color. Sexism, racism, and classism push black, Indian, mulatta, and mestiza women to the farthest margins of political, economic, and social power in Latin America. Residing in the least desirable urban barrios or the hunger-filled countryside, poor women of color constitute the most impoverished and oppressed social group in Latin America. Hence, in the *orixás*, *lwas*, and Holy Spirit, these women find all the supernatural power they need to struggle against their social, political, and economic disempowerment. Imbued with the power of the Holy Spirit, for example, the demons of deprivation no longer seem invincible.

An important by-product of the power derived from communion with the pneuma is authority. The spiritual gift of prophecy, which is almost exclusively received by women in Pentecostal and Charismatic congregations, converts women into respected moral authorities whose divine revelations can challenge the authority and conduct of brothers in the faith. In fact, the prophecies received by women frequently revolve around the transgressions of men. And although they risk alienating or even losing their husband or partner, CCR and Pentecostal women can exercise their spiritual authority at home in an attempt to expel the demons of drink, infidelity, violence, and gambling, among others, from their men. In the best-case scenario for the woman, the errant husband or partner comes to realize his wicked ways, repents, and then converts to Pentecostalism or joins a Charismatic community.

The authority claimed by diasporan priestesses is not so much a moralistic one but one that derives from their expertise in communication with the *guias* and *lwas*. The success of any medium in attracting clientele is largely a function of her ability to receive efficacious spirits that are capable of resolving clients' problems. Of course, as head priestesses of their own *terreiros*, female devotees of diasporan religions exercise spiritual and sacerdotal authority to a degree that is practically unimaginable for Pentecostal and CCR women.

Healing the Other

The second major product of Latin America's three premier religious groups has an even stronger appeal to women. Faith healing, more than any other product, is the one that initially leads prospective religious consumers to the door of the *terreiro* or temple. Having failed to resolve their affliction through secular resources, millions of Latin American men make their way to Pentecostal churches, Charismatic prayer circles, and Umbanda *terreiros* in search of supernatural succor for their drinking problem, illness, or employment woes. Likewise, women knock on the same doors attempting to resolve their poverty-related maladies. It is sickness and domestic strife, however, that leads them there more often than alcoholism or employment problems. But the relative importance of these afflictions in compelling religious consumers to sample pneumacentric products does not explain *cura divina's* unique appeal to women from rhe popular glannon, Rathe· the explanation lies in the gendered nature of health care and parenting.

Whereas men seek divine intervention for their own personal problems, women are just as likely to be imploring the spirits to resolve the illness of their son, daughter, or husband as they are to be seeking their own cure. This concern for the welfare of others, particularly family members, is what researcher Carol Ann Drogus found to be the salient feature of female religiosity among a diverse group of members of Brazilian Base Christian Communities (182). Diasporan, CCR, and Pentecostal women have more immediate concerns, such as health crises, to worry about than issues such as social justice that require a long-term perspective. Nevertheless, that women belonging to such radically different religious traditions as the pneumacentrists and the CEBs share what Drogus calls an "other-oriented" religiosity points to a common cultural denominator.

In Latin America, as in most of the world, patriarchal cultural norms assign mothers the primary responsibility of parenting. While the father is supposed to be the family's chief breadwinner, the mother is to take charge of raising the children. Mothers are charged with the physical, emotional, and moral welfare of their children. The role of nurturer and caregiver is a decidedly feminine one from Chile to Mexico. That two of the professions most strongly associated with these qualities, nursing and teaching (at the elementary level), are almost exclusively female in Latin America bears testimony to the gendered division of labor. In reality, a large percentage of mothers, especially single ones, bear the double burden of childrearing and breadwinning. In any case, whether married, in a consensual union, or single, mothers are expected to resolve the wide array of crises that their children may suffer. From bed-wetting to substance abuse, mothers must often single-handedly attempt to resolve their children's problems. When the crisis exceeds maternal and familial resources, it is the mother who is expected to seek assistance outside the home.

The range of secular options for poor children in crisis is limited in Latin America. The private clinics and institutions that attend to the physical and emotional needs of middle- and upper-class children are normally prohibitively expensive. Public resources, such as health clinics, are meager and often of dubious quality. Thus, it is typically after a failed attempt to resolve a son's or a daughter's crisis that an afflicted mother makes her way to one of the three religious groups in question in search of healing. In the context of inadequate familial and social resources for responding to the physical, emotional, and psychological crises of disprivileged youth, the healing power offered by the diasporan spirits and Holy Spirit becomes an attractive, if not the only, alternative source of healing. If the product of divine curing proves effective by healing the child's affliction, the mother will probably become a regular customer of the *terreiro* or church that facilitated the cure. Therefore, it is the convergence of gender roles and poverty that makes the product of supernatural healing so popular among women from the disprivileged classes in Latin America. Religious enterprises without such a product will not thrive in the popular market of faith.

Unique Products: The Virgin, Conversion, and Amorality

In addition to these two standard products, each of the three religious groups has its own unique good or service that is particularly appealing to female consumers. The Virgin of the CCR, the conversion experience of Pentecostalism, and the relative amorality of diasporan religions are products that are especially, though not exclusively, attractive to women and serve to complement the two aforementioned standard products. Brief consideration of each will further illuminate the reasons for the great success of these pneumacentric religions among Latin American women.

Having It All

The dynamic presence of the Virgin in the CCR allows Charismatic women to have the best of both worlds. Like their Pentecostal sisters, Charismatics enjoy the ecstatic masculine power of the Holy Spirit. Unlike Pentecostals, however,

Procession of the Virgin of Transit in Patzcuaro, Mexico

women of the CCR also have access to the feminine strength of the Virgin Mary in her myriad Latin American manifestations. While she does not offer the explosive force of the third person of the Trinity, she represents the ideal of maternal strength and sacrifice in the face of extreme adversity. Millions of Catholic women in the region find hope, inspiration, and compassion in Aparecida, Guadalupe, Luján, Nazare, and other national and regional incarnations of the Virgin. As a poor mother who suffered the ultimate loss, the death of one her children, Mary is able to console and empathize with afflicted Catholic women from the popular classes like no other Christian figure. Again, this is not to imply that she does not appeal to Catholic men—rather, that her femininity and maternity are especially attractive to those Catholics who share the same characteristics.[2] As explained in chapter 4 of this volume, it is the CCR's virgophilia that most differentiates it from its virgophobic Pentecostal rival.

Born Again

While Pentecostal churches do not offer any good or service comparable to the Virgin, they do produce another product that is of special interest to disprivileged Latin American women. The doctrine of conversion, which is peculiar to salvationist religion, calls on those who wish to affiliate with a Pentecostal church to "accept Jesus" and to reject their sinful past through spiritual rebirth. In sociological terms, religious conversion can be thought of as a process in which a person experiences a positive transformation in his or her individual identity and self-worth. Stark and Bainbridge have pointed out that religious conversion holds the greatest appeal among those individuals and groups who have been negatively evaluated or stigmatized by society (197). Poor Latin American women of color undoubtedly figure among those who have been appraised most negatively by Latin American societies. Since their lives have been more difficult than those of most other social groups, many are all too ready to jettison their past for a future filled with the hope and happiness of eternal salvation.

Perhaps more than other products, the doctrine of conversion gives Pentecostalism a competitive edge over its two main rivals in the contest for female souls. Conversion in most Pentecostal churches involves rejecting one's worldly past for a godly present and future. More specifically, the asceticism and ideological dualism of classical and modern Pentecostalism demand that converts renounce the pleasures and vices of the street for the joy of church and family life. In demonizing the street, Pentecostalism condemns the very type of behavior and activity that brought many women to the temple doors in the first place. After sickness, it is behavior associated with male prestige complex or "machismo" that most often compels afflicted women to seek divine assistance. The alcohol abuse, physical and verbal abuse, infidelity, gambling, and prostitute-seeking of their husbands or partners figure among the main afflictions that impel poor Latin American women in search of divine healing.

Their new faith teaches them that their husbands or partners are captive to demonic forces and furnishes them with several strategies to deal with the problem. The most obvious and comprehensive solution is the spouse's conversion, which though often difficult is a real possibility given that approximately half of married *crente* women share the same faith with their husbands. However, if she is unsuccessful in converting her husband to the fold, she has access to networks of sisters in the faith who provide spiritual and psychological support in the intimacy of prayer circles and other church groups for women. Of course, many of her spiritual sisters have experienced or are experiencing the same type of marital conflict with their own husbands. Finally, in addition to the newfound moral authority discussed previously, Pentecostal women have the option of making either Jesus or the Holy Spirit, or both, the primary object of their desire. The love and affection they once might have showed toward their husband can be redirected toward a super(natural) masculine figure that empowers rather than disempowers her.

Another reason for the unique appeal of Pentecostal conversion to women lies in the degree of rupture with secular norms and roles. Because of Pentecostalism's demonization of "vices" associated with the male prestige complex, the degree of rupture with secular society is generally much greater for Latin American men. In effect, conversion requires nothing less than a reformulation of masculine identity. The camaraderie that involves drinking binges, extramarital sex, and gambling and constitutes an important part of masculine identity is viewed as demonic behavior in Pentecostal churches. Millions of Latin American men have converted to Pentecostalism exactly because of the radical rupture, but for many others, particularly those whose afflictions are not so overwhelming, the admission price is too high. For women, in contrast, who are generally less involved in the "vices" of the street, the degree of rupture is less. It is sufficient to offer the positive transformation that many women are seeking, but not so great that it requires them to reconstitute their gender identity. If anything, Pentecostalism reinforces many aspects of Latin American *marianismo*. Hence, the Pentecostal product of conversion appears to provide an optimal level of tension with secular society for vast numbers of poor women. And if the tension at a particular denomination or congregation is either too high or too low, the free religious market provides believers with hundreds of Pentecostal alternatives.

Weapon of the Weak

The success of diasporan religion demonstrates that significant numbers of religious consumers are not looking for a dose of conversion in their quest for healing. Many who frequent the *iles* of Santería and the *terreiros* of Umbanda are simply looking to resolve their problems and are not interested in acquiring a new religious identity that could require significant changes in their lifestyle. As explained in chapter 5 in this volume, it is diasporan religion's relative doctrinal amorality that allows for supernatural *cura* without conversion. In a highly competitive market where pneumacentrism and divine healing have become standard products among the most prosperous firms, it is this product that most distinguishes diasporan groups from their Christian rivals. The question that arises here, then, is the special appeal of doctrinal amorality to women.

Along with sickness, what most impels women to consult with the spirits at a diasporan center is strife with their spouses or partners. More specifically, in her study of Umbanda in Porto Alegre, Patricia Lerch found infidelity to be the principal problem of married women (256). Both patriarchal cultural conditioning and the fear of losing a possible source of income typically result in the jilted wife directing most of her hostility toward the other woman who is trying to "steal" her husband. Since male infidelity is more tolerated (if not condoned) than female and occurs more often, it is to be expected that many more women than men would be seeking supernatural intervention for such a problem. The amoral Exús and other liminal spirits of diasporan religion, in contrast to the moral Jesus and Holy Spirit of the CCR and Pentecostalism, are more than willing, for the right price, to declare spiritual warfare on a spouse's lover. In fact, Pomba Gira, the Umbandista patroness of prostitutes, is a specialist in "getting romantic rivals out of the way."

For ages, sorcery has functioned as a "weapon of the weak" in which those on the margins of social, economic, and political power turn to magic and religion in an attempt to exercise control over their own lives and influence their social superiors. As one of the most historically oppressed social groups in much of the world, women have had a greater need for sorcery than men had had. In stark contrast to its main rivals, diasporan religion through its product of relative doctrinal amorality offers female clients the option of resolving their own problems through the spiritual neutralization of rivals and enemies. For many Caribbean and Brazilian women suffering from their husbands' infidelities, it would seem more cost and time effective to contract an Exu to "remove" the other woman than it would be to pray to Jesus for the conversion of her husband or romantic rival. In any case, diasporan religion's unique product of doctrinal amorality gives female religious consumers a distinctly non-Christian alternative for dealing with marital strife.

Home Marketing

As attractive as these religious products are to female consumers, they must be packaged, distributed, and displayed in a manner that entices spiritual shoppers to purchase them. All three of the religious groups under consideration have developed marketing strategies (or evangelization, in the ecclesiastical idiom) that hold a unique appeal to Latin American women of the popular classes. Above all, it is the marketing of pneumacentric products in the private realm of home and family that unites diasporan religion, the CCR, and Pentecostalism in their great proselytic success among women. Although millions of disprivileged women work outside the home, the historical cultural dichotomy in urban Latin America between the masculine (public) world of the street and the feminine (private) domain of the home endures. In advertising their goods and services to potential female consumers in the privacy of their own homes or in ritual spaces that resemble their own houses, these three pneumacentric groups are better able to vend products that promise to heal domestic affliction. Once the product is sold, the purchaser, in turn, often becomes an important amateur marketing representative by touting its benefits among afflicted female relatives.

The preceding chapters have shown that all three religious enterprises are most successful in marketing their products along the lines of preexisting social networks, particularly kin, despite the fact that several Pentecostal denominations and the CCR have invested heavily in mass media as a tool for evangelization. Since family life largely pertains to the private, feminine sphere, women who have benefited from the consumption of pneumacentric products are more likely than men to advertise them among both immediate and extended kin. Men tend to spend less time with their families and are thus less available to either vend religious goods and services to family members or purchase products from them. Any religious group that aims to increase its numbers in Latin America must develop a marketing strategy that targets female consumers as propagators of the faith among family lines.

Both of the Christian enterprises have developed evangelization strategies that take the news of their doctrine and worship services directly to the homes of prospective believers. From the beginning, door-to-door proselytism has been the cornerstone of Pentecostal evangelization strategy. And more often than not, both those knocking on flimsy doors and those opening them have been women. In order to compete with their Protestant rivals, Catholic Charismatics began their own "visitation ministry" (as it is called in Brazil) or "rescue" missions (as they are known in Chile) in the 1980s. In the shantytowns and "lost cities" (*ciudades perdidas*) of Latin America, there is a good chance that women afflicted by the pathogens of poverty will allow the Charismatic or Pentecostal proselytizers into their home. For it is within these four walls that sickness and family strife are experienced most intimately and ~~amply fulfilled~~ evangelists will ~~listen to the prospective~~ convert's story of trials and tribulation and then offer the Jesus and Holy Spirit of their denomination, as the cure for her ailment. Such entrée into the potential consumer's domestic domain gives Pentecostal and Charismatic sales representatives a strong competitive advantage in marketing the faith among poor Latin American woman.

Diasporan religions lack both the evangelical zeal and organizational structure that are requisites for the type of planned, systematic proselytization conducted by their Christian competitors. Nonetheless, they too market their doctrine and worship services in a manner that is especially appealing to Brazilian and Caribbean women. Whereas Pentecostal and Charismatic sales representatives advertise their products in the homes of potential consumers, diasporan priests and priestesses offer spiritual healing in a sacred space, the *terreiro* or *ile*, that is familiar because as the actual home of the mother or father-of-the-saints, it often resembles the religious client's own house. The *ile* ("house" in the Yoruba language) and the *terreiro* are domestic spaces that offer female clients much of the familiarity of their own homes. Subsequent sections will explain how the domesticity of diasporan religion is further strengthened by its sales representatives and organizational structure.

Spirited Rhythms

To varying degrees, these three religions of the spirit(s) also successfully advertise their products to women through the medium of music. Despite its feminine gender in the romance languages, of course, there is nothing inherently feminine about music per se. Rather, it is the type of rhythms and lyrics played and sung in the CCR, Pentecostalism, and diasporan groups that are especially attractive to afflicted women. Until very recently, Pentecostal churches were the uncontested masters of marketing the faith to female consumers through lively music. Highly emotional hymns blaring from radios, televisions, and speakers mounted on temple facades invite listeners to surrender their earthly afflictions to Jesus. While Pentecostal music, ranging from funk to old-time gospel, is the most diverse in the religious marketplace, the most common type is the evangelical ballad, a highly sentimental, saccharine pop tune with sacred lyrics. Recalling that patriarchal cultural norms place the emotional and spiritual in the feminine domain, it is not surprising that women would be more moved by the pathos of Pentecostal hymns. My previous research in Belem, in fact, confirmed the special significance of sacred songs for women. *Crente* women in the Amazonian metropolis cited church music as their greatest joy in life, in third place after church and family. Male believers, in contrast, did not mention it in sig-

nificant numbers (Chesnut 102). Once Pentecostal products have been purchased and women become regular consumers, they participate in worship services in which at least half of the time is devoted to hymns, ballads, and instrumental rhythms.

To keep up with the Pentecostals, the CCR has also turned to music as a
major marketing tool among women. The Brazilian CCR even has a cadre of
"dancing priests" led by the telegenically good-looking superstar of the Renewal,
Padre Marcelo Rossi. Singing and dancing to the fado and other popular
rhythms, these Charismatic young clerics attract the attention of nominal
Catholic women in a way that a sexagenarian priest never could. And with
Brazilian pop superstar Roberto Carlos joining the CCR and playing at mass
rallies, the movement has even greater appeal to women and girls. The music
played at rallies and mass gatherings is as lively as that at Pentecostal revivals but
tends to be more subdued and contemplative at smaller prayer meetings. The
mellower CCR sound no doubt reflects middle-class tastes and aesthetics. It is
likely that as the CCR continues to expand among the popular classes, it will
also start to play funk and other musical genres of the urban margins. The importance of music as a marketing tool is particularly striking on Redevida, the
Brazilian Charismatic television network, where CCR bands and vocalists
claim a significant amount of airtime.

The most musical religion of Latin America, the diasporan, also utilizes its
African-derived rhythms as a marketing tool to attract female clientele, albeit it
on a much smaller scale than its Christian rivals. While much of the popular
music in the Caribbean and Brazil owes its heritage to the sacred drumming of
Candomblé, Santería, and Vodou, there has been very little commercialization
of explicitly sacred diasporan music. There are no equivalents of Padre Marcelo
or Nelson Ned (a famous Brazilian, evangelical balladeer) among diasporan
groups whose disks sell by the hundreds of thousands, even millions in the case
of the former, and are played on hundreds of radio stations throughout Latin
America. Nonetheless, the hypnotic drumming of Santería's *bembe* or Candomblé's *batuque* rarely fails to attract newcomers and passersby drawn to the
rhythm of the spirits driven by skilled percussionists. In fact, with little access to
mass media, music is one of the main ways that diasporan groups advertise
their products.

The unique appeal of diasporan music to female religious clients, in contrast
to its pneumacentric rivals, is found in its pulsating power. Here there are no
sweet sentimental hymns accompanied by electric guitars and synthesizers that
invite women to surrender to the spirits. Rather, the hypnotic drumbeat is a
rhythm of power. For it is to the rhythm of the *tambor* that the spirits reveal
themselves in the dances of their human mediums. In the rhythms of the
batuque and *bembe*, casual female clients experience the power of the spirits.

Mulatas and *negras* figure among the most socially, economically, and politically powerless groups in Brasil and the Caribbean. Thus, diasporan music both announces and demonstrates one of the precious few sources of power that is available to poor women of color.

A Starring Role

Beyond marketing the faith through music, there is a final proselytization tool that sets one of the three religious groups apart from the others in its appeal to women. In the Virgin, the CCR not only possesses a unique product but also an incomparable marketing agent. Of course, the appeal of Guadalupe and Aparecidas is universal among Catholic women in Mexico and Brazil, for example. However, as demonstrated in chapter 4, the Renewal has embraced her especially tight in an effort to preserve the Catholic identity of a movement that many bishops have criticized as Protestant-influenced. From a marginal role in the early years, the Virgin has moved into a starring role in CCR evangelization campaigns in Latin America. Her image graces the cover of CCR journals, appears frequently on Redevida, and leads mass rallies and meetings organized by the Renewal. By emphasizing Mary in their effort to recruit nominal Catholic women, CCR evangelists offer a singular mix of religious rupture and continuity. The Virgin, as the greatest symbol of Latin American Catholicism, reinforces traditional religious ties, while the Holy Spirit offers a powerfully new way of being Catholic.

Women to Women: Sales Representatives

The unrivaled success that these three religious groups have had among female consumers is also due to the composition and efforts of their sales representatives. Despite their differing and even opposing views on female clergy, diasporan religion, the CCR, and Pentecostalism are united in having a predominantly female sales force. In the Christian market, both Pentecostalism and the CCR, with a few exceptions by the former, exclude women from the clergy. However, this does not present a problem in vending the goods and services to female consumers because most of the sales in the two Christian competitors are made by dedicated amateurs, who are predominantly women. Umbanda and its sister religions, in marked contrast, not only allow but encourage women to join the professional sales force to the extent that female mediums outnumber their male counterparts.

Ironically, it is partly due to patriarchal cultural norms that women dominate the diasporan priesthood. African-derived religions, reflecting prevailing gender roles in the Caribbean and Brazil, believe women to be more open to matters of the spirit. Time and time again among my Pentecostal informants in Belem, I listened to both male and female believers explain the predominance of women in church as a function of their greater sensitivity to the Spirit. The gendered conception of spirit possession in which the human medium is penetrated and possessed by the spirit parallels traditional heterosexual relations in Latin America.

Here, however, the focus is not so much on the reasons for which women become mediums or heads of their own centers but on their role as vendors of diasporan products. The sale of diasporan goods and services is made much easier by the common gender, in addition to class, compatriotism, and educational levels, shared by mediums and their clients. More often than not, a *consulta* consists of a woman client consulting with a medium of the same sex. Besides sharing similar socioeconomic conditions with her client, the *santera* or *iyalorixa* identifies with her through their common experiences as wives, partners, mothers, sisters, and daughters. This is especially important given the nature of the afflictions that are brought to *iles* and *terreiros* by the millions each year.

Sickness is the leading ailment brought to diasporan centers for healing, and as mothers and wives, priestesses, like their clients, are responsible, according to dominant cultural norms, for the health of their families, in addition to their own. Thus female mediums are in a much better position than their male counterparts to comprehend and empathize with the client who is suffering a health-related crisis. Chances are the *mae-de-santo* herself has felt the desperation of not being able to restore the health of a sick son or daughter through secular channels.

The same applies, perhaps even more so, to the next most common type of problem, domestic strife. Strained relations with husbands, boyfriends, and sons and daughters send millions of Brazilian and Caribbean women to consult with the spirits. Once again, in the priestesses of diasporan religion, female clients find the empathy and compassion of those who have suffered similar, if not the same, afflictions and interpreted them according to common gendered perspectives. A *mae-de-santo* is much more likely than a *pai-de-santo*, for example, to have suffered abuse at the hands of an alcoholic spouse. In theory, of course, none of this should matter, as the medium is merely a vessel for the *guia* or *lwa*. However, in practice, the medium and her personality have great influence on the spirits, and according to nonbelievers and skeptics, they are entirely responsible for the comportment and diagnoses of what are passed off as "spirits." In effect, the consultations between diasporan priestesses and female clients are therapy sessions in which one of the two impoverished women of color invokes the spiritual power of the *orixás* to heal the earthly afflictions of the other.

While the two Christian empires don't possess the advantage of having women among their professional sales force, a dedicated army of mostly female amateurs is probably responsible for more individual sales of Pentecostal and Charismatic products than are male pastors. In the Brazilian Assemblies of God, the largest Pentecostal church in the world, the biggest and most active mission brigade is the entirely female group known as the *visitadoras* (visitors). It is these women, eager to share their faith with others, that make most of the denomination's home visits to both potential and recent converts. Likewise, women constitute the great majority of Charismatics involved in the movement's "visitation ministry" or "rescue missions," which target Latin America's vast sea of nominal Catholics. Many of these amateur evangelists, of course, adhered to their faith through affliction, and thus, like diasporan mediums, they are in a unique position to comprehend and empathize with the suffering of the women they are evangelizing.

Model Husbands and Spirited Clerics

Charismatic priests and Pentecostal pastors, the professional sales agents, don't have the advantage of shared gender in selling their goods and services to female consumers; nevertheless, they possess attributes that are especially attractive to women. For women afflicted by abusive husbands, Pentecostal ministers can serve as models of spousal responsibility. These are men who don't spend a significant portion of their paycheck on liquor, gambling, and other women and who presumably treat their wives in a godly manner. The Pentecostal preacher represents the ideal type of man that abusive husbands could become if they were to join their wives in converting to the faith. Thus, by serving as a role model for spousal responsibility, the pastors of Prince of Peace and the Foursquare Gospel Church, among others, not only encourage women to purchase Pentecostal products but also motivate them to share them with their husbands.

Charismatic priests obviously can't serve as spousal role models, but they can appeal to female religious consumers in other ways. Priests associated with the Renewal represent a new breed of Catholic clergy in Latin America. They tend to be younger, charismatic, enthusiastic, and more secularly savvy than non-Charismatic priests. These are not bespectacled older priests whose monotones and lack of eye contact with parishioners make for a somniferous Mass. Rather, they are clerics more akin to Marcelo Rossi, the telegenic former aerobics instructor, and Padre Zeca, the surfer priest from Rio de Janeiro who attracts thousands of young cariocas to his Gospel concerts. Buoyed by the Holy Spirit, these dynamic young priests are diametrically opposed to the traditional cleric whose Masses favor the psyche over the soma. The singing, dancing, and chanting of their Charismatic Masses involves the body in a lively liturgy. The charisma, physicality, and even sex appeal of many CCR priests make them far more attractive sales representatives to nominally Catholic women than are their more staid non-Charismatic confreres.

Structuring the Appeal

Sales representatives, of course, are part of an organizational structure or polity, the fourth determinant of the fate of any given religious firm. Not surprisingly, the three groups under consideration possess certain organizational elements that are particularly appealing to female religious consumers. Organizational models that allow for high levels of lay participation in church life are what unite the two Christian groups in their success among Latin American women. In contrast, the attraction of diasporan polities to female clients is found in organizational structures that mirror kinship and household relations in Brazilian and Caribbean societies. Moreover, in allowing for female clergy, diasporan polities afford women mediums the opportunity of supplementing their household income.

An Office of Their Own

Despite prohibiting women from the clergy, both Pentecostalism and the CCR offer numerous ecclesial groups and offices in which female believers can participate. In fact, without their service as group coordinators, Sunday school teachers, prayer circle leaders, and so on, neither the CCR nor the Pentecostal churches could function. Lay women run the Charismatic Renewal from top to bottom. At the base of its organizational structure, the great majority of prayer groups are coordinated by Charismatic women. They are also well represented at the upper echelons of the Renewal. At the beginning of this decade, women headed both regional and national CCR offices in Latin America. Ligia de De Leon was coordinator of the Central American Catholic Charismatic Council (CONCACE), while Sheny de Góngora served as president of the Guatemalan Council. In Brazil, women headed four of the fourteen secretariats of the National Commission of the Charismatic Renewal, while renowned Charismatic María Lucia Vianna served as the Brazilian representative to the movement's international council (ICCRS) in Rome.

Pentecostal women in Latin America generally do not hold such high administrative offices as their Charismatic sisters, but they are able to participate in and hold office in a wide range of church groups. In addition to conducting most of the door-to-door evangelizing as *visitadoras*, female *crentes* lead prayer circles, sing in the choir, teach Sunday school, expel demons, and even preach. With the notable exception of the Foursquare Gospel Church, Pentecostal doctrine allows only men to deliver sermons in church. In practice, however, sisters in the faith, especially in the poorest congregations of the urban margins, often preach to their fellow believers. To avoid doctrinal contravention, the verb "to preach" (*pregar* in both Spanish and Portuguese) is rarely used to describe female sermonizing. Instead, female preaching is often referred to as "offering a word" (dando uma palavra in Portuguese).

Such polities that encourage high levels of lay participation are especially appealing to women from the popular classes because of their severely limited opportunities for engagement in secular organizations and institutions. At the bottom of the socioeconomic pyramid, poor women of color rarely serve as presidents, directors, or coordinators of secular groups as they do in Pentecostal churches and the CCR. These two Christian enterprises thus provide impoverished female believers with unrivaled opportunities to develop their leadership, administrative, and communication skills. Moreover, since many church groups, such as prayer circles and the visitors are overwhelmingly, if not exclusively, female, CCR and Pentecostal women can develop their skills in an environment of sororal solidarity. There are no men in these groups to monopolize positions of power and authority. True, they remain barred from becoming professional sales representatives of their faith, but believing women have far more opportunities to actively participate and hold office in the Catholic Renewal and in Pentecostalism than in secular Latin American society.

A Family Affair

The same opportunities exist for women in diasporan religion, but only for the clergy. Organized lay groups are not a part of diasporan tradition. For the millions of regular and occasional female clients, the unique appeal of diasporan polity doesn't lie in an active, organized laity but in an organizational structure that mirrors kinship and household relations in Brazil and the Caribbean. In chapter 5 in this volume, I explained how the polity of diasporan religion is patterned on primary kinship relations. Mothers and fathers of the saints head the *terreiros* and *ounfos* and are assisted by elder sisters, *ebomim* in Candomblé, who rank above the "children-of-the-saints." The reflection of secular society is sharpened by the fact that most diasporan houses of worship are headed by priestesses. More than other Latin America women, Brazilian and Caribbean mothers often head fatherless households. Thus as clients at an *ile* or *terreiro*, women often encounter the religious version of the structure of their own household and familial relations. This spiritual reproduction of the Caribbean and Brazilian domestic spheres provides a phenomenological bridge for women who are seeking to relieve their afflictions through the diasporan spirits.

Pesos and Prestige

For the mothers, sisters, and daughters-of-the-saints—the female clergy—the advantages of diasporan organizational structure are numerous. *Maês-de-santos* with their own worship center are in effect spiritual entrepreneurs who operate a religious business. Like their commercial counterparts, they manage staff, organize services and events, and service customers. The fees earned through consultations with clients are a significant source of income in Caribbean and Brazilian economies that provide poor *negras* and *mulattas* with few employment opportunities. In addition to the financial rewards, the prestige associated with being a successful medium grants the diasporan priestess a status level that as a poor woman of color would be harder to attain in secular society. Diasporan polity allows these woman who take orders as domestic servants and shop clerks, among other low-paying jobs, to empower themselves as professional agents of the spirits and heads of their own spiritual businesses.

Strategically Practical

Any attempt to understand the fate of a given religious enterprise in Latin America's new free-market economy must take into account the tastes and preferences of the largest group of spiritual consumers—women. Since women represent at least two-thirds of religious consumers, spiritual enterprises interested in prospering must develop and market products that fulfill the particular needs and desires of female believers. In the case of poor Latin American women, these interests tend to be extremely practical, such as issues of family and health. If Pentecostalism, the CCR, and diasporan religion have come to corner the region's free religious market in the past three decades, it is largely because, in their own manner, they all have designed and marketed goods and services that respond to the practical interests of poor women. Religious enterprises that have failed to develop and market products that heal the feminine wounds of poverty find themselves on the margins of the Latin American market.

Conclusion

Ex Uno Plura (Out of One, Many)

During the 1980s, the progressive Catholic Church and Base Christian Communities dominated the study of Latin American religion. This "new way of being church" with its preferential option for the poor captured the hearts and minds of many North American and Latin American social scientists. While such studies continued into the ensuing decade, it was a radically different religious group that grabbed the academic spotlight in the 1990s. Scholars David Stoll and David Martin in 1990 informed us that while sectors of the Latin American church had been "opting for the poor" since the late 1960s, the poor themselves in far greater numbers had been opting for Pentecostalism. With its provocative title, *Is Latin America Turning Protestant?*, Stoll's book, in particular, brought Pentecostalism in from the academic margins and thrust it onto center stage. In fact, it was Stoll's timely question that prompted me to examine Latin American Pentecostalism at its epicenter in Brazil.

At the beginning of this new decade, research continues on the Pentecostal boom, and there are still those who insist on looking for signs of life in the progressive Catholic Church. However, at the start of the twenty-first century, there is growing realization that beyond the rise or fall of any one particular religious organization, the greatest transformation of the Latin American religious landscape in the past half-century, if not the past half-millennium, is the transition from a monopolistic religious economy to a free-market one. Of such significance is the development of religious pluralism that the fate of any faith-based organization during the past five decades cannot be understood without understanding its position in this new unregulated spiritual economy. From 1500 to the 1940s, Latin Americans lived under a huge sacred canopy in which a single religion, Catholicism, provided spiritual goods and services. If there was any choice at all, it was essentially whether or not to consume the official product.

The disestablishment of Catholicism as the official state religion in Latin America between the middle of the nineteenth century and the first quarter of the twentieth provided the legal foundation for religious pluralism. Mainline Protestant denominations from the United States were pioneers in taking advantage of the new religious freedom in the region, but it wasn't until the arrival of Pentecostalism in the first decades of the twentieth century that the popular classes had a culturally appropriate alternative to Catholicism. In short, the separation of church and state erected the legal foundation for an unregulated religious economy, mainline Protestants built the first temples of religious pluralism, and Pentecostals almost single-handedly developed a popular religious marketplace in which the former monopolist now had to compete with other religious groups for the souls of poor Latin Americans.

Rational Faith

The logic and configuration of both the old and new religious landscape are best understood through the theoretical tools of religious economy. Eschewing the notion that religion and faith-based organizations are inherently irrational, religious economy reveals the importance of rational choices made by both organizations and individual believers in their attempt to maximize their spiritual and material rewards. During its four-century hegemony in Latin America, for example, the Catholic Church operated in the same fashion as commercial monopolists. Since they have a guaranteed market, monopolists are naturally lazy and enjoy the luxury of manufacturing uniform products that don't need to conform to consumer demand. Indeed, the tastes and preferences of consumers are largely irrelevant in a monopolistic economy, whether commercial or religious.

Thus, religious economy enables us to understand that the region's vast population of nominal Catholics is but the logical result of monopoly. Since its monopoly was guaranteed—first by the Iberian crowns and with independence by the Latin American states—the institutional church logically adopted a preferential option for the privileged in which ecclesiastical resources were predominantly invested in the state and in elite individuals. Since the state protected the church from competition and paid clerical salaries, the bishops had a compelling interest to focus much of their ecclesiastical energy on currying favor with high-ranking government officials. Likewise, the church had a strong incentive to minister preferentially to the Latin American elite, as it was wealthy ranchers, planters, and merchants who filled church coffers through their generous bequests upon death. The institutional church quite naturally largely ignored the great majority of its parishioners, black slaves, Indians, mestizos, and mulattoes who had precious few material resources to contribute. Generally ignored by church fathers who spent most of their time on the haciendas, on plantations, and in government offices, the large majority of Latin American Catholics were left to their own spiritual devices. Thus, beyond the pale of the ecclesia, the popular classes developed their own brand of syncretic, priestless Catholicism that centers on pilgrimages, processions, and the saints and Virgin.

It was not until the 1950s, when the Latin American church faced serious religious competition for the first time in its four-and-a-half-century history, that the vast population of popular Catholics appeared on the institutional radar screen. And then suddenly, by the end of the 1960s, in a revolutionary transformation, certain national churches not only abandoned their age-old preference for the privileged but adopted a preferential option for the poor. Applying the tools of religious economy to the national episcopacies' stance toward the military dictatorships that plagued Latin America from the 1960s to the 1980s, Anthony Gill demonstrates that in countries such as Chile and Brazil, where Pentecostal competition was stiff, the bishops' conferences opposed authoritarian rule as inimical to the interests of the poor whose loyalty to the church was in question as millions converted to Pentecostalism. There was no Pentecostal boom in neighboring Argentina, so the episcopacy there gave benediction to one of the period's most brutal regimes that murdered some thirty thousand Argentines.

Beyond its application to episcopal politics, religious economy is an indispensable tool for comprehending the region's new free market in faith that has rapidly developed over the past five decades. An understanding of the basic operational principles of unfettered religious competition allows for better understanding of the fate of any given spiritual enterprise and overarching trends that give definition to the market. The fundamental organizing principle of a competitive religious economy is that religious organizations interested in member maximization must market and sell their faith to customers who are free to purchase the goods that most appeal to them (Berger 138). While proselytizing religions such as Islam and Christianity are especially interested in having more followers than less, even many religions that lack the missionary zeal of the two great monotheistic traditions are interested in the growth of their membership or clientele. Hence, in an unregulated economy in which consumers are free to purchase the religious products that most appeal to them, spiritual firms must produce goods in accordance with consumer tastes and preferences.

Despite its explanatory power and parsimony, religious economy has generally received a cool reception from the few Latin Americanist scholars of religion who are familiar with it. Most of their criticism echoes that of certain U.S. scholars who have been involved since the early 1990s in the spirited debate on the application of religious economy in the United States. Brief consideration of the principal charges made against religious economy by Latin Americanists will contribute to the emerging debate on the nature of religious pluralism in the region.

The most common criticism leveled at religious economy is its alleged reductionism. Burdick charges religious economy with failing to account for the fact that Brazilians often refuse to consult with certain religious specialists or join specific religious organizations and that it ignores the question of "whether some religious options work more often for some kinds of people than for others, and if so why" (8–9). In a similar vein, another Brazilianist, Manuel Vásquez, argues that the reductionism of the model cannot account for either the complexity of religious organizations or the "messiness" of personal affiliations and choices (6).

These two scholars would have us believe that the choices and affiliations of individual believers are so messy and complex that they defy the allegedly reductionist analysis of religious economy. Indeed, there is much "messiness" and complexity in the choices and affiliations of individual believers but not to the point that they escape market-based analysis. In correctly pointing out that many Brazilians refuse to sample the products of certain religious organizations, Burdick ignores the crucial element of consumer tastes and preferences. In no way does the existence of a free market in faith imply that religious consumers engage in comparison shopping with all brands of faith. Rather, in a competitive religious market, comparison shopping takes place according to consumer tastes and preferences, which vary according to social class, gender, age, and individual experience. Tastes, preferences, and even biases are a crucial part of both the religious and commercial economies, and the fact that both spiritual and material consumers do not sample and compare all brands in no way challenges the validity of the model. Furthermore, this study has demonstrated that the tastes and preferences are not so varied as to defy categorization and analysis. Pneumacentrism and faith healing are standard products in Latin America's popular religious marketplace. And it is the development of the unregulated marketplace that has faciliatated the standardization of these two goods. Consumer demand for spirit-centered worship and supernatural healing existed prior to the advent of the new religious economy but was not supplied by the monopolist church. Indeed, faith healing and spirit possession did occur during the long era of religious monopoly but took place on the margins, often clandestinely, beyond the pale of the ecclesiastical institution. Thus, it is the competitive economy that has allowed them to evolve from marginal and unofficial goods to products that today are the sine qua non of mass appeal among religious forum. Moreover, the great popularity of these two goods among certain groups of people—namely, impoverished urban women in Latin America—addresses the question of whether some religious options work more often for some "kinds" of people than for others. As my study has shown, analysis of consumer demand and tastes and preferences can and should be an integral part of the study of religious economies.

On the supply side, Manuel Vásquez asserts that while the "methodological individualism" of religious economy may prove useful in understanding religious competition at the local level, it cannot capture the complexity of the behavior of religious organizations that cannot be reduced to the actions or choices of individuals (Vásquez). Indeed, Vásquez is correct in his assertion that institutional behavior is irreducible to the choices and actions of individuals. However, as demonstrated in this study and in Gill's, the unit of analysis in religious economy can be corporate and does not have to be limited to the individual and the local. Admittedly, religious organizations are complex, but again, their complexity is not so great that their behavior in a pluralist environment is incomprehensible. In a competitive economy, religious groups interested in growing or just holding their own will rationalize their organizational structures in an attempt to recruit new members more efficiently. For example, religious economy illuminates the rationale behind the Latin American Catholic Church's decision to embrace the Charismatic Renewal. Despite personal distaste for Charismatic spirituality on the part of many individual bishops, episcopacies throughout the region integrated the movement into the church as a strategy to retain members and compete with surging Pentecostalism. Hence religious economy proves as useful in comprehending the choices and actions of religious organizations as it does individual believers.

Another major charge against religious economy is its alleged lack of relevance to societies of the developing world. Satya Pattnayak, for instance, argues that since the model was derived mainly from the experiences of advanced capitalist societies, it is naturally irrelevant to Latin America (7). While it is the case that most religious economy theory has been derived primarily from the U.S. landscape and secondarily from the European, this in and of itself does not render it irrelevant to other societies. Latin America, on both the regional and national levels, obviously has its own unique religious history. However, many of the features of its historical religious landscape such as monopoly and pluralism are universal and as such easily lend themselves to models of global application. Simply because it was the religious landscapes of the United States and Europe that led Berger and Stark to discover that the pluralist environment is one governed by competition does not mean the principle is inapplicable to other societies. In fact, an astute student of Latin American religion without any knowledge of the work of Berger and Stark could have developed the same principle based on the operation and logic of religious pluralism in the region over the past five decades. Turning the theoretical table on its head, it would appear that the ethnocentrism lies with those who deny that individual believers and religious organizations in Latin America and other parts of the developing world characterized by religious pluralism make rational choices about the production and consumption of faith.

The Spirit(s) of Competition

Finke and Stark have demonstrated that the fate of any given religious firm in a competitive economy depends on four factors: the product, marketing, sales representatives, and organizational structure. Pentecostals, Catholic Charismatics, and African diasporan groups are the most successful religious enterprises in the Latin American market because they possess appealing products. But behind the products are skilled sales representatives who package and advertise the goods and services of efficient religious firms. Systematic analysis of these four elements, along with religious consumer profiles, have revealed the keys to success of these three religious groups. As different as they are from each other in many regards, all three groups possess the common marquee product of pneumacentrism. Pentecostal and CCR beliefs and practice center on communion with the Holy Spirit, while Umbanda and Santería, among other diasporan groups, focus on the *guias* and *orixás*, or spirits, that possess their human mediums. In fact, such is consumer demand for spirit-centered religion in the popular marketplace that pneumacentrism has become a standardized product among successful firms that attempt to distinguish themselves from the competition through marginal differentiation of pneumacentric goods and services. For example, in choosing between a Pentecostal church and the CCR, spirit-centered worship is a given. The main choice to be made, then, is whether the prospective consumer prefers a virgophilic or virgophobic brand of pneumacentric religion. Similarly, in electing between Umbanda, for instance, and the CCR, the prominence of the pneuma is taken for granted. Rather, the choice is whether to commune with just one (Holy) spirit or many.

That spirit possession and faith healing are the two leading goods and services for all three groups under consideration provides further evidence of product standardization and marginal differentiation. Again, religious consumer demand for direct communion with the Spirit or spirits and for divine healing of their earthly afflictions is such that those faith-based organizations that do not offer these very appealing two products will have a hard time competing in the popular marketplace. In the case of spirit possession, the CCR and Pentecostalism offer an almost identical product in the phenomena of baptism in the Holy

Spirit and in charismatic such as speaking in tongues. The intensity and frequency of manifestations of the Spirit constitute the only appreciable difference between the two Christian pneumacentrists. Greater differentiation occurs between the Christian and African diasporan products. Whereas just one Spirit who is the manifestation of a single omnipotent God fills Charismatic Christians with his presence, hundreds of different *orixás*, *lwas*, and *guias* "ride" their human "horses" in the *terreiros* and *iles* of diasporan groups.

But the plurality of the diasporan pneuma is not the only distinguishing feature. The most salient differentiation of the diasporan product is the nature of the spirits. In marked contrast to the Christian Holy Ghost, which is a manifestation of pure good, many diasporan spirits are notably amoral and willing to perform services that most Latin American Christians would consider immoral, if not evil. Millions of Brazilian and Caribbean religious consumers, however, come to diasporan worship centers precisely because they are interested in contracting for services that Christian churches do not provide. For example, a jealous wife intent on harming her husband's lover can contract an Exú (liminal trickster spirit), for the right price "to remove the woman from her spouse's path." Thus diasporan groups have found a profitable niche market in providing amoral spiritual services to Caribbean and Brazilian religious consumers.

The premier pneumacentric product of faith healing is the religious service that has contributed the most to the dominance of these three firms in the popular marketplace. More than any other product offered in the temples and *terreiros* of the region, supernatural healing is the service that entices popular consumers to first sample the diasporan, Pentecostal, or CCR product and is also the one that maintains them as regular customers. Demand for divine healing is strong in a region plagued by the world's highest levels of socioeconomic inequality and violent crime and relatively high indices of poverty, unemployment, and inadequate housing. In the absence of adequate health care, both physical and mental, and a social safety net for large sectors of the population, tens of millions of Latin Americans turn to organized religion to heal their earthly afflictions. Thus, the socioeconomic context practically guarantees marginalization for any religious firm that fails to prominently offer faith healing in the popular market.

Marginal differentiation of the faith healing product allows each of the three firms to distinguish itself in the crowded religious marketplace. Pentecostal churches tend to specialize in the curing of physical ailments and exorcism, while the Catholic Charismatic Renewal has historically focused on "inner healing." Much of the difference lies in social class. While impoverished Pentecostals seek first to heal their ailing corpus, middle-class Charismatics focus on afflictions of the psyche, such as early childhood trauma. However, as the CCR has expanded among the popular classes over the past decade and a half, it has followed the Pentecostal lead in offering exorcisms to tormented Catholics.

Across the Christian divide, diasporan priests and priestesses offer divine healing for most of the same afflictions that Pentecostals and Charismatics treat. However, the diasporan brand of supernatural curing distinguishes itself for its amorality and continuity with secular society. The amorality of diasporan doctrine can mean that one client's healing is another person's suffering. In other words, the sorcery that may relieve a businessman of his competition could come at the spiritual expense of his competitor. Moreover, disaporan groups do not require conversion to the faith for healing to take place. Even occasional clients with sufficient faith in the power of the spirits can access the restorative energy of the *guias* or *lwas*. Since many religious consumers are not necessarily looking for a dose of religious conversion with their faith healing, Vodou, Umbanda, Santería, and Candomblé serve as attractive options for those who prefer continuity rather than rupture with their secular identities.

No matter how attractive, though, none of these products sells itself. Rather, as in the commercial economy, religious products must be marketed through advertising and packaging to target audiences. Marketing can be thought of as evangelism in the Christian idiom. As proselytizing faiths, the two Christian groups employ a combination of low-tech and high-tech marketing strategies. To ensure maximum exposure of their product, both the CCR and Pentecostal churches broadcast their messages on radio, television, and even the Internet. Radio, though less visible than the other two media, reaches the largest number of religious consumers and is far more economical to operate than TV. Many Pentecostal churches that could only dream of marketing their products on the small screen can afford to rent a few hours of radio time a week to broadcast their message to potential consumers.

Until the inauguration of the Redevida, Brazil's Catholic television network, in 1995, Pentecostal televangelists held a near monopoly on religious broadcasting in Latin America. Following the lead of their U.S. brethren, many larger Pentecostal denominations went beyond purchasing air time to sell their goods and services to viewers and in a few cases actually bought their own station. The Universal Church of the Kingdom of God's acquisition of the Brazilian network Rede Record gave the church a potent new medium for both marketing its goods and services and filling church coffers through the sale of air time to commercial clients. Controlled by Brazilian Charismatics, Redevida attempts to compete for religious consumers through programming that combines upbeat music, healing and conversion testimonials, and soap operas with sacred themes.

If diasporan groups are able to compete with their two Christian rivals, it is because low-tech marketing induces more Latin Americans to purchase CCR,

Pentecostal, and African-Latin products than do TV and radio. The most efficacious manner of advertising the faith is through preexisting social networks,
particularly along family lines. It is one thing to hear the conversion testimonial of a stranger on television and quite another to actually witness the positive transformation of a family member due to her purchase of religious goods
and services. Across the board, new consumers most often first come into contact with these three prosperous religious firms through relatives, friends, or
coworkers.

Pentecostal and CCR sales representatives also systematically market their
products through home visits. As zealous proselytizers, Pentecostal evangelists
pioneered the practice of door-to-door sales in the region, and since the 1980s,
Catholic Charismatics have followed suit with the creation of "rescue" missions
aimed at nominal Catholics, who are the most likely group to convert to Pentecostalism. Door-to-door marketing brings the pneumacentric products into the
privacy of a prospective consumer's own home, the place where the afflictions
that compel Latin Americans to seek supernatural healing are often felt most
acutely.

In lieu of the organized marketing campaigns of the two Christian firms, diasporan groups advertise their products in sacred spaces that recall home and
family. More often than not, the *terreiro* is a room or backyard of the *mae-de-
santo*'s own home, a house that is typically similar to that of the client who has
come for a consultation. The iconography of the sacred space with familiar
Catholic saints makes the client feel at home. To further compensate for their
incapacity to systematically market their products, diasporan groups package
their goods and services more colorfully than their Christian rivals do. The
hypnotic drumming and sensual dancing that accompany the *orixás* and *lwas*
in their possession of their human mediums makes for unrivaled religious
drama. At many diasporan sessions, a significant number of those in attendance, especially on Friday nights in Brazil, when the Exús manifest themselves, are onlookers.

Marketing, of course, is only as good as the sales representatives who package and advertise the products. The three religious firms under consideration,
to varying degrees, happen to employ enthusiastic and talented individuals as
their vendors. Both Pentecostalism and the CCR, but especially the former,
enjoy an important competitive advantage over their religious rivals in possessing both dedicated and skilled professional and amateur sales forces. For both
groups, it is zealous laypersons who both as individuals proselytizing at home
and as members of ecclesial mission groups make most of the sales of pneumacentric products. Without their brigades of *visitadoras* who do most of the
knocking on Latin American doors, Pentecostals and Charismatics would
probably not enjoy their same commanding position in the religious market-

place. Historically, sales for amateur Pentecostal vendors have been made easier by the common bonds of social class, compatriotism, and gender that unite them with prospective consumers. However, as the CCR continues to expand among the region's popular classes, the difference in social class between amateur sellers and potential buyers will narrow. Since organized laity do not exist in diasporan religions, they must rely on professionals or the clergy to produce and sell their goods and services.

Above all, it is gender that sets professional diasporan vendors apart from their Christian cohorts. The four main African-derived religions not only allow for women clergy but are characterized by a preponderance of houses of worship headed by priestesses. Thus, in addition to the commonalities of class and nationality shared with their clients, shared gender brings the mother-of-the-saints closer to her clients. In effect, many consultations between diasporan priestesses of Brazil and the Caribbean and their clients are spiritual therapy sessions in which one poor women of color counsels another. The personal attention that diasporan priests and priestesses give to clients during such consultations is hard to match in the popular religious marketplace.

Even more than their Pentecostal cohorts, who are renowned for their entrepreneurial spirit, diasporan clerics are religious entrepreneurs. In the economy of scarcity in which most mothers and fathers-of-the-saints operate, the fees and gifts collected for spiritual service rendered represent a significant contribution to the cleric's income. Thus, priests and priestesses possess a natural incentive to expand their clientele. Indeed, the most successful heads of diasporan worship centers earn enough from their religious work to make ends meet, if not more.

Pentecostal pastors are also religious entrepreneurs in that their ability to collect tithes and offerings from church members is a major determinant of their salary and professional advancement in many denominations. Nowhere is this more the case than in the Universal Church of the Kingdom of God whose top-ranking clerics are gifted fundraisers. In addition to entrepreneurship, the shared bonds of social class and nationality give professional Pentecostal sales representatives a competitive advantage over their Catholic rivals. The great majority of Pentecostal preachers are Latin American men from humble origins, and as such they can more easily relate to popular religious consumers than do the North American and European priests who constitute the majority of the Catholic clergy in the region. Moreover, professional Pentecostal vendors far outnumber their Catholic cohorts as the educational requirements for the latter are far higher than for the former.

Though they cannot compete in terms of entrepreneurial zeal, numbers, and social and cultural proximity to popular religious consumers, priests affiliated with the Charismatic Renewal tend to be a new breed of Catholic cleric who are younger, more dynamic, and even scaler than their non-Charismatic confreres. Padre Marcelo Rossi, the thirty-something superstar of the Brazilian Renewal, is the paragon of the CCR priest. The telegenic former aerobics instructor electrifies Brazilian Charismatics, especially women, with his highly innovative samba-inspired song and dance routines. His recordings of sacred songs to a pop beat have topped Brazilian music charts, and over the past few years he has been a regular guest on the country's most popular talk shows. In such priests, the Latin American Catholic church has found professional sales representatives who compete head to head with the best Pentecostal evangelists.

The job of the sales representative is easier for those who work for efficient religious firms. In economies characterized both by competition and scarcity, firms with efficient organizational structures have the upper hand over those that do not. The organizational models adopted by diasporan groups, the CCR, and Pentecostalism have contributed significantly to their success in the Latin American religious marketplace. Of the three, Pentecostalism is harder to pin down in terms of polity as there are hundreds of different denominations, some with radically different organizational structures. The two largest Brazilian denominations, for example, stand at opposite ends of the Pentecostal organizational spectrum. Rare among Latin American Pentecostals, the Universal Church of the Kingdom of God (IURD) follows an extremely hierarchical episcopal polity that concentrates ecclesiastical power in the hands of the bishops and greatly restricts lay participation. In fact, IURD polity is reminiscent of the pre-Vatican II Catholic Church. Despite strong authoritarian tendencies, Latin America's Pentecostal behemoth, the Brazilian Assemblies of God, are found at the opposite end of the organizational continuum with a presbyterian model of governance that encourages high levels of lay participation. The fact that most crente churches fall closer to the Assemblies of God on the organizational spectrum and that the CCR also exhibits high levels of lay participation (probably the highest among Catholic ecclesial groups) points to strong consumer demand in the Christian market for more participatory forms of polity.

However, the spectacular growth of the IURD over the past two decades demonstrates the existence of a sizeable niche market for popular consumers with a taste for ecclesiastical authoritarianism. Accustomed to hierarchical relations with their social superiors, not all Latin Americans from the popular classes are seeking more democracy and egalitarianism in their churches. And, of course, it is the extreme differentiation of the Pentecostal market with hundreds of different denominations and thousands of churches that allows for such variances in consumer tastes and preferences. Finally, Pentecostal polities that prefer pastoral charisma over theological training give their churches a major competitive edge over their Catholic and Protestant rivals. The much lower educational requirements translate into a much larger pastorate, as even a man with only a primary school education can pastor a congregation in many Pentecostal denominations.

The CCR in its organizational structure shares the participatory authoritarianism of the Assemblies of God. As a group within the Catholic Church, the CCR offers its members the hierarchicalism of an episcopal polity. However within an authoritarian church, the CCR offers more opportunities for lay participation than do the other ecclesial groups. Beyond participation in prayer groups, lay Charismatics direct the Renewal from the lowest to the highest levels of organization. Priests and bishops serve as advisors to the CCR but seem to be less dominant than they were in Base Christian Communities, which were meant to be the maximum expression of the progressive church.

Across the Christian divide, lay participation is not one of the fortes of diasporan polity. However, there are a number of advantages to the organizational structure of diasporan religions. While national and regional federations exist, they exert little control over autonomous worship centers that are run like small family businesses. As entirely self-supporting enterprises, the fate of *iles* and *terreiros* largely depends on the number of ritual clients and the fees paid for religious goods and services. Since the prosperity of the worship centers are directly dependent on customer satisfaction, the mother or father-of-the-saints has a strong incentive to provide attractive and efficacious religious products. Diasporan polity also provides a familiar environment to its clients through a sacerdotal structure organized along family lines. Mothers and fathers-of-the-saints preside over elder sisters and sons and daughters-of-the-saints. More specifically, the predominance of *maes-de-santos* over *pais-de-santos* reflects the abundance of matrifocal households among the popular classes in Brazil and the Caribbean. Clients, women in particular, can feel at home when purchasing diasporan products in such a familiar setting.

Finally, the loose organizational structure of diasporan groups at the national and regional levels allows for a rich variety in ritual and belief. In Umbanda, for example, many priestesses practicing a more Kardecist-influenced variety avoid the liminal Exú spirits at all cost, while others actually make them the protagonists of their centers. As in Pentecostalism, the differentiation of diasporan religion gives religious consumers a wide range of options.

A Preferential Option for Women

If these three pneumacentric religions dominate the popular marketplace, it is also because they have catered to those who constitute the great majority of religious consumers—women. At least two-thirds of all consumers of organized religion in Latin America are women. To ignore their specific tastes and preferences, which are often heavily influenced by gender, is to guarantee marginal ization in the marketplace. In different manners and to varying degrees the products, marketing, sales representatives, and organizational structures of the CCR, Pentecostalism, and the diasporan religions hold special appeal to female consumers. However, the appeal is not found in any challenge to the hegemonic gender system in the region, as some have argued, but rather in the pragmatism of these religious firms. The attraction of the groups arises from the crises and affliction that results from the inability of women to realize their practical interests, such as family and health, in the face of endemic poverty. Any religious firm interested in increasing its share of the Latin American popular market must produce and market goods and services that conform to the strategic pragmatism of poor women.

Spirit of the Times

The development of a market economy and the growth of pluralism in Latin America are not limited to religion only. Rather, they are general historical trends of which religion is a specific part. The development of commercial market economies and evolution of cultural and political pluralism have taken place concurrently with the transformation of the Latin American religious landscape. On the cultural front, diverse ethnicities have always existed in the region, but until the twentieth century, Latin Americans of African and indigenous descent were repressed by those of predominantly European ancestry. While racism remains a problem at the beginning of the twenty-first century, in the past few decades blacks and Indians throughout the region have created their own organizations and movements aimed at promoting ethnic pride and achieving social, political, and economic equality. And beyond the three historic ethnicities, immigration during the past century from Europe, East Asia, and the Middle East has contributed to a degree of cultural pluralism that was unimaginable during colonial times.

On the political front, the development of pluralism is more obvious. With the exception of Cuba, all Latin American nations have evolved from monarchy in the colonial era into democratic republicanism. Of course, the democratic credentials of many Latin American republics can be questioned, but several nations, such as Mexico and Brazil, offer voters more political parties and a greater ideological range than the oldest of American republics, the United States.

Finally, in the economic sphere (which most closely parallels the religious), the monoculture and monopoly of Iberian mercantilism gave way to the statist developmental nationalism of the middle and late middle twentieth century, which, in turn, has been replaced by the current wave of neoliberalism that swept through the region in the 1980s and continues to dominate the economic landscape today. Following the prescriptions of U.S.-trained economists, governments from Mexico to Chile have privatized thousands of state-owned industries, cut social spending, and lowered barriers to trade in a belief that relatively laissez-faire capitalism is the most efficient and fastest way to grow, if not develop their economies. Thus, as is the case in the religious marketplace, consumers in the commercial economy are offered a panoply of products, from telephone service to soft drinks. Ultimately, the fate of these commercial firms depends on their appeal to Latin American consumers.

As an important part of the overarching trend toward pluralism, Latin America's competitive religious economy is here to stay. Despite lingering resentment over the loss of their spiritual monopoly, many Catholic leaders are beginning to realize that the church has actually benefited from competition. The Charismatic Renewal, which itself is a product of religious competition, has revitalized the church in many countries. Beyond the rise and fall of any one particular group, continued development of the new free market in faith should lead to even greater religious vitality in Latin America.

Notes

Introduction

1. Seeing laity as religious consumers does not mean that they cannot engage in spiritual production on their own, beyond the pale of specialized producers such as priests. Rather, the concept is meant to capture their primary role in organized religion as customers or clients who purchase spiritual goods from those who specialize in religious production. In religious economies, like commercial ones, the fundamental dichotomy is between producers and consumers.

2. The *terreiro* is the sacred space, often a believer's back yard, where the rites of African-Brazilian Umbanda and Candomblé are conducted.

3. The Cabocla Mariana (Half-breed Mary) is a ribald *guia* (or spirit) of Umbanda whose possession of female believers often leads them to dance suggestively and down liberal doses of distilled spirits. In many parts of Brazil she is especially popular among prostitutes.

4. The website, hosted at Providence College, offers more of a partisan denunciation than a debate of Gill's book.

5. Religious capital is "accumulated symbolic labor" (Bourdieu), including the skills, experiences, and goods that a religious consumer has acquired and that enables her both to consume and produce spiritual stock (A. Gill 198).

Chapter 2

1. Of course, beyond the pale of the limited reach of the church, indigenous peoples and African slaves, depending on the region and circumstances, were able to preserve many elements of their own belief systems through surreptitious worship and syncretism with Catholicism. Nevertheless, the overarching trend during the three-century colonial

period was Catholicism's increasing penetration of and acceptance among those who had been conquered and enslaved by the Iberians.

2. The Jesuits were the largest institutional slave owners in Brazil (Lockhart and Schwartz 391). The forced labor of African slaves made the Jesuit sugar plantations, cattle ranches, and farms the most prosperous in the colony.

3. In New Spain, the struggle for independence was also fought on the devotional front with the mestiza Virgin of Guadalupe blessing the independencistas, while the Spanish Virgen de Remedios protected royalist troops.

4. Chile in 1925 and Ecuador in 1937 consummated the process of disestablishment they had both initiated decades earlier.

5. Article 130 of the Constitution of 1917 called for the registration of all priests with municipal authorities (Mecham 388).

Chapter 3

1. At the same time that historical Protestantism was establishing itself in the second half of the nineteenth cenury, African diasporan religions, such as Candomblé and Santería, were organizing *terreiros* in the cities of Brazil and Cuba. However, the syncretic nature of these faiths—in which Catholic saints are worshiped and Catholic identities are typically maintained—meant that, unlike Protestantism, African-Latin religions did not offer a truly non-Catholic alternative.

2. The ISER survey included mainline Protestants whose higher income and educational levels raised the mean. If only Pentecostals had been surveyed, the gap between believers and the general population would have been substantially larger.

3. If the ISER study had focused exclusively on Pentecostals, as opposed to Protestants in general, the percentage of believers converting through illness would have been significantly higher.

4. A search in January 2001 found the following churches to be running their own websites: the IURD, the Assemblies of God in Brazil, Luz del Mundo–Mexico (Light of the World), Deus é Amor–Brazil (God Is Love), Iglesia del Evangelio Cuadrangular–Mexico (Forsquare Gospel Church), El Shaddai-Guatemala, and Iglesia Crisitian Verbo-Guatemala (Church of the Word).

Chapter 4

1. *Pagode* is an infectiously saccharine variant of samba and is popular among the urban working classes.

2. When not derisively referring to them as "sects," Latin American bishops also employ the term "separated brethren" for Pentecostals and other Protestants.

3. The *Cursillo* (little course) movement was founded in 1949 in Spain by Monseñor Juan Hervas. In Latin America, it sought to organize and train middle-class laity with the overarching goal of Catholicizing the workplace and society in general.

4. As explained in chapter 3 of this volume, historic Protestant churches and fundamentalist faith missions had been operating in the region for over half a century, but as

Virginia Garrard-Burnett demonstrates in this study of Protestantism in Guatemala, they were never able to successfully adapt their religious product to Latin American tastes and preferences.

5. Priests are usually not present at prayer group meetings.

6. Despite frequent assertions to the contrary, numerous studies have proved that the great majority of Pentecostal converts are recruited from the Catholic population, especially those whose faith is nominal. The largest study of Latin American Protestantism of its kind, the 1996 analysis of Rio de Janeiro's Evangelical population, conducted by ISER (Institute of Religious Studies), found that 61 percent of Protestant converts were ex-Catholics. In contrast, only 16 percent of converts described themselves as former practitioners of the African-Brazilian religions of Umbanda and Candomblé (ISER 18).

7. Entitled "Ecumenism and Charismatic Renewal: Theological and Pastoral Orientations—Malines Document II," the document stands as one of the most important on the role of ecumenism in the CCR.

8. The Chilean CCR conceives its labor of evangelizing nominal Catholics as a "rescue mission" (*un trabajo de rescate*) (Galilea 31).

9. Sociologist Brenda Carranza reports two hundred CCR prayer groups operating in Brazil in the mid-1970s. Conservatively estimating the average size of prayer groups at thirty members translates to a CCR community of approximately six thousand during the period.

10. The exorcism mass is not the only type of religious service that Charismatic priests have imported from Pentecostalism. In July 1998, while waiting for an interview with Padre Zeca, one of the young Brazilian stars of the CCR, I noticed that the Church of the Resurrection, the parish church of Rio de Janeiro's famous beach district, Copacabana, was holding *missas dos dizimistas*, or tithers' masses, on the second Saturday of every month. Masses aimed at recruiting and rewarding faithful tithers are a direct import from the Universal Church of the Kingdom of God, which pioneered in offering weekly *cultos dos dizimistas* (or tithers' services).

11. Known as *comunidades de alianza* (*aliança* in Portuguese), covenant communities are CCR groups that live communally and often take vows of poverty, chastity and obedience. Members are predominantly middle class, and some communities have been instrumental in creating Charismatic foundations and associations, many of which are heavily involved in mass media work (Carranza 49).

12. Cenacles are named after the locale in which the Holy Spirit descended among the Apostles "in tongues of fire" on the day of Pentecost (fifty days after the resurrection of Jesus), causing them to preach in unknown languages.

13. In 1976, the Cardinal of Santiago and an episcopal compatriot drafted a pastoral letter of endorsement of the CCR (Chordas 144). National episcopacies gave a green light to the Renewal in the following order: Puerto Rico (1977), Costa Rica (1979), Honduras (1984), and Guatemala (1986).

14. The CNBB's rather tardy approval of the Brazilian Renewal in 1994 is explored in a subsequent section.

15. Sociologist of religion Peter Berger posits standardization and marginal differentiation as two major effects of consumer influence on religious production in unregu-

lated religious markets. Berger points out that the similar religious "needs" of believers belonging to the same social strata will result in a standardized religious product, such as pneumatic spirituality in the Latin American case. Marginal differentiation arises from the need for religious producers to distinguish their standardized product from that of their competitors (148–149).

16. Numerous church studies of the "sectarian invasion" conducted in the 1980s, such as the one commissioned by Central American bishops in 1988, found that the greatest evangelizing activity of the Protestant competition was home visits (Secretariado Epoiscopal de America Central 1995).

17. Among Padre Eduardo's "novelas" are Irmã Catarina (Sister Catherine, running 24 chapters), O amor do Pai (Love of the Father), A vinda do Messias (The Coming of the Messiah), A ultima semana (The last week), Ele vive (He lives), A verdadeira história do Papai Noel (The true story of Santa Claus), and Antônio dos Milagres (Anthony of miracles) (Carranza 201).

Chapter 5

1. The Hatian Creole orthography, "Vodou" avoids the negative connotations of the English "Voodoo."

2. Xango and Jurema are the regional diasporan faiths of Recife and its hinterlands.

3. Their number have probably been dwindling over the past two decades, but a significant number of middle-class, Spiritist-influenced Umbanda centers proscribe ritual drumming as an element of African primitivism.

4. The Foursqure Gospel Church is the major exception among Latin American Pentecostalism and Catholicism in allowing women to be ordained as pastors.

5. Kardedicist spiritism is a pneumacentric religion codified by the Parisian school teacher know by the pseudonym Allan Kardec and imported to Brazil by elite Brazilians at the end of the nineteenth century.

Chapter 6

1. On Pentecostalism see Brusco; Burdick; Chesnut; Flora; Gill, "Like a Veil"; Machado; Mariz, Coping with Poverty; Pepper; Steigenga and Smilde. On the CEBs, see Burdick; Drogus; Hewitt; Machado; Mariz, Coping with Poverty.

2. See chapter 4 for the development of the Virgin's role in the CCR. Here suffice it to say that in the CCR's first decade, she was a peripheral figure due to Pentecostal influence in the movement. As episcopal pressure mounted to ensure the CCR's Catholic identity, the Virgin began to move toward center stage, to the point today where Charismatics are often the largest and most enthusiastic organizers of celebrations for the day of their national patroness.

References

Adriance, Madeleine C. 1995. *Promised Land.* Albany, N.Y.: State University of New York Press.

Aguilar, Edwin Eloy, Kenneth Coleman, José Sandoval, and Timothy Steigensa. 1993. "Protestantism in El Salvador: Conventional Wisdom versus the Survey Evidence." In *Rethinking Protestantism in Latin America,* ed. Virginia Garrard-Burnett and David Stoll (pp. 111–142). Philadelphia: Temple University Press.

Amatulli, Flaviano. 1986. *La iglesia católica y las sectas.* 2nd ed. Mexico City: Apostoles de la Palabra.

Annis, Sheldon. 1988. *God and Production in a Guatemalan Town.* Austin: University of Texas Press.

Assman, Hugo. 1987. *La iglesia electrónica y su impacto en América Latina.* San José, Costa Rica: Editorial DEI.

Barret, David, ed. 2001. *World Christian Encyclopedia.* 2nd ed., Vol. 1. Oxford: Oxford University Press.

———. 1982. *World Christian Encyclopedia.* Nairobi: Oxford University Press.

Bastian, Jean-Pierre. 1992. "Protestantism in Latin America." In *The Church in Latin America: 1492–1992,* ed. Enrique Dussel (pp. 313–350). Maryknoll, N.Y.: Orbis.

Benedetti, Luiz Roberto. 1988. "Templo, Praca, Coração: A articulação do campo religioso catolico." Ph.D. diss., Universidade de São Paulo.

Beozzo, José Oscar. 1992. "The Church and the Liberal States (1880–1930)." In *The Church in Latin America: 1492–1992,* ed. Enrique Dussel (pp. 313–350). Maryknoll, N.Y.: Orbis

Berger, Peter. 1969. *The Sacred Canopy.* Garden City, N.Y.: Anchor Books.

Berryman, Phillip. 1996. *Religion in the Megacity.* Maryknoll, N.Y.: Orbis.

Blancarte, Roberto. 1992. *Historia de la iglesia católica en México.* Mexico City: El Colegio Mexiquense.

Bord, Richard, and Joseph Faulkner. 1983. *The Catholic Charismatics.* University Park: Pennsylvania State University Press.

Boudewijnse, Barbara. 1991. "The Development of the Charismatic Movement within the Catholic Church of Curação." In *Popular Power in Latin American Religions,* ed. A. F. Droogers et al. (pp. 175-195). Saarbrucken, Germany: Breitenbach.

Bourdieu, Pierre. 1991. "Genesis and Structure of the Religious Field." *Comparative Social Research* 13: 1-44.

Brasil Cristao. Revista da Associação do Senhor Jesus. 1997-1998.

Brown, Diana. 1986. *Umbanda: Religion and Politics in Urban Brazil.* Ann Arbor, Mich.: UMI Research Press.

Brumana, Fernando Giobelina, and Elda Gonzalez Martinez. 1991. *Marginalia sagrada.* Campinas, Brazil: Editora da Unicamp.

Bruneau, Thomas. 1974. *The Political Transformation of the Brazilian Catholic Church.* New York: Cambridge University Press.

Brusco, Elizabeth. 1993. "The Reformation of Machismo: Asceticism and Masculinity among Colombian Evangelicals." In *Rethinking Protestantism in Latin America,* ed. Virginia Garrard-Burnett and David Stoll (pp. 143-158). Philadelphia: Temple University Press.

Burdick, John. 1993. *Looking for God in Brazil.* Berkeley: University of California Press.

Canton Delgado, Manuela. 1998. *Bautizados en Fuego: Protestantes, discursos de conversión y política en Guatemala.* La Antigua, Guatemala: Centro de Investigaciones Regionales de Mesoamérica.

Carranza Davila, Brenda. 1998. "Renovação Carismática Católica: Origens, mudancas e tendencias." Master's thesis. Universidade Estadual de Campinas, Brazil.

Chesnut, R. Andrew. 1997. *Born Again in Brazil.* New Brunswick, N.J.: Rutgers University Press.

Chordas, Thomas. 1980. "Catholic Pentecostalism: A New Word in a New World." In *Perspectives on Pentecostalism,* ed. Stephen Glazier (pp. 143-175). Washington, D.C.: University Press of America.

Cleary, Edward. 1994. "Protestants and Catholics: Rivals or Siblings?" In *Coming of Age: Protestantism in Contemporary Latin America,* ed. Daniel Miller (pp. 205-227). Lanham, Md.: University Press of America.

Comunicado Mensal da Conferencia Nacional dos Bispos do Brasil. 1957-1997.

Conferencia Episcopal de Guatemala (CEG). 1997. *Al Servicio de la vida, la justicia y la paz: Documentos de CEG 1956-1997.* Ciudad de Guatemala: Ediciones San Pablo.

Conferencia Episcopal de Honduras (CEH). 1984. *Exhortación pastoral de los obispos de Honduras sobre la renovación carismatica.* Tegucigalpa: Central Impresora.

Conferencia Episcopal Latinoamericana (CEL). 1979. *Evangelizacao no presente e no futuro da America Latina: Conclusões da Conferencia de Puebla.* São Paulo: Edições Paulinas.

Conway, Frederick. 1980. "Pentecostalism in Haiti: Healing and Hierarchy." In *Perspectives on Pentecostalism: Cases Studies from the Caribbean and Latin America,* ed. Stephen Glazier (pp. 7-26). Washington, D.C.: University Press of America.

Delgado Varela, José Maria. 1975. "Renovación Carismática Católica en Guatemala." *Estudios Teológicos* 4: 227-260.

Desmangles, Leslie. 1992. *The Faces of the Gods: Vodou and Roman Catholicism in Haiti.* Chapel Hill: University of North Carolina Press.

di Paolo, Pasquale. 1979. *Umbanda e integração social.* Belem, Brazil: Universidade Federal do Para.

Díaz de la Serna Braojos, Maria Cristina. 1981. "El movimiento de la Renovación Carismatica como un proceso de socialización adulta." Licentiate Thesis, Universidad Autonoma Metropolitana, Unidad Iztapalapa, Mexico City.

Documentacion e Información Católica (DIC). Boletin semanal de la Conferencia Episcopal de México. 1972–1997.

Drogus, Carol Ann. 1997. *Women, Religion, and Social Change in Brazil's Popular Church.* Notre Dame, Ind.: Notre Dame Press.

Dussel, Enrique. 1981. *A History of the Church in Latin America.* Grand Rapids, Mich.: William B. Eerdmans.

Fernandes, Rubem Cesar. 1992. *Censo Institucional Evangélico.* Rio de Janeiro: Instituto Superior de Estudos da Religião.

Fernandes, Silvia Alves. 1996. "Movimento de Renovação Carismatica Católica" *Revista Universidade Rural, Serie Ciencias Humanas* 18(1/2): 109–124.

Finke, Roger, and Rodney Stark. 1992. *The Churching of America, 1776–1990.* New Brunswick, N.J.: Rutgers University Press.

Flora, Cornelia Butler. 1976. *Pentecostalism in Colombia.* Cranbury, N.J.: Associated University Presses.

Freston, Paul. 1993. "Brother Votes for Brother: The New Politics of Protestantism in Brazil." In *Rethinking Protestantism in Latin America,* ed. Virginia Garrard-Burnett and David Stoll (pp. 66–110). Philadelphia: Temple University Press.

Frost, Robert C. 1971. *Aglow with the Spirit.* Plainfield, N.J.: Logos International.

Galilea, Carmen. 1992. *Católicos carismáticos y protestantes pentecostales.* Santiago: CISOC-Bellarmino.

Garrard-Burnett, Virginia. 2001. "Salvation or Liberation? Roman Catholicism in El Salvador." Unpublished manuscript.

———. 1998. *Living in the New Jerusalem.* Austin: University of Texas.

Gill, Anthony. 1998. *Rendering unto Caesar.* Chicago: University of Chicago Press.

Gill, Leslie. 1990. "Like a Veil to Cover Them: Women and the Pentecostal Movement in La Paz." *American Ethnologist* 17 (Nov.): 708–721.

Hebrard, Monique. 1992. *Os carismáticos.* Porto, Portugal: Editorial Perpétuo Socorro.

———. 1991. *Les Charismatiques.* Paris: Cerf-Fides.

Hennelly, Alfred, ed. 1993. *Santo Domingo and Beyond.* Maryknoll, N.Y.: Orbis.

Hewitt, Ted. 1991. *Base Christian Communities and Social Change in Brazil.* Lincoln: University of Nebraska Press.

Houk, James. 1995. *Spirits, Blood, and Drums: The Orisha Religion in Trinidad.* Philadelphia: Temple University Press.

Instituto Superior de Estudos da Religião (ISER). 1996. *Novo nascimento: Os evangelicos em casa, na igreja e na politica.* Rio de Janeiro: ISER.

International Catholic Charismatic Renewal Services. Available at www.iccrs.org/CCR%20worldwide.htm; accessed January 17, 2000.

Jesus Vive e é o Senhor. A Revista da Renovação Carismática Católica. 1977-1998.

Lampe, Armando. 1998. "The Popular Use of the Charismatic Movement in Curação." *Social Compass* 45 (3): 429-436.

Leacock, Seth, and Ruth Leacock. 1972. *Spirits of the Deep.* Garden City, N.Y.: Doubleday Natural History Press.

Lerch, Patricia. 1982. "An Explanation for the Predominance of Women in the Umbanda Cults of Porto Alegre, Brazil." *Urban Anthropology* 11 (2): 237-261.

Lima, Samarone, and Thais Oyama. 1998. "Católicos em transe." *Veja.* Available at www2.uol.com.br/veja/080498/p_092.html; accessed December 14, 1998.

Lockhart, James, and Staurt B. Schwartz. 1988. *Early Latin America.* New York: Cambridge University Press.

Machado, Maria das Dores. 1996. *Carismaticos e Pentecostais: Adesão Religiosa na esfera familiar.* Campinas, Brazil: ANPOCS.

Mariano, Ricardo. 1999. *NeoPentecostais: Sociologia do novo pentecostalismo no Brasil.* São Paulo: Edições Loyola

Mariz, Cecilia. 1995. "Pentecostalismo, RenovaçãoCarismática, Comunidades Eclesias de Base." In *Pentecostalismo, CEBs e Renovção Carismatica no Rio de Janeiro* (pp. 22-48). Rio de Janeiro: CERIS.

——. 1994. *Coping with Poverty: Pentecostals and Christian Base Communities in Brazil.* Philadelphia: Temple University Press.

Martin, David. 1990. *Tongues of Fire.* Oxford: Basil Blackwell.

McDonnell, Kilian. 1980. *Presence, Power, Praise: Documents on the Charismatic Renewal,* 3 vols. Collegeville, Minn.: Liturgical Press.

McGuire, Meredith. 1982. *Pentecostal Catholics.* Philadelphia: Temple University Press.

Mecham, J. Lloyd. 1966. *Church and State in Latin America.* Chapel Hill: University of North Carolina Press.

Miguez, Daniel. 1999. "Exploring the Argentinian Case: Religious Motives in the Growth of Latin American Pentecostalism." In *Latin American Religion in Motion,* ed. Christian Smith and Joshua Prokopy (pp. 221-234). New York: Routledge.

Molyneux, Maxine. 1986. "Mobilization without Emancipation? Women's Interests, State, and Revolution in Nicaragua." In *Transition and Development,* ed. Richard Fagen et al. (pp. 280-302). New York: Monthly Review Press.

Moreno, Pedro. 1999. "Evangelical Churches." In *Religious Freedom and Evangelization in Latin America,* ed. Paul Sigmund (pp. 49-69). Maryknoll, N.Y.: Orbis.

Muñoz Rios, Alma. 1997. "Movimiento de la Renovación Carismática Católica." Liccentrate thesis, Escuela Nacional de Antropologia e Historia, Unidad Chihuhua.

Murphy, Joseph. 1994. *Working the Spirit: Ceremonies of the African Diaspora.* Boston: Beacon Press.

——. 1993. *Santería: African Spirits in America.* Boston: Beacon Press.

"Não sou artista, nem quero ser ídolo de ninguém: Meu sonho era jogar futebol." 1998. *CARAS,* December 4.

"Nao sou milagreiro." 1997. *Isto É,* December 24.

Negrão, Lisias Nogueira. 1996. *Entre a cruz e a encruzilhada: Formação do Campo Umbandista em São Paulo.* São Paulo: Edusp.

Ofensiva Nacional 1998. São José dos Cumplos, Brazil. Edições com Deus and FUN-
DDC

Oliveira, Pedro et al. 1978. *Renovação Carismática Católica: Uma análise sociológica, in-
terpretações telológicas*. Petrópolis, Brazil: Vozes.

Oro, Ari. 1996. *Avanco pentecostal e reação católica*. Petropolis, Brazil: Vozes.

Pattnayak, Satya. 1995. "Social Change, Political Competition, and Religious Innovation
in Latin America: An Introduction." In *Organized Religion in the Political Transformation of Latin America*, ed. Satya Pattnayak (pp. 1–14). Lanham, Md.: University
Press of America.

Pedrón-Colombani, Sylvie. 1998. *Le Pentecotisme au Guatemala: Conversion et identite*.
Paris: CNRS Editions.

Pepper, Joanne L. 1991. "The Historical Development of Pentecostalism in Northeastern
Brazil, with Specific Reference to Working Class Women in Recife." Ph.D. diss.,
University of Warwick, U.K.

Pike, Frederick, ed. 1964. *The Conflict between Church and State in Latin America*. New
York: Knopf.

Poblete, Renato. 1970. "The Church in Latin America: A Historical Survey." In *The
Church and Social Change in Latin America*, ed. Henry Landsberger (pp. 39–52).
Notre Dame, Ind.: University of Notre Dame Press.

Prandi, Reginaldo. 1997. *Um sopro do espirito*. São Paulo: Edusp.

Prien, Hans-Jürgen. 1985. *La historia del Cristianismo en América Latina*. Salamanca,
Spain: Ediciones Sigueme.

Reich, Peter Lester. 1995. *Mexico's Hidden Revolution: The Catholic Church in Law and
Politics since 1929*. Notre Dame, Ind.: University of Notre Dame Press.

Santagada, Oswaldo. 1986. *Las sectas en América Latina*, 4th ed. Buenos Aires: Editorial
Claretiana–CELAM.

Secretariado Episcopal de América Central (SEDAC). 1995. *El paso de algunos católicos a
las sectas fundamentalistas en Centroamérica*. Guatemala City: SEDAC–Universidad Rafael Landivar.

Soneira, Abelardo Jorge. 1998. "La Renovación Carismática Católica en la Argentina."
Revista del Centro de Investigación y Acción Social 477: 473–486.

Stark, Rodney. 1996. *The Rise of Christianity*. Princeton, N.J.: Princeton University
Press.

Stark, Rodney, and William Bainbridge. 1987. *A Theory of Religion*. New York: Peter
Lang.

Stark, Rodney, and James C. McCann. 1993. "Market Forces and Catholic Commit-
ment: Exploring the New Paradigm." *Journal for the Scientific Study of Religion* 32
(2): 111–124.

Steigenga, Timothy J., and David A. Smilde. 1999. "Wrapped in the Holy Shawl: The
Strange Case of Conservative Christians and Gender Equality in Latin America."
In *Latin American Religion in Motion*, ed. Christian Smith and Joshua Prokopy (pp.
173–186). New York: Routledge.

Stoll, David. 1990. *Is Latin America Turning Protestant?* Berkeley: University of California
Press.

Tennekes, Hans. 1985. *El movimiento pentecostal en la sociedad chilena*. Iquique, Chile: Centro de Investigación de la Realidad del Norte.

United Nations Development Program (UNDP). "Human Development Report for Brazil," ch. 4, "Education and Health." www.undp.org.br/HDR/HDR96/hdr4.htm, accessed January 3. 2003.

Uribe Jaramillo, Alfonso. 1991. *Renovación carismática y pastoral*. Bogotá: Centro Carismático Minuto de Dios.

Vásquez, Manuel. 1999. "Toward a New Agenda for the Study of Religion in the Americas." *Journal of Interamerican Studies and World Affairs* 41 (4): 1–13 (ProQuest electronic version).

Wafer, Jim. 1991. *The Taste of Blood: Spirit Possession in Brazilian Candomblé*. Philadelphia: University of Pennsylvania Press.

Williams, Philip. 1997. "The Sound of Tambourines: The Politics of Pentecostal Growth in El Salvador." In *Power, Politics, and Pentecostals in Latin America*, ed. Edward Cleary and Hannah Stewart-Gambino (pp. 179–200). Boulder, Colo.: Westview Press.

Wilson, Bryan. 1973. *Magic and the Millennium*. London: Heinemann Educational Books.

www.adherents.com/religions-by-adherents.htm#yoruba; accessed May 15, 2001.

Index

171

CPSIA information can be obtained at www.ICGtesting.com
Printed in the USA
BVOW070709100712

294798BV00001B/38/A

9 780195 314861